TWENTY BRITISH FILMS

D1546249

MANCHESTER
1824

Manchester University Press

Other books by Brian McFarlane include:

Class-Act: The Remarkable Lives and Careers of Googie Withers and John McCallum

The Encyclopedia of British Film: Fourth Edition (ed.)

Real and Reel: The Education of a Film Obsessive and Critic

Michael Winterbottom (with Deane Williams)

The British 'B'Film (with Steve Chibnall)

Screen Adaptations: Charles Dickens' Great Expectations

The Cinema of Britain and Ireland (ed.)

Lance Comfort

The Oxford Companion to Australian Film (with Geoff Mayer and Ina Bertrand)

An Autobiography of British Cinema

Novel to Film: An Introduction to the Theory of Adaptation

Sixty Voices: Celebrities Recall the Golden Age of British Cinema

New Australian Cinema: Sources and Parallels in American and British Film (with Geoff Mayer)

Viewpoints on the Nineteenth-Century Novel (ed.)

Viewpoints on Film (ed.)

Australian Cinema

Cross-Country: A Book of Australian Verse (ed.) (with John Barnes)

Words and Images: Australian Novels into Film

Martin Boyd's 'Langton Novels'

Twenty British films

A *guided tour*

Brian McFarlane

Manchester University Press

Published by Manchester University Press
Altrincham Street, Manchester M1 7JA

www.manchesteruniversitypress.co.uk

British Library Cataloguing-in-Publication Data
A catalogue record for this book is available from the British Library

Library of Congress Cataloging-in-Publication Data applied for

ISBN   978 0 7190 8713 4   hardback
ISBN   978 0 7190 8714 1   paperback

First published 2015

Typeset
by Carnegie Book Production, Lancaster
Printed in Great Britain
by Bell & Bain Ltd, Glasgow

For my old friends Rhyll and Alan Nance,

with thanks and love

Contents

List of figures   *p.* ix

Acknowledgments   xiii

Introduction   1

1 Ladies on a train: Hitchcock's *The Lady Vanishes* (1938)   7

2 Shaw's Cinderella on screen: *Pygmalion* (1938)   22

3 Pulling together for *The Way Ahead* (1944)   34

4 The long-lasting *Brief Encounter* (1945)   47

5 Two from the Comfort zone: *Great Day* (1945) and *Temptation Harbour* (1947)   61

6 *It Always Rains on Sunday* (1947) – and other things go wrong too   74

7 *The Third Man* (1949) and several more   86

8 *Genevieve* (1953): old cars and 'the other thing'   98

9 Double bill: *Private Information* (1952) and *Cash on Demand* (1963)   109

10 *A Kind of Loving* (1962) – and of living   121

11 *The Servant* (1963): things fall apart   133

12 Sex, talk, men and *Women in Love* (1969)   146

13 Hard men: *Get Carter* (1971)   158

14 From life: *A Portrait of the Artist as a Young Man* (1977)   170

15 Alice in the real world: *Dreamchild* (1986)   181

16 Guests and others at *Four Weddings and a Funeral* (1994)   192

17 Families and other disasters: *Secrets & Lies* (1996)   204

18 In search of *Wonderland* (1998)   217

19 Giving and taking *Last Orders* (2002)   228

20 In your face: *In the Loop* (2009)   240

Cast and credits   251

Further reading   259

Index   261

Figures

The Lady Vanishes

1 On the set with Sally Stewart (Julie), Margaret Lockwood (Iris), Alfred Hitchcock and Googie Withers (Blanche). Courtesy of the Steve Chibnall Collection.   13

2 Naunton Wayne (Caldicott), Margaret Lockwood (Iris), Dame May Whitty (Miss Froy), Michael Redgrave (Gilbert), Basil Radford (Charters) and Cecil Parker (Todhunter). Courtesy of the Steve Chibnall Collection.   17

Pygmalion

3 Leslie Howard (Professor Higgins), Wendy Hiller (Eliza Doolittle), Ivor Barnard (bystander), Scott Sunderland (Colonel Pickering) and Everley Gregg (Mrs Eynsford Hill). Courtesy of the Steve Chibnall Collection.   27

4 Wendy Hiller (Eliza Doolittle) and Leslie Howard (Professor Higgins). Courtesy of the Steve Chibnall Collection.   28

The Way Ahead

5 James Donald (Lloyd) and David Niven (Jim Perry). Courtesy of the Steve Chibnall Collection.   42

Brief Encounter

6 Celia Johnson (Laura Jesson) and Trevor Howard (Alec Harvey). Courtesy of the Steve Chibnall Collection.   49

7 Celia Johnson (Laura Jesson), Avis Scott (waitress) and Trevor Howard (Alec Harvey). Courtesy of the Steve Chibnall Collection.   51

8 Celia Johnson (Laura Jesson) and Trevor Howard (Alec Harvey). Courtesy of the Steve Chibnall Collection.   53

Great Day

9 Eric Portman (Captain Ellis) and Flora Robson (Mrs Ellis). Courtesy of the Steve Chibnall Collection.   63

10 Eric Portman (Captain Ellis) and Sheila Sim (Margaret Ellis). Courtesy of the Steve Chibnall Collection.   66

Temptation Harbour

11 Robert Newton (Bert Mallinson) and Simone Simon (Camelia). Courtesy of the Steve Chibnall Collection.   70

12 Robert Newton (Bert Mallinson) and Simone Simon (Camelia). Courtesy of the Steve Chibnall Collection.   72

It Always Rains on Sunday

13 John McCallum (Tommy Swann), Patricia Plunkett (Doris Sandigate) and Googie Withers (Rose Sandigate). Courtesy of the Steve Chibnall Collection.   76

14 John McCallum (Tommy Swann) and Googie Withers (Rose Sandigate). Courtesy of the Steve Chibnall Collection.   81

15 John McCallum (Tommy Swann) and Googie Withers (Rose Sandigate). Courtesy of the Steve Chibnall Collection.   83

The Third Man

16 Joseph Cotten (Holly Martins) on the set of *The Third Man*. Courtesy of the Steve Chibnall Collection.   89

17 Joseph Cotten (Holly Martins) and Orson Welles (Harry Lime). Courtesy of the Steve Chibnall Collection.   94

Genevieve

18 Kay Kendall (Rosalind Peters) and Kenneth More (Ambrose Claverhouse). Courtesy of the Steve Chibnall Collection.   100

19 Kay Kendall (Rosalind Peters). Courtesy of the Steve Chibnall
    Collection.   103

Private Information

20 Jill Esmond (Charlotte Carson), Carol Marsh (Georgie
    Carson), doctor and nurse uncredited. Courtesy of the Steve
    Chibnall Collection   112

A Kind of Loving

21 Alan Bates (Vic Brown) and June Ritchie (Ingrid Rothwell).
    Courtesy of the Steve Chibnall Collection.   126

22 Alan Bates (Vic Brown) and Thora Hird (Mrs Rothwell).
    Courtesy of the Steve Chibnall Collection.   128

The Servant

23 Dirk Bogarde (Hugo Barrett) and James Fox (Tony).
    Courtesy of the Steve Chibnall Collection.   137

24 Dirk Bogarde (Hugo Barrett) and James Fox (Tony).
    Courtesy of the Steve Chibnall Collection.   141

Women in Love

25 Jennie Linden (Ursula Brangwen) and Glenda Jackson
    (Gudrun Brangwen). Courtesy of the Steve Chibnall
    Collection.   149

26 Oliver Reed (Gerald Crich) and Alan Bates (Rupert Birkin).
    Courtesy of the Steve Chibnall Collection.   155

Get Carter

27 Film poster for *Get Carter*.   159

28 Bryan Mosley (Cliff Brumby) and Michael Caine
    (Jack Carter).   162

Dreamchild

29 Coral Browne (Mrs Alice Hargreaves). Courtesy of the
    Steve Chibnall Collection.   184

Four Weddings and a Funeral

30 Kristin Scott Thomas (Fiona) and Hugh Grant (Charles) in a
     promotional shot. Courtesy of the Steve Chibnall Collection.   194

Secrets & Lies

31 Marianne Jean-Baptiste (Hortense) and Brenda Blethyn
     (Cynthia). Courtesy of the Steve Chibnall Collection.   209

32 Timothy Spall (Maurice) and Brenda Blethyn (Cynthia).
     Courtesy of the Steve Chibnall Collection.   211

Wonderland

33 Gina McKee (Nadia). Photo by Marcus Robinson. Courtesy
     of the Steve Chibnall Collection.   221

Last Orders

34 Ray Winstone (Vince Dodds) and Sally Hurst (Mandy).
     Courtesy of the Steve Chibnall Collection.   230

35 Bob Hoskins (Ray Johnson) and Michael Caine (Jack Dodds).
     Courtesy of the Steve Chibnall Collection.   233

In the Loop

36 A promotional poster featuring Peter Capaldi (Malcolm
     Tucker).   242

Acknowledgments

First, I thank Matthew Frost at Manchester University Press for expressing an interest in this slightly unusual project and to MUP for taking it on. I also thank Matthew for providing helpful comments on the manuscript along the way. Because my intention was to write a book about films I admire, indeed *love*, rather than an academic text, it was important to ensure that the result was attractive to interested audiences. In this matter, I am greatly indebted to friends who read chapters, in several cases read *all* the chapters, and constituted the sort of readership I hoped for – that is, those with a real but non-specialist interest in British film. They include Brenda Niall, Jonathan Croall, Ian Britain, Rhyll and Alan Nance, George Wood, Rose Lucas and, an authority on British film, Andrew Spicer. I am most grateful for the time they took, for their careful reading, and for all their suggestions.

Introduction

What? No Michael Powell? A chapter on 'B' films? In a book about twenty British films to cherish? *What* is going on here?

There will inevitably be something strongly personal about any such choice – and about any *defence* of that choice. It is based on the notion of films that have remained fresh and provocative for me after multiple viewings. These are films that stay in the mind, sometimes over decades, when hundreds of others are forgotten. They are films that speak of a rich national cinema too often undervalued as if it were a poor relation of Hollywood. This book, then, will have some element of celebration, but its aim is also to look closely at these twenty films both in their contexts and as individual achievements. There are at least another twenty I'd like to have included: of course it would have been good to include *A Canterbury Tale* or a later David Lean, or any number of others. Sometimes, I've been motivated to write about a film that doesn't seem to me to have had the attention it deserves; and sometimes I've decided not to write about a film that has been much discussed but about which I felt I didn't have anything new to add.

I should like the book to be useful to anyone who might be studying these films but above all to be readable and accessible to a much wider audience that has an interest in and affection for British film. A friend with a keen but non-specialist interest in film said after reading a couple of chapters that they seemed like 'a guided tour' of the films and where they belong in British cinema. I was happy with such a judgment, hence the book's subtitle. The book is meant to be enjoyable. It was all very well for Milton to say that his aim in writing *Paradise Lost* was to 'justify the ways of God to man', but I'll bet Jane

Austen had something less lofty – like pleasure – in mind when she wrote *Pride and Prejudice*.

My book is not intended to gather together 'the twenty best British films ever' or even 'my favourite British films'. Lists like those can, in any case, change from year to year, or perhaps more often. Rather, each of the chosen films highlights something about British cinema that seems important to me. This may, for instance, reflect its strong ties with literature, or it may represent a high spot in British comedy or crime drama, or it could be a matter of rescuing a 'B' film from obscurity and critical condescension, or of celebrating a star performance.

To be more specific, I begin with *The Lady Vanishes* because it reflects the best of British cinema of the 1930s, a matter of stylish, unpretentiously swift story-telling, and because Hitchcock's pre-Hollywood cinema often seems to me underrated (sometimes with his own collusion). I end with *In the Loop* to suggest how far British film comedy has come, not just in the non-stop profanity of the dialogue, but in its ruthless engagement with the slippery facts of political life. Elsewhere, because of my long-term interest in the adaptation of literature to film, an interest clearly shared by British cinema over many decades, several of my choices offer very classy examples of how film can take a notable novel – for instance *Women in Love* – and make something new and compelling, perhaps sending us back to re-read the novel from a different perspective. And British cinema's dealings with literature took an original and beguiling turn with the neglected *Dreamchild*.

I wanted also to represent what have been some of the recurring genres in British cinema. So, there are chapters on such hugely successful romantic comedies as *Genevieve* and *Four Weddings and a Funeral* and on crime thrillers as potent as *The Third Man* and the amazingly sombre *Get Carter*. These are not just supremely accomplished examples of their genres but are also fascinating for what they reveal about the times in which they were made. On another matter, the British 'B' film, the pre-interval attraction in the days of the double-bill, has generally had such an undeservedly poor reputation that I wanted to do justice to a couple of superior productions at this modest level. *Private Information* and *Cash on Demand* each have ideas and a star performance that would have been commendable in their 'betters' after the interval.

While I wasn't setting out to be quirky, the list of films selected, because of the personal element in their choice, isn't meant to correspond to anyone else's idea of the most important British films, let alone represent widespread agreement. Each has been attractive to me over a long period and my aim is to communicate that attractiveness to readers. Of course, as I say, the choices will be strongly personal. I've loved British films since post-war childhood – or, to be more specific, since I saw Lance Comfort's *Great Day* as a 'supporting film' to a Hollywood eastern extravaganza I was desperate to see. There was never a question as to whether Lance Comfort would be represented here; not just because of my *Great Day* experience, but because he has always seemed to me the most seriously underrated director in British film history.

I'd like to know what others who have also loved British cinema might offer as their twenty films to cherish and why. The 'why' is important in this book; otherwise the result might be a mere list or mere opinion, too arbitrary to interest anyone else, whereas if you can see where opinion has come from you can use this to make up your own mind.

Over the last couple of decades I've read a good many proposals for often-admirable academic books on aspects of British cinema. Normally, and often convincingly, it will be suggested that everyone teaching in the field will want a copy and that the book will be widely prescribed for graduate and/or undergraduate courses. Almost as a matter of routine this will be followed by a statement suggesting that, 'It will also appeal to the general reader with an interest in British film', when it is perfectly clear that the 'general readers' who would be interested in such a book could be counted on the fingers of a damaged hand.

My target audience with *Twenty British films* is in fact the general reader who shares my zeal for British film, wants something more substantial than newspaper-review length about a particular film, but who might find the wilder shores of academic theory a bit off-putting. I don't mean for a moment to be dismissive of academic writing, I have in fact contributed to it in the past. I'm very happy for academics to read this book, especially if they've bought it, but it is not primarily intended for them. Film theory has been immensely valuable over the last few decades. It has helped the study of film to take its place among that of the other arts; indeed, it has helped film itself to acquire this status. And I admire those achievements. However, it now seems to me that much valuable academic work could usefully be made accessible to a wider reading public by writing about it in non-specialist terms that might attract that legendary creature, 'the general reader'. I hope the style of this book will communicate an enthusiasm for the films highlighted and that it will lead readers to a reconsideration of these films and those that come trailing in their wake.

While such readers may well have a special interest in and affection for this or that film, it is possible that this kind of personal response may also be enriched by exposure to some of the relevant contexts to which an individual film may belong. On *A Portrait of the Artist as a Young Man*, for example, the connection of the film to a particular kind of coming-of-age novel or to the phenomenon of Anglo-Irish film cooperation, or how *A Kind of Loving* belongs to a crucial upsurge of realist filmmaking whose roots may be found in the novels and plays of the 'angry young man' era. Such connections may be resonant for those to whom these films matter, as they have to me across several decades.

But readers should not expect a theoretical framework applied consistently over these twenty disparate films. In dealing with each film, I have started from a point that strikes me as significant in relation to that particular title. The coherence I aim at is in relation to each film in its turn, not to some overmastering concept. My first criterion for each chapter is to get at the essence of pleasure each of these films has for me, and then to account for this in terms that make this pleasure clear and perhaps to lead readers to reconsider the sources of their own delight in these films – or to strengthen their bases for disagreement. It's not just a matter of mere indulgence but of forcing indulgence to account for itself in ways that are stimulating to others of like or unlike mind about the twenty films highlighted here.

I hope the reasons for the inclusion of each film will be clear, but this clarity is not to be achieved by adopting a uniform approach throughout. For instance, I admire *A Portrait of the Artist* for the way it brings Joyce's great novel to such visual life in the film medium – and to its *daring* to submit the filmgoer to so much *argument* about ideas of art and religion and sex. I hope each chapter will make plain, and justify, its reasons for the inclusion of each film.

Above all, these are films that have remained – and grown – in the memory, films that have indeed enriched life. Mine, at least. Lean is there, so are Hitchcock and Carol Reed (twice), though not necessarily for their most famous works, but it wasn't my aim to produce a list of works by the canonical figures of British cinema. Nor, though the films are arranged chronologically, are they intended to be read as a mini-history of British cinema, even if they will sometimes suggest particular strengths of their period of production. On a couple of occasions, keen-eyed readers will notice, I've squeezed two films into a particular chapter: after all two 'B' movies only really add up in length to one long 'A' film; and I simply couldn't decide which of the two Lance Comfort films I could bring myself to leave out. Convincing reasons?

Certain recurring notions asserted themselves while I was writing the book. For instance, how much *talk* there is in British films, and often such rewarding talk. Think of films as diverse as *Pygmalion, Women in Love, Secrets & Lies* and *In the Loop.* This doesn't mean the films are somehow 'uncinematic'; on the contrary, it suggests how audacious they are in seeking to hold our attention in this way. Again, and this is hardly a new idea, I was struck by how many – well over half – of my chosen films were derived from literature or drama, so perhaps the level of talk and its quality are not so surprising. The cinema, and not just British cinema, has always ransacked literary and theatrical sources, sometimes indeed even improving on the original (my own view of *Brief Encounter*).

As well as reflecting these matters, my choices also drew my attention to other aspects of British film over the seventy years they cover. Some of these aspects of this richly rewarding cinema only became clear to me as I worked on the book. Though I didn't intend this at the outset, it began to appear that these choices achieved a kind of representativeness, testifying to the richness and diversity of British cinema. (Even the preponderance of films from the 1940s seemed to reflect accurately its history.) Many of the twenty are in the realist tradition of much great British filmmaking; in almost all, the quality of the acting is remarkable and across several generations of acting styles; some show a director at the peak of his powers; others offer unobtrusively but persistently a commentary on the sheer *Englishness* of British film across the decades. I became fascinated by what my choices were revealing about the changing social mores, in matters of class and sex and language, as I moved from, say, *Brief Encounter* to *Secrets & Lies,* and on a minor level the fondness for multi-story plotting in films as diverse as *The Way Ahead, Four Weddings and a Funeral* and *Wonderland.* Could this latter element attest, I wonder, to some kind of multi-perspective tolerance as well as just a narrative strategy for shifting the focus of attention?

The book may well prove to be one that readers will prefer to dip into, focusing on this or that particular film, ideally in conjunction with a re-viewing of it. The rewards of this kind of reading will be different from (not necessarily less or greater than) those to be had from reading straight through. If there is a preponderance of films in, say, social realist mode or derived from literary sources, it may reflect my own preferences but, equally, it could be said to reflect areas of ongoing distinction in British cinema. The rest is up to the reader.

1   Ladies on a train:
Hitchcock's *The Lady Vanishes*
(1938)

Was there ever a more beguiling train-set thriller in film history than Alfred Hitchcock's 1938 version of Ethel Lina White's *The Wheel Spins*? There is something irresistibly compelling about the idea of dark deeds being enacted in a confined space: think of all those country-house thrillers by Agatha Christie, Marjorie Allingham and the like, with their play on the idea of someone on the premises who is dangerous to the rest of the cast. A train has this sense of confinement but has as well the attraction of moving headlong through changing terrain, with the possibility of strange people boarding at sinister night stops and limited opportunities for escape once the train is in motion. You could move from compartment to corridor to dining-car, but so could potential assailants. If all this is set against the backdrop of a continent beginning to seethe with political discontents that, with the benefit of hindsight, were shortly to erupt into large-scale war, the tensions gain a special resonance.

Trains and films

Trains have been the setting for a large number of films, and I wonder what makes them so attractive to filmmakers as they have been since the very earliest days of cinema – at least from Edwin S. Porter's pioneering narrative, *The Great Train Robbery* (1903). Some of the train-set films have been comedies, such as Howard Hawks's *Twentieth Century* (1934), but more often they have been thrillers which make the most of the confined space, and preferably on major expresses because this limits the opportunities for escape. Certainly in *The 39 Steps* Robert Donat did jump from a moving train as it crossed the Forth Bridge, but in general once the passengers are assembled there is the gratifying sense that they are stuck there, whatever they are up to, until the next (closely-observed) stop. There is also from the outset the pleasing demand on our attention as we sort out which of the many persons on the train are to be 'characters' with roles to play in the ensuing drama, as distinct from the many who are largely irrelevant – irrelevant in terms of plot, that is, their function being that of realism, so that we accept that this is an 'actual' train. Third, and as suggested above, there is that frisson of excitement that goes with the apparent contrast of stasis and movement that makes equally for dangerous opportunity and severe limitation.

There have been big star-studded train-set dramas, from Joseph von Sternberg's *Shanghai Express* (1932), with Marlene Dietrich as Shanghai Lil entangled with Clive Brook and a bunch of Chinese revolutionaries, to Sidney Lumet's *Murder on the Orient Express* (1974), with Vanessa Redgrave, John Gielgud, Wendy Hiller, Ingrid Bergman, Anthony Perkins and others plunging knives into the sleeping body of Richard Widmark. But some less pretentious numbers have been at least as much fun. Think of Sherlock Holmes in *Terror by Night* (1946), one of Universal's series drawing on the name of the master sleuth, if little else, from Conan Doyle, or Richard Fleischer's taut programmer, *The Narrow Margin* (1952, and remade to more lavish and lesser effect by Peter Hyams in 1990). And there were a couple of nifty British 'B' films, too, in the post-war era, including Michael McCarthy's *Mystery Junction* (1951), Guy Fergusson's *The Gold Express* (1955) and, best of all, *The Flying Scot* (1957), directed by Compton Bennett long past his *Seventh Veil* fame but doing some of the smartest work of his career.

Nearer home for Hitchcock in the 1930s was Bernard Vorhaus's *The Last Journey* (1935, combining strong personal drama with the more usual train-thriller suspense) and perhaps Hitchcock's most obvious predecessor in this setting, Walter Forde's *Rome Express* (1932), a strongly cast Gaumont–British production that puts a motley group on a train and involves them in murder and theft, and, like *The Lady Vanishes*, has Sidney Gilliat as co-screenwriter. It was remade in 1948 as *Sleeping Car to Trieste* (directed by John Paddy Carstairs), in which the blend of suspense and comedy is maintained, a blend which Hitchcock mastered to perfection in his 1930s thrillers. Forde, incidentally, finished the decade with a remake of *The Ghost Train* (released March 1941, a decade after his earlier version of Arnold Ripley's stage thriller).

The titles listed here by no means exhaust the films that have used the train setting to shrewd effect, milking the stasis/motion dichotomy for effect both oddly comforting *and* disconcerting. If there is something cosy about the setting of a long-distance train journey, there is also something potentially alarming about the very limitations of that cosiness, the possible proximity of dangerous contact, the difficulty of escape. At the time of *The Lady Vanishes*, air travel was a much less established fact of life and the spatial opportunities of aeroplanes are perhaps less conducive to the unfolding of mysteries than the big train is with its more varied negotiable spaces. In 1937 Britain, Robert Stevenson directed his then-wife Anna Lee in *Non-Stop New York*, but, despite its diversity of casting and incident, the plane setting never really adds much to the tension. Having suggested a preference for train travel as a site for screen mayhem, I should however refer to the harrowing *Flightplan* (2005), in which Jodie Foster plays a distraught mother whose child vanishes as she flies from Berlin to America, and which draws on aspects of both *The Lady Vanishes* and *So Long at the Fair* (1950) – that is, of mysterious disappearance and unfriendly collusion.

Hitchcock and the 1930s

1930s British cinema is hard to envisage without Hitchcock, whose achievement in the decade towers over his nearest compeers, such as Anthony Asquith or Victor Saville – or the emerging Michael Powell still more or less occupied by second features. Those entertainments Hitchcock made in that decade remain delectable for their wit, their fast-moving narratives, for what now looks like profligate casting and for the subtle ways in which they reflect the decade's growing sense of unease. Probably, none ticks as many of these and other boxes as *The Lady Vanishes*. Hitchcock of course went on to the indisputable US triumphs of *Vertigo*, *Psycho* and others, but it is arguable that nothing ever had quite the unquenchable zest and dexterity of touch that this train-set thriller has. It is sexy, comic and exciting, with a sense of real threat hovering over all – and the threat has to do with the film's timing in relation to European affairs as well as to the inventiveness of its source novel, or even of Launder and Gilliat's screenplay.

That run of lively, largely unpretentious thrillers which made Hitchcock's name in the 30s established him as the key director of the decade. His only serious rival is Victor Saville, even more prolific than Hitchcock and possibly still awaiting major reappraisal, who scored notable successes across several genres (musicals, romantic melodrama, regional studies, portmanteau narrative). It may well be that Hitchcock's ascendancy grew from the honing of his particular skills in relation to a single genre. *The Lodger* (1926), of which he said to François Truffaut in the famous book-length interview, 'In truth, you might almost say that *The Lodger* was my first picture'.[1] It was a thriller of murder and mistaken identity and, as well, introduced Hitchcock as a confident stylist, whose thematic and narrative interests and stylistic effects would be refined in the series from 1934's *The Man Who Knew Too Much* to *The Lady Vanishes* four years later.

The two that most clearly anticipate *The Lady Vanishes* are *The 39 Steps* (1935) and *Young and Innocent* (1937). All three share the strongly kinetic element that derives from a sense of rapid movement from place to place; all three involve disguise of true identity; and in subtly different ways all are concerned with the establishment of a romantic couple and with the sort of sexual by-play that confidently leads us to expect a gratifying sense of closure to the romantic as well as to the mystery elements that underpin the narrative in each case. The other Hitchcock films of this period, thrillers all though they are – *The Man Who Knew Too Much, Secret Agent* (1936) and *Sabotage* (1936) – are more sombre in tone, less obviously exhilarating than the other three, but still tarred with the same filmmaker's brush by which stories are unfolded with exemplary speed, as much clarity as he deemed necessary, and a master's feeling for tensions in character and event.

The 39 Steps, Young and Innocent and *The Lady Vanishes* are all based on popular novels and in each case Hitchcock takes what he wants and proceeds, in his own words to Truffaut, to 'forget all about the book and start to create cinema'.[2] In the two earlier films, he is in fact much more ruthless in jettisoning the twists and turns of plot than he is in *The Lady Vanishes*. In adapting *The Thirty-Nine Steps*,[3] John Buchan's 'yarn' of 1915, Hitchcock sets his hero Richard Hannay on a northern pursuit after his being involved in a death in his London flat, but thereafter most of what Hannay gets up to derives from Hitchcock and his screenwriter rather than from Buchan. In the case of *Young and Innocent*, based on Josephine Tey's *A Shilling for Candles* (1936), film and novel share the narrative starting-point – the death of the woman who, from humble beginnings, has become a famous film star – but Tey takes much more interest in creating a background for her than do Hitchcock and his screenwriters. Next morning, a young man sees her body on the beach and then runs from the scene. Whereas in the novel Tey offers a quite witty appraisal of film star celebrity, in *Young and Innocent*, Christine's death is little more than the means of setting the plot in motion, and literally the chase is on.

Hitchcock has never been associated with the adaptation of major literary works, perhaps because they have seemed to him to have a status and integrity that he would not venture to compete with or that would not allow him the scope for reimagining. Certainly he has never been daunted by the novels he has chosen to adapt, and in fact most of his films have been derived from novels, usually of the 'popular' kind. *Sabotage*, adapted from Joseph Conrad's *The Secret Agent*, may well be the nearest he has come to dealings with 'literary' fiction. With the kinds of novels he chose as his starting-points, he has obviously felt free to take an idea or a striking event and then to head off in his own direction. In the case of *The Lady Vanishes*, he has followed the contours of Ethel Lina White's thriller much more closely than was his wont.[4] Originally entitled *The Wheel Spins* when it appeared in 1936, it remains an attractive thriller, overhung with a sense of political threat in contemporary Europe and marked by some sense of its heroine's moral development. If that sounds like a promising scenario for Hitchcock, the resulting film would seem to bear this out. Compared with the Christies and Allinghams and Heyers of the decade, White seems at least as assured and a little more substantial in her dealings with personal and more widely international relations.

While allowing that Hitchcock is more indebted than usual to his literary source (and few directors have been more ungenerous in acknowledging such indebtedness), I'd still want to argue that he makes *The Lady Vanishes* very much his own film. By this I refer to such matters, among others, as: the use of the 'MacGuffin', the motivating device which actually has no more importance in the plot than as an initiator of the ensuing action; the growth of romantic attachment between a couple, one of whom has difficulty in persuading the other of, say, veracity or accuracy of information or of probity of intention; the use of dubious or duplicitous identity; and the eye (and camera angle) for the heart-stopping moment. All these elements would resurface in more portentous circumstances in the big Hollywood films, but it is arguable that they were never more deftly blended than here, in spite of the way in which so distinguished a critic as Robin Wood tended to dismiss Hitchcock's British films as 'prentice work.

Ladies, and others, on a train

In 1945 Universal Studios released a film actually called *Lady on a Train*, starring Deanna Durbin and based on a story by crime writer Leslie Charteris. Apart from the appositeness of its title, it shares with *The Lady Vanishes* a debutante-type heroine who has trouble getting anyone to believe her. The first-billed of Hitchcock's ladies is Margaret Lockwood who plays Iris Henderson, leader of a social 'crowd', who is leaving her two friends at the Alpine resort to travel back to England to marry, for no very good reason other than that she feels she's done everything else. The other principal lady on this train is Miss Froy (Dame May Whitty), the middle-aged, tweed-clad governess who is returning to England with an important message relating to international affairs entrusted to her.

The film opens in an unspecified snowbound mountain setting and as the camera pans over this – and the credits – it gradually comes down to pick out a railway station, a village (possibly some skilful model work here), and finally settles on an inn. The plot is set in motion by an *obstacle* to motion: there's talk of an avalanche and everyone in the inn's reception area is harassing the manager about the possibilities of getting on the train as planned. Many of the film's main characters are introduced here. Miss Froy establishes at once an air of brisk, good-humoured common sense. The next pair we meet are those archetypal Englishmen, Charters and Caldicott (Basil Radford and Naunton Wayne), created especially for the film by screenwriters Launder and Gilliat, and you could say that there are elements here of stereotypical characterisation in this sequence, with excitable foreigners and rather superior Brits. These two are not pleased when three young Englishwomen, Iris and her chums Blanche and Julie (Googie Withers and Sally Stewart), come breezing in, immediately assuming priority attention for themselves. These three, of whom Iris is the obvious leader, order food to be served in their rooms and generally conduct themselves as if the world is there to do their bidding. It is important to note how supremely confident they are, attractive and charming enough but utterly certain about their rightful place in the world. Also hovering in this sequence is the somewhat prickly couple, 'the Todhunters' (Cecil Parker and Linden Travers), whose adulterous adventure will have its part to play in the drama of the train and the vanishing lady.

Two crucial relationships are telegraphed in this early part of the film. First, there is a meeting on an upstairs landing between Iris and

1   On the set with Sally Stewart (Julie), Margaret Lockwood (Iris),
Alfred Hitchcock and Googie Withers (Blanche).

Miss Froy: as they go to their respective rooms, they appear briefly together in a shot which, in hindsight, will prove a pivotal moment. Miss Froy, in her own room, listens appreciatively to a song coming up from below, showing herself again as sensitive to the country she is in, and thus at some remove from Iris's spoilt hedonism. (Shortly after, the singer will be strangled by a pair of disembodied hands and we will remember this next morning when an unseen hand pushes a pot-plant off a window ledge and knocks Iris out.) They share another moment at the top of the stairs when each comes out of her room to investigate the cause of a thumping noise – feet stamping on the floor overhead as it will prove to be – and Iris, used to having her wishes attended to, bribes the manager into getting the noise stopped. I stress these moments because of Miss Froy's subsequent importance in Iris's moral growth.

The second important relationship referred to is that between Iris and, as it transpires, the instigator of the overhead thumping. Musicologist Gilbert Redman (Michael Redgrave) is the film's equivalent, in terms of his plot functions, of the novel's Hare: 'a young man... of rather untidy appearance with a pleasant ordinary face and large hazel eyes', with some grasp of the language of the European country in which they find themselves and some eccentric opinions. Making Gilbert a musicologist has a couple of significant bearings on the narrative. First, he has been recording the noisy local music and dancing which puts him and Iris at loggerheads to start with – as so many of Hitchcock's leading couples are – and it is the means of providing the film's anticlimax in relation to Miss Froy's activities as a spy for the British Government. At the inn, Gilbert, for all his breeziness, is not about to give in to Iris's spoilt self-centredness. The romantic-comedy strain of the film is set in motion when he bursts into her room, claiming that he has come to share it unless she gives in and phones the manager to restore his own room.

As the train moves on

In plot terms, then, the basis for Iris's development from heedless socialite to more serious young traveller is laid in her concern for what will subsequently happen to Miss Froy on the train. The initial antagonism between her and Gilbert will similarly deepen as, on the train, she tries to persuade him that she is not imagining the disappearance of Miss Froy, of whom she has become fond. In fact, those early sequences *before* the train appears next morning lay the ground most skilfully for what follows. As well as the Iris-Miss Froy and Iris-Gilbert connections, what we see of Charters and Caldicott and 'Mr and Mrs' Todhunter will also help to influence the events on the train. Charters and Caldicott are cricket-mad and when they speak of the condition of 'England' they refer not to the nation at large but to its Test team.[5] Their desperation to get back to Manchester for the match and the illicit nature of the Todhunters' liaison mean that they will prove unreliable supporters for Iris's quest to establish what has happened to Miss Froy on the train.

I don't propose to go through the events of the film in this kind of detail: those who are familiar with the film will know them already and those who are not won't want to have their pleasure spoiled. But it is important to see how cleverly, and apparently casually, Hitchcock sets in place the basis for what follows. Something faintly mysterious is established about Miss Froy; she is not just another Englishwoman abroad and the shot of her listening almost rapt to the singer below seems to signal this difference. As for the other chief lady-on-the-train, Iris is set up as someone to whom something significant must happen if she is ever to be more than the vapid pleasure-lover she appears to be. Just before boarding she is hit on the head by the flower-pot pushed from an upper-storey window, as she goes to help Miss Froy, for whom, we later realise, it was no doubt intended. Could it be the work of the same unseen hand that strangled the singer the night before?

Once the train starts, the scene is set for the film's major drama. When Iris comes to in her compartment, Miss Froy is sitting opposite her, the others in the compartment being, as we shall discover, involved in the conspiracy that leads to Miss Froy's disappearance. When, after having tea with Miss Froy, who writes her name in the dust/mist on the window, Iris sleeps again, she wakes to find Miss Froy gone. The central section of the film is taken up with Iris's attempts to persuade fellow-passengers, especially Gilbert, that she is not suffering from concussion but that in fact Miss Froy *was* on the train. The Charters-Caldicott pair and the Todhunters, for self-interested reasons of their own, fail to support her though they have all seen Miss Froy in the dining-car and elsewhere, and the other members of Iris's compartment, for some reason never made clear (and this doesn't matter), go along with the opinion that she is deluded. As in both *The 39 Steps* and *Young and Innocent*, the mystery will involve an element of disguise as the conspirators, including the seemingly urbane Dr Hartz (Paul Lukas), all testify that the woman who has assumed Miss Froy's seat and wears her clothes is she whom Iris has mistaken for Miss Froy.

Once we get on the train, we are pretty much confined and there are very few outside shots, but every now and then we get a glimpse of the countryside that reminds us that we are indeed involved in a sort of race against time, that we are moving across Europe. And there are shots of train wheels relentlessly turning to the accompaniment of the characteristic sounds of a steam locomotive. When the train arrives at a station, Dr Hartz, accompanied by a nun, brings on a patient swathed in bandages, and this is a crucial moment in the plot, and this figure being brought on will be a replacement for Miss Froy. On the matter of 'disguise', of false identity so common to Hitchcock's films, one might note here the 'nun', whose aberration of dress will later give her away. The two major strands of the plot become wholly intertwined as the train's journey gets underway. The obvious thriller element lies in the mystery of Miss Froy's disappearance and the increasing frustration of Iris when she is unable to get other passengers to corroborate her story. The other strand is that of the growing rapprochement between Iris and Gilbert, and there are a couple of key moments which clinch his belief in her story.

Iris grows

What makes *The Lady Vanishes* so richly satisfying a piece is that it offers a good deal more than might be expected of a mere thriller. Even of a 'mere thriller' with a romantic couple evolving, though this is by no means negligible in itself. The development of the Iris-Gilbert relationship recalls many such in the Hitchcock filmography: it begins in antagonism, is acted out initially in cynicism on his part and outrage on hers, and via the events on the train leads to the mutuality we have been anticipating. When Gilbert has incontrovertible evidence that Iris's story about Miss Troy is true (the tea-label which flattens itself on a window is the turning-point in this respect), he commits himself to helping her: 'You're right. Miss Froy *is* on this train... We're going to search this train'. But it's not just this piece of clinching evidence that has brought him around to Iris's cause. He, like us, has seen the self-centred girl grow in stature as she pursues a matter which she could easily, and with far less trouble to herself, have simply let pass.

It sounds a bit solemn, perhaps pompous, to be talking about 'moral growth' in the context of what might easily be taken as a light-hearted comedy-thriller, but in my view this element is what goes on making the film a compelling experience long after one knows exactly where the big moments of suspense and surprise are coming. Iris has responded to something in her brief acquaintance with Miss Froy, a sense of character and purpose outside her own narrow social range, and in turn is herself imbued with a new firmness of character and purpose when she suspects a dangerous conspiracy at work. In fact, I think this is the film's chief interest. How much do we know really about Miss Froy's espionage activities? Or about those of the conspirators? Or what sort of international agencies are involved? Very little, I suggest, and more it *matters* very little.

What matters more to the viewer, at least to the viewer familiar with the outcome of the plot manoeuvres, is this sense of Iris's maturing until the relationship between her and Gilbert seems to have a certain rightness, a sense of equality, about it. Further, the texture of the film is made immeasurably richer by the ways in which certain of the other characters are revealed as the mystery of Miss Froy's disappearance and its aftermath is revealed. 'Mrs' Todhunter (Linden Travers), after seeming first to capitulate to her jittery lover and to claim that the false Miss Troy is the real thing, eventually finds her nerve and throws in her lot with Iris, while the pompous and pusillanimous Todhunter meets

2   L to R: Naunton Wayne (Caldicott), Margaret Lockwood (Iris),
Dame May Whitty (Miss Froy), Michael Redgrave (Gilbert),
Basil Radford (Charters) and Cecil Parker (Todhunter).

a sticky end; the cricket-mad duo of Charters and Caldicott, appalled at the idea of Iris's search as a stumbling-block to their arriving home in time for the Test match, put aside their obsession long enough to act like 'real Englishmen' in the final showdown with the forces of the conspirators when the train is stopped in the woods; and Dr Hartz's assistant, the 'nun' (Catherine Lacey), whose un-nunly high heels are given an identifying close-up, rebels against the idea of being part of a conspiracy against an Englishwoman. In other words, there are many and much more interesting things going on than just the finding of the vanishing lady. If that were all, the film would scarcely repay so many repeat viewings.

The film remains such a rich experience because it works so satisfyingly on several levels, integrating the personal (Iris's maturing; the development of the romantic couple), the thriller events (where is Miss Froy?; why has she vanished?), the pervasive sense of a tense international situation which might erupt (even if the details of this are by no means clear) and some witty satirical observation of the English abroad. The irresistible texture thus created is the more fully appreciated when one considers the dire remake of 1979. Forty years earlier, all the elements had fused with apparently effortless grace and precision.

Hitchcock and others

In accounting for the film's high pleasure quotient, I want to draw attention to the function of some of Hitchcock's key collaborators, even if that was not his own common practice. The behind-camera personnel include some of the key names of the decade. Jack Cox, director of photography, from the outset confers a handsome, luminous sheen on the proceedings, whether in the confines of the mountain inn or in the constricted spaces of the train. Notice, too, how clearly and beautifully Margaret Lockwood is lit as she comes to in the compartment of the moving train after her mild concussion. The fakery involved in shooting the train and in rendering it credible, as well as in creating the mountain village, also drew on the expertise of legendary art director, Alex Vetchinsky. As Alfred Roome, assistant editor (cutter, as he is billed; R. E. Dearing is 'editor'), recalled, 'The Lady Vanishes was made by Gainsborough, over at Islington. All the model train stuff was done in a disused garage, and we got some train footage in the south of France'.[6] And on the matter of editing, Roome also said, 'Hitchcock shot his stuff so well that it scarcely needed editing. It went together so that it only needed some final trimming up here and there'.

Perhaps the most significant of Hitchcock's collaborators, however, was the screenwriting team of Sidney Gilliat and Frank Launder, who would go on as a producing and directing team for several decades from the early 1940s. In the 30s, Gilliat had already been part-author of the screenplay for several train-set thrillers, most notably *Rome Express*, but also *The Ghost Train* (1931) and *Seven Sinners* (1936), sharing the writing credit for the latter with Launder. But it is *Rome Express* which sets up the most interesting comparisons with *The Lady Vanishes*. This is no place for a detailed discussion of these but just note some of the elements in the earlier film which will echo in Hitchcock's: the satire at the expense of the ultra-Englishman abroad, this time golf- rather than cricket-mad, is there in Gordon Harker's plus-foured bore; there is a warily adulterous couple (Harold Huth and Joan Barry) who will be echoed in the Todhunters; the central idea of the 'missing' Van Dyke is a sort of precursor to the missing Miss Froy; there is the same neat editing of exteriors (train wheels, bridge, mountains) and the confinement on board the train itself; soldiers of indeterminate nationality appear when the train makes a night stop and there is a reference to Mussolini to remind us of what was happening in Europe in the 1930s. Some of this is no doubt attributable to Clifford Grey's novel, but at least Gilliat had been thinking about how to vary thrills and comedy, movement and stasis in a train setting. When the film was remade in 1948 as *Sleeping Car to Trieste*, it adopted many of the motifs of the earlier film, again to enjoyable effect.

As to those in front of the camera, Michael Redgrave and Margaret Lockwood were near the start of their film careers. *The Lady Vanishes* was Redgrave's first starring role and he would not often be cast in leading-man roles such as Gilbert, though he was the star of the following year's *The Stars Look Down*, again with Lockwood. He brings the right amused insouciance to the role of Gilbert who has to be convinced that there is more to Iris than meets even an appreciative eye. Lockwood was already pretty well established as a leading lady. She got off to a goodish start in the 30s in such films as *Lorna Doone* and *Dr Syn*, and would go on to become Britain's most popular female star in the 40s, in such famous melodramas as *The Man in Grey* and *The Wicked Lady*, but it is just possible that *The Lady Vanishes* is her most attractive work on film. She conveys admirably the gradual adjustment from heedless socialite to purposeful young woman with the bit between her teeth, and the growth of feeling between Iris and Gilbert is achieved with subtlety and persuasiveness, the number of two-shots in which they appear increasing as their mutual regard does.

The supporting cast is rich in notable character players, notably Dame May Whitty, who went on to have a prolific career in Hollywood and whose Miss Froy gives a firmly realised centre to Hitchcock's film, and Paul Lukas (Dr Hartz) who had played leading romantic roles in his native Hungary but was most often cast as villains in English-speaking films. He made several films in Britain but is probably best remembered now for *Watch on the Rhine* in the US in 1944, for which he won an Oscar in a sympathetic role. But as with Herbert Lom in later years, his film roles tended to build on the notion among Anglophone audiences of foreigners' inevitably being sinister. In a very short role in the film's pre-train sequences, Googie Withers plays with the engaging swagger that would mark her out for some major leads in the next decade, while Cecil Parker and Linden Travers as 'the Todhunters' would be involved in another illicit liaison ten years later in 'The Colonel's Lady' sequence of *Quartet*. Their playing in *The Lady Vanishes* provides an effective counterpoint to the Lockwood-Redgrave pairing: as the latter are being drawn together in mutual trust, so the Todhunters' deception is gradually leading to the disintegration of their relationship. An adulterous affair could hardly be seen to prosper in 1938 cinema.

The happiest writing and casting stroke was probably in Launder and Gilliat's creation of the cricket bores, Chalmers and Caldicott, whose tunnel-vision obsessiveness would be put to the test (as it were). As incarnated by Basil Radford and Naunton Wayne, these two assumed iconic significance as Englishmen abroad determined not to let anything broaden their horizons or interfere with their obsession. These characters were successful enough to reappear in Carol Reed's *Night Train to Munich* (1940), another thriller set in a Europe fraught with conflict and also scripted by Launder and Gilliat; in John Baxter's comedy-thriller, *Crooks' Tour* (1940); and – in a wartime, home-front setting this time – in Launder and Gilliat's first feature as writers and directors, *Millions Like Us* (1943). These characters, not in the original novel, were retained for Anthony Page's lamentable 1979 remake of *The Lady Vanishes* when they were played by Arthur Lowe and Ian Carmichael, and there was a TV series actually called *Charters & Caldicott* in 1985, with Robin Bailey and Michael Aldridge in the title roles. The point of giving this information is to suggest the hold these two had on the public imagination as a result of their inimitable contribution to Hitchcock's film.

So where does it stand?

In the Hitchcock canon, as suggested above, the British films tend to be given comparatively short shrift, though at least one DVD company[7] has recently been offering immaculate new releases of several of the British thrillers. These films may well lack the high production values and huge star names of, say, *Rear Window* or *Vertigo*, but they have an honourable place in one of the most distinguished filmographies any director has ever run up. And among these, *The Lady Vanishes* may well be the most accomplished. As we have seen, it has a good deal in common with *The 39 Steps* and *Young and Innocent*, but its texture is arguably richer than either, composed as it is of a mystery thriller strand, the engaging growth of a romantic partnership and, intertwined with both, the heroine's moral maturing. Gaumont-British/Gainsborough may not have had the financial resources of the big Hollywood studios, but the qualities of wit and pace and sheer cinematic intelligence and know-how were already in evidence in these films. In them, Hitchcock was establishing himself as the supreme master of the genre which he would work in for most of his professional life.

Notes

1 François Truffaut, *Hitchcock* (New York: Simon and Schuster, 1966), p. 31.

2 Truffaut, *Hitchcock*, p. 49.

3 Buchan spells out and hyphenates *Thirty-Nine*; the 1935 and 1959 films give it as *39*; the 1978 film has *Thirty Nine*.

4 *The Wheel Spins* was published by Collins in Britain in 1936 and as a paperback under the title of *The Lady Vanishes* by J. M. Dent & Sons in 1987. Other novels of White's to be filmed were *Some Must Watch* (1933, filmed as *The Spiral Staircase* in 1946 and 1975, and for television in 1961 and 2000), and *Midnight House* (1942, filmed as *The Unseen* in 1945).

5 This running joke had previously appeared in Chapter VI of A. G. Macdonell's *England Their England*, published in 1933.

6 'Alfred Roome' in Brian McFarlane, *Autobiography of British Cinema* (London: Methuen, 1997), p. 498.

7 Madman Entertainment, Directors Suite label, Australia, released in 2011: *The Lodger, The 39 Steps, Young and Innocent, The Lady Vanishes*.

2 Shaw's Cinderella on screen: *Pygmalion* (1938)

Though *St Joan* or *Major Barbara* or *Heartbreak House* may find George Bernard Shaw tackling loftier issues, it is at least arguable that no play of his has exerted such a hold on audiences as *Pygmalion* has. Certainly not in my own case: it was the first of his plays I ever saw performed (in a semi-professional production), and among several subsequent sightings the two most recent were those with Peter O'Toole as Higgins and Jackie Smith-Wood as Eliza in 1984 at London's Shaftesbury Theatre, and Peter Hall's rendering at the Theatre Royal, Bath, and later the Old Vic, in 2007–8 with Tim Pigott-Smith's Higgins and Michelle Dockery's Eliza. As well as innumerable stage revivals since the play first appeared nearly a hundred years ago, there have been half a dozen television versions (first in 1948 with Ralph Michael and Margaret Lockwood), the hugely successful musical comedy adaptation, *My Fair Lady* (1956), which ran for years on Broadway and the West End stages, and which became in turn an award-winning film in which Rex Harrison won an Oscar for repeating his stage performance on screen. There was even a German film in 1935. All of these notwithstanding, for me at least the 1938 British film version remains definitive, and I now must try to account for this view.

People

Shaw

The greatest British playwright of the first half of the twentieth century, an assessment with which he would undoubtedly have concurred, Shaw was very interested in seeing his plays on the screen. 'Interested' is not in it: he was mad keen to reach the sort of audiences that only the cinema could command. "'I am extremely anxious," he said in 1933, "to have all my plays filmed before I die."'[1] He was very alert to the screen's potential for the dissemination of his works and their ideas, but he was also absolutely obdurate about how this should be done. He had in fact no real grasp of the screen's specific strategies for putting its stories before its audiences. 'Shaw wanted the cinema to become an extension of the stage' wrote Donald Costello, the chief commentator on Shaw's dealings with film,[2] and this no doubt accounts for the early film failures derived from his plays.

Director Cecil Lewis, a fervent admirer of Shaw's plays, made the first two film versions of his plays.[3] These were *How He Lied to Her Husband* (1930) and *Arms and the Man* (1932), and neither apparently had anything other than curiosity value. Shaw had insisted on sticking to the dialogue, not allowing a changed word, and refusing to accept that there was any essential difference between the strategies available to stage and screen. These films cannot have helped Lewis's career either, but fortunately he won distinction in other fields[4] and, still with Shaw, was one of the screenwriters credited on *Pygmalion*. And *Pygmalion* remains Shaw's one indisputably triumphant brush with the cinema he both hankered after and despised. What he saw as its real purpose was to make his work available to the populace at large, and on *his* terms rather than the cinema's.

Gabriel Pascal

'He didn't make any money for himself; he was just an old bumbler-on with great charm and a certain appreciation of good acting and Shaw.'[5] This was how Wendy Hiller remembered Gabriel Pascal, the Hungarian producer of the *Pygmalion* film, fifty-odd years later. This view of Pascal seems to have been supported by others who worked with him, including Harold French, uncredited director of Pascal's next go at filming Shaw, with *Major Barbara* (1941), claiming that Pascal 'knew nothing at all about directing and in the end he paid me quite a lot of money *not* to have my name mentioned as a director of it'.[6]

What Pascal had going for him was Shaw's ear: he beguiled Shaw with his obvious admiration for his work and Shaw was amused by him. In her biography of her husband, Valerie Pascal employs as an epigraph Shaw's famous comment on Pascal, which begins: 'Gabriel Pascal is one of those extraordinary men who turn up occasionally – say once in a century – and may be called godsends in the arts to which they are devoted'.[7] From very obscure parentage and Hungarian background, he had a career that included military school, acting in Hamburg, a Hussar cavalry officer in World War One, looking after horses in post-war Denmark where he first became involved (by chance) with film, prior to starting as a director in Italy. He met Shaw when they both turned up, swimming naked, at a buoy off the beach at Antibes, and some years later he took Shaw at his word and fetched up at his house. Shaw's secretary, Blanche Patch, said of Pascal, 'GBS never met a man who entertained him more'.[8]

Whatever the legends surrounding Pascal's dealings with Shaw, the fact remains that Pascal did succeed where others had failed, though getting *Pygmalion* financed was by no means easy, the previous films derived from Shaw having failed utterly with the public. However, Pascal secured the support of Richard Norton, head of Pinewood Studios, and finance was arranged, Norton having the business head and contacts Pascal so signally lacked. Those backers can only have been pleased when the film became an enormous critical and commercial success, a success which Shaw generously attributed to Pascal.

Anthony Asquith

Perhaps underrated now, Anthony Asquith was one of the few British directors whose early talkies had been well received, having acquired a name for genuinely cinematic flair in such films as *Shooting Stars* (1928), *A Cottage on Dartmoor* (1930) and, especially, *Tell England* (1931). However, his career had entered a doldrums phase in the middle 30s before being triumphantly resuscitated by *Pygmalion*. On this, he is technically listed as co-director with Leslie Howard, but Wendy Hiller, 'as one who was in practically every day's shooting... wouldn't have known Leslie was co-directing until the day when we were shooting the tea-party scene'.[9] She had not found Howard sympathetic, whereas, like so many other British actors of the next couple of decades, she felt Asquith was a discreet artist and craftsman, not at all flashy but with a real feeling for what would work on cinema.

Asquith directed many films from plays: after *Pygmalion*, which ushered in his period of highest distinction, came others such as *Quiet Wedding* (1941), *The Winslow Boy* (1948), *The Browning Version* (1951) and *The Importance of Being Earnest* (1952), but these were not essentially stagy in effects. All were remade but never as well. He seems to have been a director who liked and respected actors. Even small part players get a close-up and chance to establish a character, as Ivor Barnard does as a nosy bystander in the opening sequence of *Pygmalion*. Asquith would film two more Shaw plays – *The Doctor's Dilemma* (1959) and *The Millionairess* (1960) – with less success, but his work on *Pygmalion* remains impressive for its unobtrusive cinematic rendering of his theatrical material.

Wendy Hiller

One of Shaw's greatest services to the screen was his insistence that Wendy Hiller should play Eliza Doolittle in the film. He had been impressed with her performance in the West End in her husband, Ronald Gow's, play, *Love on the Dole*, and then at the Malvern Festival when she'd played *St Joan* and *Pygmalion* in celebration of Shaw's eightieth birthday. Her only film work to that time had been in the little-seen *Lancashire Luck* (1937), scripted by Gow and directed by their friend Henry Cass, so that the filmmakers – and their financial backers – were taking a chance on a newcomer with no 'name' in terms of film. As it happened, the chance paid off handsomely and Wendy Hiller became the definitive Eliza for a generation or two. Eloquent of face, with wonderful cheekbones and eyes, and distinctive of voice, she has an unassailable place in British cinema history, in spite of having made barely a dozen films. Everything she did was memorable, including another Shaw protagonist in/as *Major Barbara* (1941) and the determined heroine of Michael Powell's *I Know Where I'm Going!* (1945). If being a star is to be one of a kind, then Wendy Hiller abundantly qualifies: to whatever role she afterwards played, she brought an indefinable but palpable quality that was uniquely her own. She had her own kind of beauty allied to a shrewd intelligence, an unbeatable combination which the screen would doubtless have made more use of if she hadn't also wanted to pursue a theatre career. But if she'd done nothing more than Eliza, graduating from the 'squashed cabbage leaf' of the early scenes to the graceful beauty who descends the embassy stairs in the ball sequence, her star's stature would have been assured.

From page to sound stage

Getting round Shaw

Given Shaw's intransigent attitude to how his plays were to be filmed, with every line of dialogue to be retained and nothing 'Hollywoodish'

to be added, there was obviously a severe challenge to be faced by
the filmmakers. Ultimately, though, he did accept the possibility of
extending settings and locations in the interests of 'showing' what in the
theatre is merely described as happening off-stage. The major addition
is the ball scene which I'll return to, but there are over a dozen other
scenes of varying length and importance that have been created for the
film and which contribute to its smooth flow.

I don't plan to make my way through all the additions and changes
that somehow Pascal and the other filmmakers prevailed on Shaw to
accept, but it is worth noting that subsequent editions of the play, such
as the 1964 Penguin I am using, carry a 'Note for Technicians' between
Shaw's 'Preface' and the start of Act 1. Its opening sentence is:

> A complete representation of the play as printed for the first time in
> this edition [1946] is technically possible only on the cinema screen or
> stages furnished with exceptionally elaborate machinery. For ordinary
> theatrical use the scenes separated by rows of asterisks are to be
> omitted.

Montage: a cinematic strategy

The opening sequence offers an example of film's invention, though as
it scarcely involves dialogue, it is not marked off by asterisks. For some
minutes before Shaw's dialogue begins with Miss and Mrs Eynsford-
Hill (Leueen McGrath and Everley Gregg) complaining about the rain
and Freddie's ineptness in finding a taxi, the camera prowls around
the Covent Garden market by day, alighting briefly on Eliza getting on
with her day's work and greeting a friend, and tracking the tweedy back
of Higgins as he walks through the busy market. There is a sense of
bustling life which gradually dissolves into the deserted space in front
of St Paul's Church at night. All is now silent, but the silence is broken
by the chiming of a great clock, by thunder and the ensuing rain, as the
Eynsford Hill women emerge, talking crossly. Similarly at the end of
this sequence – that is, the play's 'Act 1' – there is another insert, this
time asterisked for the notice of stage producers, as Eliza makes her way
home by taxi, walks up the alley, and enters her shabby lodgings where
she greets a little bird in a cage.

Other such scenes specially invented and scripted either by Shaw
or with his approval include that in which Higgins's housekeeper, Mrs
Pearce (Jean Cadell), carries out her employer's order when she takes
Eliza upstairs to be given a bath. Or, with even more cinema-specific
strategy, there are several brilliantly devised 'montage' sequences which

3   Left: Leslie Howard (Professor Higgins); centre: Wendy Hiller (Eliza Doolittle), Ivor Barnard (bystander), Scott Sunderland (Colonel Pickering); back right: Everley Gregg (Mrs Eynsford Hill).

encapsulate a series of actions that would be hard to emulate with the same sense of repetition and 'busy-ness' on stage. The essence of a montage sequence is to convey, through a series of rapidly juxtaposed shots, a narrative 'episode' or a building of emotions or a thematic intention, for example. It is a sort of cinematic shorthand for which the stage as a rule has no equivalent.

Shaw wrote for the post-film edition of the play: 'There seems to be some curiosity as to what Higgins's lessons to Eliza were like. Well, here is a sample: the first one'.[10] In fact, though, the lesson on the page scarcely hints at the kinetic effect of the montage on screen in which, in a rapid series of shots, we see Higgins verbally belabouring Eliza with vocal exercises (the 'rain in Spain' bit, now famous from the song in *My Fair Lady*, had its origins here in the film, rather than in the original play). She is then seen tossing in her sleep, unable to get free of his persistence. A sequence of shots such as this depends a good deal for its effectiveness on the skill of the editing and Asquith was fortunate to have David Lean as editor. Lean was possibly the most distinguished editor in British films of the 1930s, prior to becoming one of the most

4   Wendy Hiller (Eliza Doolittle) and Leslie Howard (Professor Higgins).

notable of all directors in the following decade. Indeed, according to Harold French, Lean directed 'about three-quarters' of Pascal's next Shavian project on screen, *Major Barbara*.[11]

The ball

Another such notable example is the montage of preparing and costuming Eliza for the embassy ball. By the time the film was being made, Shaw had come to accept the fact that some scenes merely referred to on stage could be shown on screen with advantage to his original play. Most notable of course is the embassy party which is transformed into a ball where Eliza is seen to put into practice all that Higgins has taught her, and this in fact becomes the highlight of the film, the moment in which the 'squashed cabbage leaf' is successfully passed off as, if not a duchess, then a lady of great distinction.

The prelude to this scene involves a montage of work, with odd camera angles indicating Higgins's domination of Eliza as he works away relentlessly on her speech, the odd angles reinforcing the element of distortion as Eliza's life is being wrenched out of its old patterns at the same time as her way of talking is being refined away from her natural street lingo. Then there is the matter of etiquette, and again Asquith employs a montage sequence to create a sense of the effort that has gone into learning modes of address and dancing. The brief appearances by Freddie, now smitten with Eliza and bearing flowers to show it, are not allowed to interrupt the remorseless training sessions. A point is made unobtrusively here: mere affection can't stand a chance against Higgins's dedication to the job in hand.

Director Asquith had said: 'We decided quite rightly that you must show Eliza and her triumph at the ball, which isn't in the play at all'. 'Out of the question' was Shaw's response, but he was taken by Asquith's saying at one point, 'Eliza comes up the stairs with the frozen calm of the sleepwalker', and Asquith added, 'from that moment he was hooked'.[12] And so he might have been, for the sequence is not only a triumph for Eliza and for Higgins but for the film as a whole. For Higgins, Eliza's performance is a vindication of his belief that how English people *speak* is a matter not merely of communication but of social placement and discrimination. What he has not taken into account of course is the sense of social dislocation and its emotional toll, but this is to move away from the embassy ball itself. It is above all the actors, and especially Wendy Hiller, who fix this scene in the memory.

Hiller, a surprisingly small woman in real life, creates centre-screen an unforgettable image of statuesque beauty and elegance as she descends the embassy stairs, holding in tension with this image the strain its achievement has imposed – and is still imposing – on her. The director's skill is in the way he ensures that the audience shares with Higgins, Pickering and the mischievous Kaparthy (Esmé Percy – the character is called Nepommuck in the play) their focused attention on this social experiment as it is exposed to public scrutiny, its triumph climaxing in Kaparthy's verdict that, 'She is Hungarian, of the blood royal. She is a princess'. The other components of the scene, especially the grandeur of Laurence Irving's production design, its scale augmented by the use of huge mirrors, and the costumes of Worth and Schiaparelli, are all brilliantly captured by Harry Stradling's gracefully fluent camera as it tracks up and down stairs, cuts between Eliza and tensely watching faces, and swirls around the dance floor.

After the ball

The play's Act IV certainly provides the basis for the post-ballroom scene, but inevitably the scene gains a good deal when it comes in the wake of our having *witnessed* Eliza's triumph as distinct from merely hearing Higgins's and Pickering's account of the way she has carried it off. Compare Eliza's return in the shadow of Higgins's sitting-room with her grand entrance in the preceding ballroom. Cinema can make such juxtapositions wordlessly eloquent. Words of course take over as the men talk of *their* success, Higgins's fervent, 'Thank God it's over!' encapsulating the extent of his involvement – and the limitation of his vision. The camera makes clear his total ignoring of Eliza at this point. Hiller's Eliza sits perfectly still in the shadowy corner of the room as the men discuss *their* nervous strain, and how, for Higgins, the strain of 'putting the job through all these months... has told on me'. He has failed to understand that surmounting the cruelties of the class system is more than a linguistic matter, unlike Eliza who now asks in real emotional stress: 'What am I fit for? Where am I to go? What am I to do?'

In the ensuing confrontation between them – and Howard captures Higgins's self-centredness as acutely as Hiller nails Eliza's wretchedness – Asquith orchestrates a montage of close-ups that reinforces the angry verbal by-play, followed by a two-shot of them locked in conflict and then a longer take as Higgins stands above her, still asserting his superiority. She anguishes about where being 'made a lady' leaves her, and Hiller achieves real poignancy as she weeps at her predicament, a poignancy intensified as she strips herself of her adornments and creeps out, after a further montage of undressing and dressing before leaving, and finding lovesick Freddie on the street. In a further insert for the film, she is seen walking through the Covent Garden market early in the morning. When a flower-seller asks her to buy, Eliza, unrecognised, realises there is now no place for her. She has stubbed her toe irrevocably against the social order – while the incomparable Wendy Hiller went on to instant stardom.

The ending

Shaw had been opposed to the casting of Leslie Howard as Higgins on the grounds that, given Howard's star reputation, the public would be expecting the film to take on a romantic note that he as author had never intended. In fact, he had wanted the forceful character actor Cecil Trouncer to play the role to obviate all suggestion of tenderness (Trouncer appears in a small role as a policeman). Howard was also associate director on the film, so presumably had some influence. In the event, few people would agree with Shaw who wrote to Pascal during the filming, 'It is amazing how hopelessly wrong Leslie is', though he concedes, 'However, the public will like him and probably want him to marry Eliza, which is just what I don't want'.[13] Almost from the start, *Pygmalion* establishes between Higgins and Eliza a connection that, accustomed as audiences were/are to the idea of the starring pair moving towards some sort of coupledom by the final moments of the film, seems inevitably likely to surmount their extraordinary differences.

Donald Costello, in his study of Shaw and cinema, can only suggest 'What kind of hypnotic powers Pascal, Asquith and Howard used over Shaw... to approve the final ending of the film only the gods can now tell us.' And Shaw himself wrote about the ending some time after the film's preview, 'It is too inconclusive... to be worth making a fuss about'.[14] There may be a suggestion of Shaw's making the best of having his ending overthrown, but actually the film's last moments are so discreetly done that it's hard to imagine even Shaw being dissatisfied with them. It is perhaps not the tough, socially astringent idea he had in mind – that Eliza might marry Freddie and run a flower shop – but it is equally not a full-blown Hollywood-style finale complete with starry clinch. Back in Higgins's house, this time when Eliza returns she is in the light, not in the shadow as after the ball. Now she is there of her own volition and the film ends on a muted note of promise for their relationship. Not how the play ends, certainly, but aptly tentative rather than an all-stops-out romantic cliché.

Parents and others

I've been writing as if only Higgins and Eliza are significant in accounting for the film's interest, but it is worth picking out from the film's distinguished cast two actors who play the protagonists' parents, Marie Lohr as Mrs Higgins and Wilfred Lawson as Alfred Doolittle. The film follows the play's lead in bringing them together on Doolittle's wedding day in Mrs Higgins's drawing-room, Higgins having gone in pursuit of Eliza. Marie Lohr, who had a very long stage career, also made over three dozen films, usually as dignified upper-class types, but able to imbue this dignity with attractive warmth and beautiful comic timing, no doubt honed on West End stages. Here she presides over the conflict between her son and his Galatea – and over Eliza's re-meeting with her father, the ex-dustman now a morning-dressed philosopher about to make an honest woman of Eliza's mother.

As for Doolittle, the earlier scene between him and Higgins is a sparring match between equally matched opponents: Doolittle's cunning logic is a match for Higgins's erudition. Here, in Mrs Higgins's drawing-room, with marriage looming for him, we realise that Eliza is not the only one to end up out of her class. Doolittle arrives lamenting his lost happiness and the triumph of middle-class morality. Eliza fails to recognise him at first, recalling his similar failure with her in the earlier scene at Higgins's house. This kind of parallelism works very much to reinforce the film's narrative strength: here the contrast between the two occasions involving an unrecognised daughter or father, but often too in brief moments such as those showing Higgins on the stairs trying to bully someone into doing what he wants, while at the end of this later scene Eliza will be seen standing over him, slumped in a chair, signifying at least her moral superiority. Wilfred Lawson, who plays Doolittle with the ripest regard for his native cunning and rhetorical flourish, was a great character actor, who was only thirty-eight at the time of the film, but he'd already played the part on stage at twenty-seven.

The rest of the large cast was filled out largely with 'names' from the theatre: Jean Cadell (in films since 1912) as a doughty Mrs Pearce, brooking no nonsense from either employer or his protégée; beady-eyed Ivor Barnard as the suspicious bystander in the opening scene; Everley Gregg as snobbish Mrs Eynsford Hill (did editor David Lean remember her when he cast her as gossipy Dolly Messiter in *Brief Encounter*, seven years later?); the eccentric Esmé Percy, noted exponent of Shaw and elected president of the Shaw Society in 1949, as Higgins's leery, devious former pupil, who 'sees through' Eliza at the ball; and even the very small role of the ambassadress is taken by Violet Vanbrugh who had a fifty-year career on the London stage. Perhaps because Asquith is associated much with the adaptation of plays to screen and is often thought of as an actor's director, everyone seems to be given a real chance to register.

Conclusion

Not many films sustain our interest in so much *talk*, however brilliantly written and delivered. That *Pygmalion* does so is no doubt attributable, not just to a dazzling stage original, but also to the cinematic skills that are brought to bear in putting this talk before us. Just watch how, for instance, characters secure ascendancy as a result of how they are framed; how the camera places Eliza higher in the frame when she has come back to Higgins's rooms at the end, but on her own terms. The film was praised by filmmaker and critic Basil Wright for turning 'what might so easily have been a photographed stage play into something essentially filmic'.[15] Pascal's further brushes with Shaw on film were never as successful and it's tempting to think he needed those superb collaborators – before and behind the camera – who make *Pygmalion* such a notable *film*.

Notes

1 Quoted in Donald P. Costello, *The Serpent's Eye: Shaw and the Cinema* (Notre Dame and London: University of Notre Dame Press, 1965), p. 21.

2 Costello, *The Serpent's Eye*, p. 22.

3 Apart from an eleven-minute fragment depicting Sybil Thorndike in the cathedral scene from *St Joan* (1927).

4 He was a celebrated flying ace in World War One and one of the founders of the BBC.

5 'Wendy Hiller' in Brian McFarlane, *An Autobiography of British Cinema* (London: Methuen, 1997), p. 295. Interview conducted in June 1991.

6 'Harold French', McFarlane, *An Autobiography*, p. 212. Interview conducted in July 1990.

7 Valerie Pascal, *The Devil and His Disciple* (London: Michael Joseph, 1971), p. 9.

8 Quoted in Pascal, *The Devil and His Disciple*, p. 78.

9 'Wendy Hiller', McFarlane, *An Autobiography*, p. 295.

10 George Bernard Shaw, *Pygmalion* (London: Penguin, 1964), p. 65.

11 'Harold French', McFarlane, *An Autobiography*, p. 212.

12 R. J. Minney, *Puffin Asquith: A Biography* (London: Leslie Frewin Publishers, 1973), pp. 94, 95.

13 Quoted in Minney, *Puffin Asquith*, p. 98.

14 Costello, *The Serpent's Eye*, p. 68.

15 *The Spectator*, 14 October 1938.

3   Pulling together for
The Way Ahead (1944)

AN ARMY – A considerable body of men, armed, organised
and disciplined, to act together for purposes of warfare.

The key words of the *Encyclopedia Britannica*'s definition are 'to act
together' – at least as far as they apply to Carol Reed's famous wartime
film, *The Way Ahead*, which quotes the definition as its opening title
after the credits. It was held at the time by some military personnel that
it was too late in the war for a film about the need for diverse individuals
to act together in the greater interest. Given that it was finally released
in June 1944, there were perhaps some grounds for such objections.
Sixty-odd years later that is of course irrelevant and what we're left with
is a brilliantly made 'war film' that evokes a period and ways of thinking
that seem almost to belong to a lost world.

Back then

British cinema of the 1930s was not often closely allied to the day-to-day
concerns of everyday lives. Its staples included film versions of West
End plays, especially of the famous Aldwych farces which look pretty
stiff and stagy on screen; numerous crime thrillers, about thirty of them
adapted from the popular fictions of Edgar Wallace; musicals set in
mythical European kingdoms; and, on a larger scale and, at the prestige
end of production, Alexander Korda's imperial adventures and the witty
thrillers of Alfred Hitchcock. As for realism, it was largely a lost cause:
the films of the music hall stars, Gracie Fields and George Formby, hugely

popular at the time, were among the few that placed working-class lives at the centre of their plots. Otherwise, plot synopses of 1930s British films reveal an extraordinary preoccupation with the doings of the wealthy and the titled. It's hard to be certain to whom these films were meant to appeal, but there seems to be evidence that Hollywood films, much more democratic in spirit, were more popular than the home-grown variety.

The other aspect of 1930s cinema, apart from the commercial arm, was the documentary film movement, led by John Grierson, and dedicated to putting on screen authentic pictures of life as it was lived by ordinary people. This movement, concerned with matters such as housing problems, addressed aspects of life remote from the world of so much commercial British cinema of the decade. During the war, these two strands, previously having little to do with each other, became intertwined to produce some of the most notable films of the early 1940s and to give a new lease of life to British film production. In the process the result was, many would claim, the finest hours in the history of British cinema.

The Way Ahead is a shining example of the ways in which documentary strategies and ethos infiltrated the fiction film during the war. There was a great deal of actual documentary filmmaking during the war, essentially for propaganda purposes, but I am more concerned here with how its influence made itself felt in films intended for entertainment. There was, too, an increasing sense that 'entertainment' was more valuable for purveying important ideas and attitudes than the more overt propaganda documentaries. Films such as *...one of our aircraft is missing* (1942, d. Michael Powell, Emeric Pressburger), *Millions Like Us* (1943, d. Frank Launder, Sidney Gilliat), *The Gentle Sex* (1943, d. Leslie Howard, Maurice Elvey), *Nine Men* (1943, d. Harry Watt) *Waterloo Road* (1945, d. Sidney Gilliat) and, above all, *In Which We Serve* (1942) bore out the wisdom of such thinking.

The way to *The Way Ahead*

The commercial and critical success of *In Which We Serve* led to a demand for a film which would do for the Army what the Noël Coward–David Lean film had done for the Navy. This 1942 film told the story of *HMS Kelly*, Lord Mountbatten's destroyer, which provided the basis for a celebration of the naval defence of Britain, while the Powell-Pressburger film, *...one of our aircraft is missing*, brought similar credit to the RAF in the same year. In the following year, Ealing Studios made *San Demetrio, London*, the stirring account of how the crew of a crippled tanker re-boarded it after a German attack and brought it safely back to harbour. It is against the background of such films that *The Way Ahead* is set. It is a less obvious 'flag-waver' than *In Which We Serve*; it is less 'documentary' than *San Demetrio, London*. It is enough to propose now that a film suggesting how ordinary men were turned into efficient soldiers, just as its predecessors showed men doing their jobs at sea, seemed timely. There was also an echo perhaps of *The Gentle Sex* in which a disparate group of young women was trained for the women's army. This kind of film, partly propaganda, partly reassurance for the public, was very much in the air in the early 1940s.

So the seed was there, but the immediate precursor of *The Way Ahead* was a short film called *The New Lot*, 'made in 1942 and generally assumed to have been "lost" until a print turned up in India last year [1996]'.[1] It subsequently attracted a large audience when it was shown at the Imperial War Museum, but it remains otherwise largely unseen. *The New Lot* was a forty-minute training film, made for the Army Kinematograph Service but never released. It seems to have grown from the perception of the Directorate of Army Psychiatry that there was serious lack of morale and self-esteem among those conscripted to the Army. 'The idea was to make something that would make disgruntled new recruits understand that primary training, while tough, had a real purpose.'[2]

It involved some of the same personnel who would work on *The Way Ahead*. One of these was the author Eric Ambler, who co-wrote the screenplay for *The New Lot* with Peter Ustinov. In his autobiography, Ambler recalls that, by the middle of 1942, 'The prevailing mood among the new intakes was becoming one of fatalistic bloody-mindedness. The psychiatrists wanted a film made specially for showing to these new intakes.'[3] When the film was shown to an audience of high-ranking military types, it met a mainly hostile reception, with claims that it showed the recruits as grumblers. The genesis and fate of *The New Lot* has been extensively canvassed in scholarly and popular sources. In one of the latter, Peter Ustinov recalled nearly fifty years later that it was 'based on the idea of a group of new recruits, who got to know each other while they learned the techniques of discipline and so on. Eventually they went to see a commercial film (a mock one) on their day off, in which Robert Donat, being extremely funny, led a charge in the 1914 war and was silhouetted on the skyline; and they all roared so much with laughter they were asked to leave the cinema. They realised how stupid that film was and that they were now different, they were trained.'[4]

Not everyone in the Army disapproved of *The New Lot* as strenuously as those who condemned it as 'subversive stuff bordering on the bolshy'[5] and there was a move afoot to produce a feature film that would cover some of the same ground, but would be more optimistic in tone. The key figures at this point are Captain Carol Reed, Lieutenant Eric Ambler and Private Peter Ustinov. The Army favoured Ambler (respected novelist, particularly of crime and espionage fiction) as the most serious of the three and wanted him to prepare the draft of the screenplay without the intervention of the other two, but inevitably they arranged meetings. Nicholas Wapshott's excellent biography of Carol Reed, one of the key names of 1940s British cinema, gives a full account of this stage of preparations for *The Way Ahead*, including the business of getting Reed out of the Army to 'make films of national importance'.[6] The film was to be made by a commercial film company, Two Cities, run by the Italian *émigré* Filippo Del Giudice, and as part of the arrangement Reed committed himself to some later filming for the Ministry of Information, which he did; his next film was the renowned documentary *The True Glory* (1945), which he co-directed with Garson Kanin.

I don't want to go into all the detailed negotiations that attended the making of this film, but just to suggest that, though it was made as a commercial undertaking, it was done with the approval of the Army, partly gained by Major David Niven's willingness to star in it. As a soldier in a respected regiment, he had the ear of Army brass, and his standing as an international film name was a guarantee of the film at least being seen. The Ministry of Information had long recognised the value of film as a medium of propaganda, especially if it was contained in a compelling fictional story. Official cooperation took such varied forms as allowing Ambler to have work space in the War Office in central London and granting permission for location-shooting in Libya, where the US Army also cooperated by providing the necessary explosions for the film's final sequences. But enough of the background and on to the film's actually getting made.

Documentary and fiction

I mentioned the location-shooting in North Africa. This is perhaps the most obvious way in which the strategies of documentary filmmaking are felt in *The Way Ahead*, but in a more general way there is a kind of realism, unusual in pre-war British film, in the settings and photography for the film as a whole, whether on location or in sequences staged in the studios. There was a good deal of exterior filming at Aldershot and on Salisbury Plain and this no doubt accounts in part for the realistic 'look' of the film. Further, Guy Green's cinematography is notably unflashy, often achieving a reality that reminds one of the newsreels of the period.

For a film whose narrative trajectory is described by the welding together of a bunch of raw recruits into a fighting unit, there is the whiff of documentary about the way the details of their training are presented. We are shown enough of the rigorous processes of the training to be convinced of its arduousness, recalling the interest taken by the documentary film movement in the actualities of work. The actor Raymond Huntley, who plays Davenport in the film, recalled forty-five years later: 'I've never forgotten that assault course! We did it all, no doubles or anything then.'[7] This perhaps accounts for its look of the real thing. As well, though, the film's screenplay is not geared to an artificial plot-line in which unwilling civilians are licked into shape prior to revealing themselves as heroes in the film's finale. Instead, the film, having shown the processes of training, then takes its rookies off to the scene of the action and lets us watch the extent to which that training has equipped them. Unlike many war films, including Hollywood jobs starring the likes of Errol Flynn, *The Way Ahead* is concerned with a group rather than with a dominant individual. Even though Niven is the star name, he really has a role scarcely more developed than any of the others. And, in a last gesture to the film's sober documentary-style intentions, there is no attempt to whip up a romantic interest which would have been common practice at the time, and the women's roles, as we shall see, are little more than sketches.

What does the film show?

This is a film with a more than usually complex production background, but interesting as this is it doesn't account for why I (or perhaps anyone) would value it so highly. The point is that its intrinsic interest is so closely bound up with the context of the times and that its underlying narrative – the welding of a group of raw recruits into a potentially effective fighting team – was so firmly related to the propaganda needs of the day that it is more important than usual to sketch in this background. It's not just 'narrative' procedures that belong so tenaciously to the period but, as well, the thematic intention of revealing the Army as something more than a soulless war machine: it is presented as an organisation with concern for its personnel. I admire the way the film, in the Ambler-Ustinov screenplay and Reed's direction, is so redolent of key elements of the period in which it was made and yet continues to compel the viewer's attention all these decades later.

Consensus and class
The issue of wartime consensus is too obvious to need detailed treatment here, but it is an inescapable aspect of those films referred to above. From whatever background men and women came, once they entered upon their involvement in the war effort they were inevitably shown to be drawn together in a common cause that transcended their differences of peacetime class and profession. It's not that such distinctions are done away with – officers will generally still talk in posher accents than conscripts and other ranks – but that they can be put aside when more pressing matters, such as the country's survival, are at issue. In *Millions Like Us*, snobbish socialite Jennifer (Anne Crawford) will learn to work in a plane factory side by side with a girl who sleeps in her underwear, and to fall for the rough-hewn foreman, Charlie (Eric Portman). In John Boulting's *Journey Together* (1945), working-class RAF corporal David (Richard Attenborough) and nicely-spoken university graduate John (Jack Watling) become friends as they train to become wartime pilots. Even in *In Which We Serve*, the captain of the 'Torrin' (Noël Coward) and his men, officers and others, cling to the same life-raft after their ship has been bombed, while the film's flashbacks fill in their respective civilian-life associations.

In *The Way Ahead*, this sort of pattern is followed, and in my view more subtly and persuasively than in any of the others of its kind. The film overtly raises the issue of class. It does this by first showing the origins of its seven key recruits in their civilian occupations and, in some cases, their relationships. None of them is shown to have come from an upper-class background, though the accents of the upper classes are heard later on among some of the officers (Reginald Tate, Leo Genn). The recruits include a rent collector, a travel agent, a stoker of the House of Commons' boilers, a car salesman, a store department manager and his assistant, and a Scottish farmer. If the film was to appeal widely, it needed to provide points of identification for large numbers of people.

There appear to be subtle gradations of class among the recruits and the film is wise enough not to suggest that the experience of war does away with the ingrained class distinctions of British life, and it may well be dangerous for an Australian to be venturing into such sensitive territory. However, class has always been the ever-interesting topic of British cinema (and literature?), and the relationship between Davenport (Huntley) and Parsons (Hugh Burden) suggests that its discriminations are likely to be upheld at any point on the scale. Huntley specialised in wintry-faced officials of various kinds, pitched between pedantry and pomposity, and this mix serves him well as Davenport, head of 'Garden Furniture' in a large store. Our first glimpse of him in his office is preceded by a brief scene between the meek Parsons and his wife (Eileen Erskine) at breakfast, he having just received his call-up papers, though Mr Davenport had told him he'd be 'safe' from this. Reed then dissolves to Davenport sanctimoniously intoning to Parsons: 'You must realise there's a war on; only key men are deferred now', smugly sure that he is a 'key man'.

In a quietly comic touch, when Parsons leaves, Davenport finds notice of his own call-up papers, and this subdued comic note is retained when the next dissolve reveals the two men sharing a compartment on their way to their military destination. Davenport, as if in a show of democratic feeling, suggests they should 'forget any differences of status' now they are in the Army, while also considering it 'thoughtless of the powers-that-be to allow such a situation to arise.' There is a world of inane class feeling at work in these two brief scenes, and part of the film's triumph is to convince us that the Army just might reduce such feeling.

Pulling together

These two and the other five recruits, all disparate in their work and class backgrounds, are revealed, through the medium of their Army training, to be gradually learning to pull together, sinking their crasser differences in the interests of consensus and the common good. *The Way Ahead* certainly doesn't offer a radical critique of the class system, but it does show how its potential for divisiveness may be set aside, or transcended, in a time of crisis, and, in doing so, it may have helped to sow seeds of permanent change. If men of all walks of life could cooperate so well in war, might not this spirit be continued in peacetime?

Let's look briefly at this diverse group thrown together as conscripts, and see what aspects of their civilian lives might be up for change. They are preceded by a caption, 'March 1939', and two old Chelsea Pensioners (John Ruddock and A. Bromley Davenport), veterans of the Duke of Glendon's regiment, the DOGs, talking about the prospect of war, and wondering gloomily, 'Where are the men to fight it? Where are they?' In their ultra-conservative way, they believe that 'Chaps now can't fight... It's all this education and machinery and going to the pictures' that have sapped the nation's strength. This is a simple but effective way of introducing the recruits, and the film will return to these two ancients from time to time to offer a commentary on the course of the action.

Brewer (Stanley Holloway), who stokes the boilers at the Houses of Parliament, is first glimpsed complaining about the late-night parliamentary sittings. Beck (Leslie Dwyer), the travel agent, with the commercial interests of his firm no doubt in mind, is seen telling customers planning overseas travel that there's no danger of war. The next dissolve reveals rent-collector Lloyd (James Donald) fending off irate complaints from a tenant on grounds of the possibility of war. 'We can't all be thinking of ourselves in times like these' he tells her complacently. These three, Brewer, Beck and Lloyd, are thus revealed in the practice of various kinds of self-interest, as in their ways are Parsons, who'd expected Mr Davenport to keep him out of the call-up, and the self-satisfied Davenport himself. These five come together on the train to Crewe, where, in the railway buffet, they are joined by car-salesman Stainer (Jimmy Hanley), half-cut and raving drunkenly about how he 'can't stand people telling [him] what to do', and the quiet Scot, Luke (John Laurie). Observing this 'new lot' as they go about their last hours of self-concerned civilian life (Davenport complains about 'appalling service') is a sergeant, Fletcher (William Hartnell), of whom they will shortly see a great deal more.

David Niven and Captain Perry
Just before the train is ready to leave, the eighth of the Army newcomers on whom the film will focus rushes in to buy cigarettes. He is Jim Perry (Niven) who has been at Dunkirk and done an Officers Training Course. This is not our first glimpse of Perry. In the sixth of the film's (mainly short) sequences, he is found in the garage where he works, serving a customer who is complaining about having only had his car for six months and now there's a danger of war and a shortage of petrol. The garage proprietor (Raymond Lovell, who played many a cravatted villain in post-war British cinema) warns Jim 'not to start looking for

5   James Donald (Lloyd) and David Niven (Jim Perry).

trouble', as Jim gets into his Territorial Army uniform when his wife comes in to drive him off.

It is important to the film that Perry is established in this way: he is not of 'the officer class', but a man who works modestly for a living. The significance of this will be clear in several later sequences. When Lloyd complains about Sergeant Fletcher to Perry, Lloyd is able to speak openly to Perry and to leave it to him to follow up the complaint. Initially the recruits are hostile to Fletcher's barking of orders, but the film makes clear in a scene shortly after, when the officers are fraternising with the sergeants, that his bark indeed conceals a real understanding of his new lot and his real hopes for them. Perry is not presented as an aloof officer. The film has been at pains to root him in the ordinary working life of the garage, and, when he and the recruits meet informally at the home of Mrs Gillingham (Mary Jerrold) who offers them tea and a hot bath on their day off, residual awkwardness gradually breaks down. In this way, perhaps, the film is anticipating a post-war egalitarian ideal, and the Army is presented as a potentially democratising force, a creator of brotherly understanding.

In all this thematic intention, if that is what it is, and narrative development, David Niven's function is significant. He was already established as a Hollywood star, with a certain box-office drawing power and, as noted above, useful connections with the military. Later in his career, he seemed to perfect a somewhat bland upper-class insouciance; in *The Way Ahead*, however, he projects the nice working guy who is attracted enough to the idea of soldiering to take a proactive approach to the coming conflict but who retains a convincing common touch. When the platoon, led by Lloyd (now Lance-Corporal), gives way to selfishness and laziness and as a result messes up a military exercise, Perry ticks them off and reminds them of the regiment's long history. Niven is able to pull off this rare 'star moment' without losing the essential humanity of the character of the garage mechanic who has become an officer.

Writing of Niven's efforts in setting up and developing the film, his biographer Sheridan Morley notes that, though 'It was the only one of his ninety-plus films of which he could genuinely be said to be the creator as well as the leading actor... Yet in the 500 pages of his collected memoirs it rates rather less than four lines'.[8] Niven recorded that it 'was not only a huge public success but for ten years after the war was used as a training film at Sandhurst'.[9] It was a shrewd touch on the part of the screenwriters to show the Perry character as one not born to superiority but as one who has worked to attain his position.

Other ranks

With the exception of Perry and brief glimpses of other officers, the film essentially concentrates on the experiences of the seven conscripts, as we note the changes in their attitudes from early disgruntlement to some recognition of what is expected of them and why. This is not to suggest the effect is too schematic and predictable, because the ways in which the recruits change is subtly enough done to avoid such criticism. They are played by a bevy of British character actors who bring them to life in a series of short scenes. Parsons, caught trying to go AWOL to help protect his wife from bullying hire-purchase officials, is made to feel that, in the Army, however little you might want to be there, you are not alone. Parsons is played with touching exactness by Hugh Burden, and his quiet growth in stature is complemented by the way in which his former superior, Davenport, played by Raymond Huntley, loses some of his smug pomposity. Jimmy Hanley, specialist in prole heroes in British films, registers convincingly the diminishing of Stainer's bragging conceit. James Donald, who would go on to play a number of quietly authoritative types, ensures our belief in Lloyd's development from being too sure of himself to becoming a reliable NCO, knowledgeable about the regiment's history and ready to defend it to a friend he meets when on leave. Cast in a more middle-class role than usual, Leslie Dwyer makes an amiable figure of the travel-agent Beck who has his moment – as, in fact, all these actors do – at the camp concert when a visiting colonel (A. E. Matthews) steals his thunder by reciting the only poem Beck knows. We know least about Luke, the farmer, but John Laurie's distinctive Scottish accent and angular face keep him clearly before us, and we do see him at work on his farm during his pre-embarkation leave. And best-known of them all, Stanley Holloway hones his familiar persona of working-man bluffness as the stoker Brewer, whose mildly know-all tendency is punctured somewhat by Mrs Gillingham's discreet comment about how he doesn't really understand how her boiler works.

I've listed all the recruits and the actors who play them because the character acting in British films has always seemed to me one of its chief glories. Perhaps it's the fact that usually these supporting players are given only brief moments in which to establish themselves that one feels a kind of concentration in their work that stars, with more time and space to develop their roles, don't need. *The Way Ahead* thrives on the interplay of these actors, who may be more familiar as faces than as names to filmgoers – and that's another reason why I wanted to name them here.

Waiting women

Women don't get much of a look-in here. There is a short sequence in which the wives of Perry, Parsons and Brewer, as members of the DOGs Women's Committee, discuss the latest news of the war and of their husband's chances of a stripe. The democratic spirit of the film is unobtrusively reinforced here with the officer's wife, Mrs Perry, easily at home with the other two. Given that Mrs Perry is played by the radiantly lovely Penelope Dudley Ward, who had all manner of posh connections in real life, this is a tribute to the playing, and the other two – Eileen Erskine (as Mrs Parsons) and Esma Cannon (Mrs Brewer) – offer nicely differentiated cameos of domestic meekness.

There are only three other women involved: Marjorie Gillingham (Renee Asherson), who serves on the mobile canteen and invites the men to tea at her aunt's house; the shrewdly kind old aunt (Mary Jerrold); and, most memorable, Tessie O'Shea, playing herself as an ENSA singer at another camp concert. This latter sequence is symptomatic of the film's over-all aim as it shows all ranks joining in singing a robust chorus to 'If you were the only girl in the world'. The ideal of consensus is most vividly conveyed in this moment of unselfconscious forgetting of individuality in preference to the group spirit at large.

To conclude: the beginning

The troopship carrying the DOGs to North Africa is struck by depth charges, and there is a symbolically crucial moment when Sergeant Fletcher gets his leg stuck on the damaged ship. In a moment of consensual effort, the Sergeant is released by the combined efforts of his Captain and a ranker, Luke as it happens, pulling together. The order is given to abandon ship and we see the conscripts when they fetch up in a village café run by Rispoli (Ustinov), who is not at all welcoming. Eventually sounds of gunfire are heard, shells explode near the village, and Perry and his men go into action. The film ends with the recruits heading off into the smoke of battle in North Africa, the men appearing one at a time as they approach the enemy lines, with fixed bayonets and no ammunition, but – the inference is – equipped with an appropriate fighting spirit. This is not the sort of film in which we expect to see the characters involved in heroic actions and poses. They have been trained now to go into battle and this is where the film ends, with the final title given as THE BEGINNING, while the elderly pensioners back at the Royal Chelsea catch up on the doings of the DOGs. They have had the answer to the question they posed about the war in the film's opening sequence: 'Where are the men to fight in it?'

Notes

1 Ben Shephard, 'A bunch of loony-bin doctors', *Times Literary Supplement*, 7 June 1996, 18.

2 S. P. MacKenzie, *British War Films 1939–45* (London: Hambledon Continuum, 2001, reprinted 2006), p. 114.

3 Eric Ambler, *Here Lies: An Autobiography* (1985) (Glasgow: Fontana Collins, 1986), p. 184.

4 'Peter Ustinov' in Brian McFarlane, *An Autobiography of British Cinema* (London: Methuen, 1997), p. 586.

5 Ambler, *Here Lies*, p. 195.
6 Nicholas Wapshott, *The Man Between: A Biography of Carol Reed* (London: Chatto & Windus, 1990), p. 163.
7 'Raymond Huntley', McFarlane, *An Autobiography*, p. 311.
8 Sheridan Morley, *The Other Side of the Moon: David Niven* [1985] (Sevenoaks, Kent: Coronet Books, 1986), p. 178.
9 David Niven, *The Moon's a Balloon* [1971] (London: Coronet Books, 1972), p. 230.

4   The long-lasting
Brief Encounter (1945)

It seems that anyone who has ever written about British cinema has had to come to terms with *Brief Encounter*. Why? I wonder. And why do I need to include it here, if it has been so much discussed elsewhere? My answer is that it seems to me almost the quintessential British film in all sorts of ways, to the point where I felt that no book about twenty British films to cherish could afford to leave it out. When I was being interviewed a few years back in connection with a book of mine on British cinema I was asked if I had a favourite British film. This was impossible to answer off the top of my head, so I fudged by saying, 'Not sure about a favourite, but the most British film ever seems to me to be *Brief Encounter*.' That is, it's hard to imagine its having been made anywhere else – and, perhaps, by British I really mean 'English'.

Does it still work?

Obviously it does. Just think of the number of times it is 'quoted' in later films. One of the most recent occurs in a brief moment in *Brick Lane* (2007), set in a house in London's East End, when the television is playing and no one is actually watching. A black-and-white film is screening and it is a scene from *Brief Encounter*, in which Fred, the prosaic husband of Laura (Celia Johnson) is asking her to turn down the music a little just after she has recalled the moment when Alec (Trevor Howard) has told her, 'I love you so'. It is all quite fleeting but this quotation subtly points us to how we should be reading Sarah Gavron's touching film in which a Bangladeshi woman, married to a kind, dull older man, falls tremulously in love with a young sewing-machine repairman. This unobtrusive moment reminded me of how often *Brief Encounter* has been called into play in other films, including, among others *A Touch of Class* (1973) and *Truly Madly Deeply* (1990), in which key extracts are glimpsed, and *The History Boys* (2006), in which two schoolboy characters act out an affectionate parody of the movie's ending. Is it the archetypal film-rendering of the unexpected love that surprises the people in *Brick Lane*, a love they turn away from, as Laura and Alec did sixty-two years earlier?[1]

Another small bit of evidence for its durability came my way in the 1990s. When I was regularly teaching a course on British cinema in this decade, I always included it and was invariably impressed with how well it was received by students all born several decades after the film's release. I was prepared for an element of cynicism, maybe even derision at how much things had changed. But the only hint of this occurred when they laughed as poor distraught Laura wanders the night streets and her voice-over says (as if to her husband), 'Oh Fred, I know you disapprove of women smoking in the street'. Twenty years later, of course, the situation would have changed so that *anyone* smoking in the street would be an object of disapproval, or worse.

I want to look more closely at why the film still works when the 1974 remake so abjectly failed to, despite its high-powered stars, perhaps *because* of its high-powered stars – Sophia Loren and Richard Burton. Could anyone possibly believe in a drama of rejected adultery starring these two: she an international sex symbol and he one of the most publicised off-screen Lotharios of the era? Their publicity must surely have got in the way of our accepting them as middle-class suburbanites whose lives are invaded by unlooked-for passion. Celia Johnson and, especially, Trevor Howard, were scarcely known as film stars in 1945. She had appeared in three films – *In Which We Serve* (1942), *Dear Octopus* (1943), and, this time starring, *This Happy Breed* (1944) – but Howard had had only an uncredited bit in *The Way Ahead* (1944) and a small role in *The Way to the Stars* (1945). At the time of *Brief Encounter* they were more or less unknown quantities to cinemagoers, but this film gave them what is probably (to use that much misused word) iconic status. Celebrated American director Robert Altman claimed that it was, 'The first film that made the difference in my mind between a movie and a film... This girl, Celia Johnson, was not pretty. She wore those sensible shoes. And suddenly I'm in love with her.'[2] A tribute indeed.

6   Celia Johnson (Laura Jesson) and Trevor Howard (Alec Harvey).

Brief Encounter and the roaring 40s of British cinema

Mention of those other popular films of the 1940s leads me to consider
Brief Encounter in that context. Wartime and immediate post-war British
film-making was a high point in the history of the national cinema.
Indeed, there is even a book which takes its title from this 'fact': Charles
Drazin's *The Finest Years: British Cinema of the 1940s*, which evokes
the period with warmth and precision, and of course has a chapter on
David Lean.[3] Lean, producer Anthony Havelock-Allan, and cinematographer Ronald Neame began an association on *In Which We Serve*
which was formalised as Cineguild in 1944, with the purpose of filming
some of Noël Coward's plays. *This Happy Breed* came first, followed by

Blithe Spirit and then, most successfully, the one-act play *Still Life* was transformed into *Brief Encounter*.

Cineguild accepted an invitation to join J. Arthur Rank's Independent Producers, a consortium that gave producers a guarantee of production funding and of distribution, but most importantly gave them remarkable creative freedom. Under the Cineguild banner, David Lean not only brought Coward to the screen but also went on to produce the two benchmark Dickens adaptations, *Great Expectations* (1946) and *Oliver Twist* (1948). Until it ceased production in 1950, Cineguild acquired a reputation for high quality, disproportionate to its slender output, and, along with other production companies operating under the Independent Producers umbrella, accounted for a good deal of the prestige of this major period of British cinema.

If Gainsborough Films' *The Wicked Lady* (1945) might be seen as the apogee of commercial success, *Brief Encounter*, along with such others as *Henry V* (1945) or the Dickens films or *The Winslow Boy* (1948), represents the 'quality' cinema of the period. Whereas Margaret Lockwood, as the eponymous wicked lady, represented melodramatically a move towards a more liberated female image, Celia Johnson's Laura can be made to suggest the reinstating of a more conventional one: that of the woman safely back in the home. The fact that these two films were released in the same month (December 1945) makes the comparison almost irresistible. But while Gainsborough was making music at the box-office, though often critically (and snobbishly) derided, Cineguild was making critical reputations for British film, at home and abroad. Critics generally fell approvingly on *Brief Encounter*, even if, as Lean was later quoted as saying, 'it did not "go" with the great new and enlightened British audience.'[4] This banner decade of British filming was much associated with literary and theatrical sources, but the decade also saw the best of British films attaining a new level of *cinematic* fluency, and this is one of the strengths of *Brief Encounter*.

David Lean and filming Noël Coward

Lean had been perhaps the most notable editor in British cinema of the 1930s and it was said that, though credited only as editor, he also directed most of Gabriel Pascal's production of *Major Barbara* (1941). His first director's credit is on the Noël Coward tribute to the merchant navy, *In Which We Serve*. Decades later one of its stars, John Mills,

7   Celia Johnson (Laura Jesson), Avis Scott (waitress)
                 and Trevor Howard (Alec Harvey).

recalled that Lean 'essentially... directed the picture even though he
and Noël are credited as co-directors. Part of Noël's genius was that
he could judge when to leave it to someone else, as he did with David.'[5]
On the next two Coward adaptations, *This Happy Breed* and *Blithe
Spirit*, Lean has the solo directing credit. I'd claim that some of the best
moments in *This Happy Breed* are the result of Lean's cutting loose from
Coward, and that he seems comparatively hamstrung into staginess by
Blithe Spirit but, with *Brief Encounter*, he is at once fully master of the
screen's possibilities and of his own craft.

The opening credit of *Blithe Spirit* announces: 'Noël Coward's *Blithe
Spirit*. A Noël Coward–Cineguild Production'. Such an announcement
also ushers in *Brief Encounter*, but seems much less appropriate here.
This is primarily *Lean's* film, from the undercurrent of urgency in the
Rachmaninoff piano concerto on the soundtrack and the opening
*noir*ish shot of the train passing through the station, even though it
is well known that Coward wrote extra scenes over and above those
contained in his long one-acter, *Still Life*. The play no longer reads

well – what may once have seemed the last word in naturalism now seems calculated and constipated. First, confining the action to a single set involves too much explanation of what has led up to each of its five scenes, and feels contrived. Second, its linear presentation is less narratively inviting than the film's flashback approach which plunges us into the heart of the matter. And third, a kind of drabness settles over the series of dialogue exchanges which, in *Brief Encounter*, are made urgent by the film's cinematography, editing and sound.

In Lean's adaptation of *Blithe Spirit*, the changes of scene serve little purpose other than to break up the monotony of the single set, whereas in *Brief Encounter* the film's mobility among places enriches our sense of Laura's life. Primarily, but not exclusively, it establishes her in her middle-class home with comfortable, decent, crossword-solving husband (and Cyril Raymond's contribution to the film in this role is significant in its good-natured ordinariness), children and largely unseen servant. Seeing her in this context, we can enter more fully into her conflict when a wayward passion threatens all she has taken for granted. As well as home, the film shows her shopping, changing her library book, lunching modestly at the Kardomah, walking confidently in the streets by day, later emotionally lost in them in the dark and rain. And the scenes directly relating to her 'affair' with Alec mean so much more for not merely being *talked* about but seen: the cinema, the posh restaurant, the jaunts to the country and the boating escapade. Both what she's tempted by and what she's in danger of losing take on an actuality that the play can barely suggest. The moment in Stephen Lynn's flat, the turning point for the would-be lovers, gives immediacy to the daring and furtiveness, and the dingy escape. The credit for how intelligently the film has expanded the play's setting and action may be at source Coward's attention to the screenplay, but it is also essentially a matter of Lean's thinking in cinematic terms. (It may be worth noting that in 2000 a stage version calling itself *Brief Encounter* was based on the film, not on Coward's original.[6])

Even more important to its success as a film is the way in which the narrative starts almost at the end of Laura and Alec's 'affair'. The quiet couple in the corner of the railway buffet while the porter and the woman behind the counter exchange words, his bantering and hers fake-refined, are joined by Dolly, a chattering friend who ruins their last moments together. The camera aligns Laura and Alec sitting side by side, faces mute with suppressed unhappiness, so that they are front-on to the viewer, while Dolly yaps in quarter-profile. Immediately, the film

8   Celia Johnson (Laura Jesson) and Trevor Howard (Alec Harvey).

sets up questions in our minds: who is this couple? why do they appear so miserable? Our attention to them is focused by the comic badinage of Albert and Myrtle and by the non-stop superficiality of Dolly's chatter. We wonder how Laura and Alec came to this point of unhappiness, and we count on the rest of the film to provide the answers. The main narrative, both *shown* and *told* (in Laura's voice-over), is revealed in a series of flashbacks, with her remembering the preceding months as she sits with unimaginative Fred in their 'library'. And as one writer has said: 'the film is her imaginary confession to her husband as he sits opposite her on the sofa... but it is all the more eloquent for being ultimately unspoken.'[7] The way in which this is put before us allows us, too, to wonder how much is a dream, a fantasising on Laura's part as suggested by her glamorous, if conventional, imaginings, and this ambiguous quality, so far from detracting from its narrative power, makes the film more intensely moving. If it has been largely a dream, that does not make it less crucial as a commentary on her life.

The resources of the cinema are exercised with an imaginative flair that neither of Lean's previous Coward adaptations had exhibited.

Take for instance such apparently simple strategies as the way the camera closes in on Laura's face when she sits at home reflecting bleakly on what has happened to her or at the moment when she knows she's irrevocably in love. Or the tilted close-up of Laura as she rushes out on to the platform in the film's penultimate sequence, a simple but persuasive strategy for suggesting a mind in turmoil. Or the disjunction between sound and image, when, for instance, Dolly's lips are snapping open and shut in close-up and Laura's voice-over is heard saying 'I wish you were a wise kind friend'. Lean again and again with effortless authority renders such kinds of emotion through means that belong entirely to the cinema. And the stage could scarcely match that great overhead shot of Laura wandering the wet night streets until she fetches up near the aggressive war memorial statue where a policeman greets her.

Some of the contemporary critical responses managed not to mention Lean's name. C. A. Lejeune in *The Observer* found it 'the most mature work Mr Coward has yet prepared for the screen', while Dilys Powell in *The Sunday Times*, attributed its 'breadth of sympathy' to Coward's participation, calling it 'his best film', without so much as mentioning Lean. Nor does waspish James Agate, who simply refers to it as 'Noël Coward's *Brief Encounter*', going on to describe Coward as 'very nearly a man of genius, and a man of near-genius should have done better.'[8] Well, times and reviewers have changed, but it still needs stressing that this is above all Lean's film. He and the Coward of the clipped, inhibited emotional utterance seem not to have been made for each other, and when he turned next to Dickens he would be in the presence of a very different sensibility.

Love and lies

Back in those pre-feminist days of the 1940s, the American critic James Agee, though liking the film, felt nevertheless that 'the same story... is told once or twice in every issue of every magazine for housewives',[9] without considering that *that* might have had its own significance. In fact it's hard to see what Agee's comment really means. At *all* levels of fiction, there are examples of people surprising themselves by falling in love in inconvenient situations – outside their marriages for instance. *Brief Encounter* is a story of ordinary middle-class people – decent, conventional, likable – who are indeed surprised, unsettled, to find themselves in love in just such an awkward place. The plot is developed through a series of meetings in commonplace venues such as a railway buffet or a café, settings at odds with the emotional upheaval they are experiencing. The film records their touching sense of quiet pain and pleasure at being together in the scene in the boatshed, their sense of guilt at the ways in which they are inevitably deceiving spouses to whom they are devoted, their movement to what Laura calls 'the edge of a precipice', the moment of failed adultery at Alec's friend's flat, and their decision not to see each other again, or to correspond once they have made the break.

Sixty or seventy years later they could possibly have gone off together without necessarily losing the audience's sympathies, but in 1945 (let alone pre-war when the film is unobtrusively set) the humiliating moments at Stephen's flat and its aftermath are enough to indicate to them where their loyalties lie. I believe the film still works today despite the radical changes that have taken place in sexual behaviour in the intervening decades. Social conventions have certainly altered out of recognition, but desires – and the potential tumult of discovering love – are as real as ever. They simply come up against different conventions, and the change in socially acceptable conventions since 1945 need not, in any case, detract from the film's power to move us.

A Freudian view of the Laura-Alec relationship would no doubt see the id, the unbidden impulses, as being repressed by long obedience to the strictures of the superego, all those aspects of the barely conscious, learned ethical code which for the most part enable us to keep desires in some sort of workable relation with reality, with the functioning ego. But we don't need this kind of psychoanalytic approach to enable us to understand how Alec and Laura are tied by claims of family, of fidelity to their spouses, and by what their whole middle-class background has built into their thinking and feeling. Neither by temperament nor background are they likely to engage in a casual sexual liaison, and Stephen's unexpected return seems like an inevitable intervention to reclaim them for the respectability of their middle-class lives.

This is not, though, to underestimate the kind and degree of pain this involves for them. The film makes plain the guilt, the pain caused by lies and deceit, that the would-be lovers experience. They actually talk of whether the lies and the furtiveness are worth a brief moment's happiness, and the shock of decent people's lying still shakes one. In the recurring voice-over, Laura says, 'It's awfully easy to lie when you're trusted implicitly'. If she did not feel the shame she does in deceiving her husband, we should not have a drama and we should not feel for her pain. And when she wonders whether Alec will tell his wife about the nice woman he met and went to the pictures with, she says in voice-over, 'I knew without a shadow of a doubt he wouldn't say a word'. Perfect trust makes deceit easy.

At one point Laura says to Alec: 'Do you know, I believe we should all behave quite differently if we lived in a sunny climate all the time. We shouldn't all be so withdrawn and shy and difficult.' In this way, the screenplay seems to be drawing explicit attention to the essential *Englishness* of the film. This is the way decent *English* people behave, it suggests. Long subservience to the ordinary domestic virtues, of *not* giving spontaneous vent to feelings, may have left them emotionally ill-equipped to deal with the sudden raw feeling that springs between Alec and Laura. It's not as if she isn't aware of alternatives to her conventional routine. There are glimpses of what she sees as alternatives to it. The library book she talks about is by Kate O'Brien, whose most famous novel, *The Ante-Room* (1934) has been described as being about 'the way people become addicted to each other, even when the addiction is hellish'.[10] If Laura's library borrowing is along these lines, it is tempting to see her reading as a means of sublimating her own unconscious passions vicariously through absorption in a much more emotionally charged world. Another contrast with the facts of her everyday life is the fantasy segment in which she imagines herself and Alec in a variety of glamorous situations, such as at the opera in Paris, in a Venetian gondola, against the rail of a ship, or dancing in a chandeliered room.

Class acts

As to the class aspect of the film which permeates it and British cinema and life at large, at the time certainly, and at every turn, *Brief Encounter* is absolutely middle- (to upper-middle) class in its approach. Noël Coward's own background is no doubt important here. He came from the lower-middle class and became famous as a chronicler of high society, the friend of royalty, the epitome of the sleek, witty sophisticate in the 1920s and 30s. When he subsequently wrote about the lower orders, there was often an element of patronage in his view of them.

In *Brief Encounter*, the lower orders are represented by Albert Godby (Stanley Holloway), the station porter, and Myrtle Bagot (Joyce Carey), who runs the buffet at the station. Their very names are a give-away as to their class and to their function in the film. They are there as comic relief. Their 'romance' is seen as a comic version of the serious emotional matters that engage their social superiors, though, more positively, they are freer than Alec and Laura in expressing their feelings. They are, though, the lower classes seen from an upper-class point of view. They are made fun of, as if they do not have emotional lives that one could possibly take as seriously as those of their social betters. In this matter, the influence of Coward can be felt. He collaborated on the screenplay with Lean and producer Havelock-Allan, who later said that Lean was 'never happy with the comic by-play'.[11]

This sort of approach to lower-class life is one of the recurring problems of British cinema of the period, even allowing for the loosening up of the class system during the war and for the fact that post-war British cinema has more connection with the realities of actual life than did pre-war films. Myrtle, played by upper-class actress Joyce Carey, and Albert, played by popular character star, Stanley Holloway, from a lower-middle-class background, are essentially presented as butts for jokes. They are placed as a crude comic counterpart to the serious affair at the film's centre. There is a nudging sexual innuendo in the jokes about Myrtle's former marriage and Albert's intentions; and Myrtle's 'refeened' accent and diction and genteel habit of primping her hair are also used to make her a parody of a lady.

The way Albert and Myrtle are presented helps to reinforce the film's overriding impression that middle-class lives, and life, are the norm, though the way gossiping Dolly is presented suggests some critique of them too. The film is set pre-war, and maybe it could be argued that the times had changed by 1945, but not all that much to judge by film (and theatre). Notice, too, all the small ways in which Laura's middle-classness is signalled, apart from the film's sense of her superiority to Myrtle, or to the lady musician, in matters such as her attitude to Hollywood films and her reading, and casual reference to servants. 'Ask Ethel to leave some soup in a saucepan in the kitchen for me,' she tells Fred. The fact that Ethel is nowhere else referred to suggests that such a servant presence is taken for granted. British cinema would have to wait for more than a decade before films such as *Room at the Top* (1959) would start taking 'lower-class life' seriously and interrogating the class system itself, though it might be argued that Lean offers a foretaste of this in his version of *Great Expectations*.

Realism and reality

There is a great deal of theory about what 'realism' means as an approach to story-telling but I want only to add that, when *Brief Encounter* was released, it was hailed as a prime example of a new realism brought to bear on what might have been thought of as conventional material. Agee, in fact, claimed that 'so many people have spoken of this [film] almost as if Noel Coward had personally invented realism', seeing this as 'a shriveling commentary... on the reality of the run of films'.[12] It still looks 'realistic' in relation to the period in which it was set and produced, and in comparison with much pre-war British cinema, or with Gainsborough's mid-1940s box-office successes, such as *The Wicked Lady*, or by comparison with most Hollywood films of the period in which the romantic leads were much more obviously sexually attractive. And, at the cinema Alec and Laura go to, there's a swipe at Hollywood when the preview for the forthcoming 'epic' *Flames of Passion*, is made to look ridiculous in its obvious exaggeration, though flames of passion may well describe what is about to engulf our pair. It still *looks* as though we're dealing with real streets and houses; the surface, that is, persuades us of the film's connection to the reality of the lives it is dealing with.

But realism is more than a matter of surfaces. The film so persuades us of the physical and social reality of Laura's life so that we can grasp the emotional convulsion into which her unexpected love for Alec plunges her. There's realism there certainly, but the film is also indebted to the influence of *film noir*, a style that was so prominent in the black-and-white cinema of the time, especially of Hollywood-based thrillers and romantic dramas. Like the great Hollywood *noirs* of the mid-40s, *Brief Encounter* makes much use of low-key lighting to heighten contrasts of light and shade, of oppressive use of sets (especially of the station platforms and corridors), of revealing close-ups and disorienting angles (to suggest emotional turmoil), and of elaborate use of flashbacks and a fantasy sequence within the flashback. It's as though the *noir* tendencies work against the realist habits of the script and the settings, and in doing so help us to understand how Laura's real world is being threatened. The sequence when she wanders the town square at night, in a state of anguish, is perhaps the key example of what I mean. Night here seems to signify Laura's no longer being certain of who and where she is. Another example of *noir* working to create unease is seen when she is sitting desolate in the train, having parted from Alec for good, while her gossipy friend's mouth is seen in close-up, prattling banalities while Laura's heart is quietly breaking.

Why do we go on watching it?

Mainly, I'd say not because of the stylistic complexities of realism and *film noir*, or even as a study of middle-class mores half a century ago. The film begins with a night shot of the railway station behind the credits and Rachmaninoff's powerfully romantic 'Piano Concerto No.2' comes up on the soundtrack, and after this I'm more or less unable to stop watching. And once the camera lights on Celia Johnson's face, eloquent with what seems – and proves to be – suppressed misery, her emotional life trapped behind those eyes, I'm utterly caught. Who are these rather ordinary-looking people, not looking at all like 'film stars', sitting at a table in the railway buffet in mute and mutually-felt pain, and what has brought them to this point? The contrast of the comic station staff and gossiping Dolly (Everley Gregg's most vivid moment on film?) with Laura and Alec, as we'll learn they are, reinforces our attention on them, as does the stillness of Johnson and Trevor Howard.

But there's more to it than night and the stars and the music. *Brief Encounter* may be absolutely a film of its time, and the specifics of the conflict in which Laura and Alec find themselves may have changed. Of course they have, but underlying those period specifics are ideas and imperatives that work as potently as ever. As a story of love at odds with everyday responsibilities and accepted conventions, *Brief Encounter* undoubtedly still has the power to move us. Alec may say, 'We know we love each other – that's all that really matters', but Laura knows better when she replies, 'It's not all that really matters. Other things matter too', and she means self-respect, as well as what is owed to others.

Ultimately Laura and Alec place the concerns for and allegiances to others over their own gratifications – we don't see Alec's wife, just hear about her, but there's a certain tender dimness in Fred that also helps Laura over her crisis, without his being aware of it. The pressures here are in Laura's romantic/sexual awakening, encoded as it is for the period, and her comfortable life style suddenly no longer seems secure. Film makes plain the awful challenge to her: the idea of throwing away a lifetime's morality and mores for the possibility of passion of a kind she has perhaps never known. That she resists this challenge, and returns to Fred, still works because it enshrines values that don't date. They have been comfortable together in ways that don't include discussion of feelings – until, very movingly at the end when the normally prosaic Fred manages a touching, 'Thank you for coming back to us'.

This is a film about some of the realities of human experience. It is made with great skill by Lean and his collaborators, but it holds the viewer because of the way it suggests the possibility of danger for the most insulated-seeming lives and the compassion with which it shows how people might behave when suddenly pushed near the edge.

Notes

1 I understand that there is also an entire episode of the British TV series, *Shameless*, which is devoted to a parodic tribute to *Brief Encounter*.

2 Quoted in Michael Zuckoff, *Robert Altman: The Oral Biography* (New York: Alfred A. Knopf, 2009), p. 55.

3 Charles Drazin, *The Finest Years: British Cinema of the 1940s* (London: André Deutsch, 1998).

4 Quoted in Hugh Hudson, 'Dreaming in the light', *Sight & Sound*, September 1991, 19.

5 'John Mills' in Brian McFarlane, *An Autobiography of British Cinema* (London: Methuen, 1997), p. 414.

6 Lyric Theatre, London, 11 September–4 November 2000, starring Jenny Seagrove and Christopher Cazenove.

7 Alison Light, *Forever England: Femininity, Literature and Conservatism between the Wars* (London: Routledge, 1991), p. 208.

8 See: C. A. Lejeune, *Chestnuts in Her Lap: 1936–1947*, second edition (London: Phoenix House, 1948), p. 161; Dilys Powell, *The Golden Screen: Fifty Years of Films* (London: Pavilion Books, 1989), p. 54; James Agate, *Around Cinemas*, Second series (Amsterdam: Home & Van Thal Ltd, 1948), pp. 161, 162.

9 James Agee, *Agee on Film* (New York: McDowell, Oblensky Inc., 1958), pp. 214–15.

10 Penny Perrick, 'On the Shelf', *The Sunday Times*, 9 November 1997.

11 Interview with the author, London, July 1990.

12 Agee, *Agee on Film*, p. 235.

5   Two from the Comfort zone:
Great Day (1945) and
Temptation Harbour (1947)

Films don't have to be masterpieces to make a profound and lasting impression, but for me it is gratifying to read a recent film historian refer to *Great Day* as 'quite simply a masterpiece'.[1] For me as a child, it began a life-long addiction to British films and, as I grew older, I became a committed admirer of its director Lance Comfort. While *Temptation Harbour* is more obviously Comfort's major work, *Great Day*, on at least a tenth viewing, seems almost perfect within the limits it sets itself. Hence, both rate attention here.

Great Day

After repeated viewing and much thinking about *Great Day*, I'm still impressed with what a rich and varied sense of life it compresses into its 79 minutes. Though its central character is the former World War One captain, Ellis (Eric Portman), what emerges is less a story of individuals than of a community. It ends on a note that confirms this: the citizenry of Denley is gathered together in public to welcome a distinguished visitor, and it is this communal image that stays with us. I'll come back to this to suggest what this ending means in terms of resolution – and what it does not.

A sense of community

The film opens with Mrs Mumford (Marjorie Rhodes) cycling round the village as she spreads the word that everyone – all the women, that is – are to assemble at the Hall for a 'secret' matter. An emergency meeting of the Women's Institute (WI) has been called at the Denley Memorial Hall, where Lady Mott (Isabel Jeans) arrives with an official from London, Miss Allen (Joan Maude), who delivers the news. Denley is to be honoured by a visit from Mrs Roosevelt as a tribute to the work of the WI, and she is spoken of as 'a natural human person', 'a woman like yourselves... a wife and mother'. She wants to 'see things as they are'. When sour-faced Miss Tyndale (Margaret Withers) wonders why Denley has been singled out, Mrs Mumford makes a brisk speech to the effect that, 'We're a community working together'.

In this opening sequence quite a lot has been established about the community. Importantly, it has been established as a site for cross-class consensus in a critical period. Mrs Mumford is the local pub-keeper with a strong organising spirit. Lady Mott, the local grandee (she is only 'Mrs' Mott in Lesley Storm's source play), throws herself into the Institute's affairs, but not in a commanding way. She refers to Mrs Ellis (Flora Robson) as the one who 'does the work', and she calls some of the women – the clearly middle-class ones – by their Christian names, and others not. This is perhaps making heavy weather of the unobtrusive way in which class differences are generally suppressed in the common cause. Denley has been chosen as representative of the war effort and the WI as a symbol of the way in which cooperation can be achieved even in the face of major differences.

In spite of this, the film doesn't idealise Denley. Community may seem to be taking precedence over individual wishes, and this is confirmed in the final sequence when the entire village gathers to welcome Mrs Roosevelt. But it is one of the film's strengths not to imply that personal desires and animosities have simply gone away. *Great Day* is not propaganda. The WI may have reason to be proud of its place in the community and of its wartime contribution (helping to keep Russian women warm with the garments they have made), but this doesn't preclude a malicious exchange between spiky Mrs Walsh (Maire O'Neill) and Miss Tyndale, who has been made vindictive by the frustrations of her life.

9   Eric Portman (Captain Ellis) and Flora Robson (Mrs Ellis).

Pressures

Against the background of the WI members working towards putting on a good show for their distinguished visitor, the personal situations of several of the main characters are wracked with problems arising from the complex network of pressures that make up their daily lives. Conflicts centred on the demands of the heart and the need for personal security keep the film constantly busy and give it a sense of lives almost jostling for attention in this pocket of rural England.

The Ellis family comprises the film's central trio. John Ellis, a captain in World War One, has found nothing comparably challenging since, and has made life difficult for his wife by constantly lamenting the more exciting past, as he sees it, and bemoaning the way the 'country's going to the dogs with a pack of women running everything.' This is not a film that is nostalgic about 'the old days': 'The old days are dead and gone,' Elizabeth asserts, 'they're nothing but a few books and a few ridiculous photos [of his old regiment]'. 'If only you had something to occupy you,' she worries at him.

The pressures on Ellis may be largely of his own making, but he feels their impact nevertheless, and it is almost as if Lance Comfort is anticipating what might be the state of things for many ex-servicemen in the years immediately ahead. The film was actually released in Britain in July 1945, and the relevance of Ellis's situation is clear: this sort of unproductive longing for the past, with its cruel and absurd distinctions, shouldn't be allowed to happen again. When Ellis has ordered a crate of wine, Elizabeth chides him with 'spend[ing] £10 we don't have on something we don't need'. His reply, 'At least one can live like a gentleman', gets the reply it deserves: 'Gentleman! I'm sick to death of the word', again perhaps pointing to the need for a more egalitarian future.

If Ellis suffers from a sense of failure, uselessness and outmoded values, he creates pressures for his wife over money matters and an ongoing insecurity that she transfers to her concern for their daughter, Meg (Sheila Sim). Meg is in love with a handsome young soldier, Geoffrey (Philip Friend), but, having watched the way her mother has struggled, she has become engaged to the prosperous but unromantic middle-aged Bob Tyndale (Walter Fitzgerald) on whose farm she works as a land girl. She's aware of the conflict this makes for her – and of the animosity it creates in Miss Tyndale, who has been used to running the household on her brother's farm, and sees this situation as being about to change.

It would be laborious to trace how each of these sets of pressure is worked out, and some of them are still hovering at the film's end. The community itself is under pressure, most specifically the WI and the men they rope in to do their bidding, to be ready to put on a good show for Mrs Roosevelt in twenty-four hours. The communal effort is not without its strains and conflicts. Harassed but kind Mrs Ellis undertakes to make a dress overnight for the little girl chosen to present a bouquet to the visitor, and she is at work on this far into the night when Ellis comes home from his encounter with police after stealing a ten-shilling note in the pub. At least suspicious of his intentions when he walks out into the night, she continues making the dress, responding to the pressure of her commitments – to children, to the WI, to the war effort, as well as to those of her marriage. Behind the communal pressure, the individual conflicts remain unabated – even in a comic moment when Miss Tyndale rebukes Mrs Beale for adding an egg to an 'eggless cake' (an example of wartime frugalities) just to make it look better for the display.

Lance Comfort maintains effective control over the busy, prolif-erating personal dramas, to greater and less extent fraught with conflicting urges, interlocking with the larger demands of a community aiming to be on its best behaviour. The balance seems to me just right: we can accept the exhilaration of the final moments when the black car bearing the visitor hoves into sight, but there are also brief individual close-ups that remind us that consensus in a common cause may be admirable but it doesn't mean that all disruptive potential has gone away.

Pastoral moments: possibilities or nostalgia?

At odds with the bustle and tensions of the village in its preparations, or with the army trucks trundling through that remind us of the still wider conflict, are the film's glimpses of the natural beauties of the surrounding countryside. These are not the object of mere pictorialism, but are worked into the fabric of this cunningly put-together film. In a sequence that reminds one of that moment shared by the same actors, Eric Portman and Sheila Sim, in Michael Powell's *A Canterbury Tale*, when on a serene hillside they contemplate birds in flight, Ellis and daughter Meg contemplate the hawks circling above. This is integrated into the pattern of the film by Ellis's contrasting the birds' freedom – 'No cages for them' – with human beings' tendency to get themselves into traps. He disapproves of Meg's working as a land-girl, and warns her not to let herself become trapped, as he is in his memories. But Meg is pragmatic enough not to be seduced by this talk and claims, 'I'd rather be a woman than a hawk, even if it is freer'. She's seen enough of her mother's anxieties not to dismiss the idea of security out of hand.

A few scenes later, while Mrs Ellis is urging this security on Meg, Ellis comes into conflict with farmer Bob Tyndale who's just shot a partridge. So, the pastoral fringe around Denley isn't just a matter of nostalgia for the past; it too can be a scene of conflict, but it does reveal another aspect of the complex, unhappy Ellis. It will also be the scene, however beautifully lit in Erwin Hillier's lustrous black-and-white cinematography, of Ellis's conflict with the present coming to a sort of climax. Following the incident of the stolen ten shillings, he has first blamed 'this stinking little village', then confessed to his wife how frightened he'd been of having wife and child dependent on him when he'd come back from war. Out by the river at night, he observes his image in the water, as if indulging in a moment's self-analysis, when Meg finds him and persuades him that, 'Sometimes it's braver to live

10   Eric Portman (Captain Ellis) and Sheila Sim (Margaret Ellis).

than to die.' In the beautiful pastoral setting, the dangerous shadows of *film noir* complicate our responses, as Meg and her father move back to the village and pause to watch as a troop convoy rolls through to deal with the larger conflict. The episode by the river at night has given us the dark side of pastoral (literally and metaphorically) without undermining its capacity for spiritual refreshment.

A film of its time

Talk of 'pastoral' reminds me of other points of comparison with *A Canterbury Tale*. Not only are the same stars – Portman and Sim – involved in a relationship in which love of the English countryside is a potent factor, but in both films there is a sense of Anglo-American connections. Certainly in the Powell masterwork, the naïve young American soldier (Bob Sweet) will play a more central role as he responds to the notions of English heritage put before him by the strangely obsessive JP, Colpepper (Portman), than does the US sergeant (John McLaren) in *Great Day*. Nevertheless, the echo is there in the scenes in which Ellis harangues the American in the pub, with his talk about how the last war was for the preserving of 'civilisation' (recalling Colpepper's passion for tradition), while the sergeant talks of Guadalcanal, of how the Americans are here to finish up the job, and of how he can't wait to get out of uniform. And of course the imminent arrival of the American First Lady merely reinforces the sort of cross-Atlantic amity that was being so much promoted at the time and which found its way into such other key films of the period as Anthony Asquith's *The Way to the Stars* (1945) and Powell's *A Matter of Life and Death* (1946).

Again, like *A Canterbury Tale* and several others of the early 1940s, *Great Day* moves towards its moment of consensus, cutting across class and national barriers. Whereas everyone fetches up at the Cathedral in Powell's film, in *Great Day* all the pressures, problems and conflicts have either been resolved or shelved in the interests of presenting a united front. What is being celebrated is perhaps a kind of courage that can put self to one side in the interests of a common cause. Other British films of the period such as *The Way Ahead* and *In Which We Serve* offer the spectacle of diverse groups of people being brought to awareness of such a commitment.

'It's no good hanging on to the past,' Meg tells Geoffrey when he tries to remind her of how things were on their last leave, accusing her of planning to marry Tyndale just for security. She is certainly right when she goes on to speak of her mother's bitterness at 'Dad's swaggering and drinking and clinging to his last war record.' But this film, like so many others of its period, insists that things can and should be different – and better – in the future. 1945 was just the year for such a message.

Temptation Harbour

Money is the undoing of both Captain Ellis in *Great Day* and signalman Bert Mallinson in *Temptation Harbour*. Ellis's swaggering in the village comes to an end when he steals a ten-shilling note from a woman's handbag in the pub so that he can go on impressing others in the bar. Bert's is a far bigger theft and leads to an even greater crime. He is essentially a decent man, and in Robert Newton's subtle and powerful performance he retains our sympathy, just as Portman's did in the earlier film. Both men are undone by a wrong decision made at a critical moment.

Perhaps *Temptation Harbour* isn't as perfectly put together as *Great Day*, but it is the more ambitious work of the two, and has some major claims to attention, so much so that it is surprising that it has never been commercially available on VHS or DVD. It belongs with a small group of distinguished, moody, *noir*-ish crime films made in Britain in the latter 1940s, including such titles as *Wanted for Murder* (1946), *Brighton Rock* (1947) and *They Made Me a Fugitive* (1948), and, in some ways, *It Always Rains on Sunday* (1947). In fact it resembles the latter most in the way it melds *noir* thriller elements with a scrupulously observed sense of the everyday, in this latter element reflecting one of the strengths of its source novel, Georges Simenon's *Newhaven-Dieppe* (French title, *L'homme de Londres*).[2]

A good man?

Bert Mallinson, a railway signalman working night-shift at a Channel ferry-port, is established very early as a decent, ordinary man. A widower, he lives with his teenage daughter Betty (Margaret Barton), who, in the opening sequence wakes him for his supper. 'You'll soon be cooking as well as your mum did,' he compliments her. Then when he finds that she has actually brought the kidneys home from the butcher's shop where she works, without paying for them, he chides her gently for this small act of dishonesty, referring to it as 'the thin edge of the wedge'. This touchingly played scene establishes the bond of affection between father and daughter *and*, though we aren't aware of it at this point, really ushers in the film's central drama. They talk of his money problems and the fishing boat he'd like to own, and we understand that he is an upright man struggling to achieve modest aims.

In the succeeding episode he will have his temptation just as Betty succumbed to the kidneys lying unattended on the butcher's slab. His signal-box on the railway line overlooks the docks at Newhaven, and shortly after his shift starts, he sees two men struggle on the wharf over possession of a small case. One of the men, with the case, falls into the water while the other heads off into the night. On instinct, Bert comes down from his box and dives into the water to try to save the man. He fails in this but does find the case, which proves to contain five thousand pounds. We know Bert is short of money, so that we expect this find to lead to some sort of crisis of conscience for a good man who hasn't let his daughter's tiny pilfering pass without comment. And prior to both these episodes, we have seen Betty making her way purposefully through a crowded carnival and recall how often carnival has stood for a sense of liberation from everyday worries and restraints. This particular carnival will also provide the basis for the second temptation in the life of this good man.

Two temptations

Bert is aware that he should report the entire incident he has witnessed. He phones his supervisor (Edward Lexy) who hasn't time to listen carefully to what has happened, so that Bert decides not to tell him about the money. 'It's for me and the police,' he tells himself, and the film has a habit of using interior monologues on the soundtrack to take us into Bert's thinking. In fact, it is arguable that this is a slight miscalculation on the filmmakers' part: Newton's performance, especially in terms of facial expression, as caught in Otto Heller's atmospheric cinematography, suggests amply the kind of battle Bert is having with his conscience, without its needing to be spelt out so explicitly as it will be here and later. 'A whole life I'd have to work and then I wouldn't have this,' his voice-over will ponder as he weighs up the courses open to him. In fact, the authors of the screenplay may have taken their lead in this matter from the film's source novel in which Simenon depicts his protagonist (Maloin in the book) as one who talks aloud to himself during the lonely hours of night duty in the signal-box, though not usually in the sorts of inner-conflict matters the film employs.

In the flush of possibly being in possession of so large a sum of money, Bert buys himself a meerschaum pipe he has coveted, then goes to see Betty at work where he is shocked to find her scrubbing the floor for her bossy employer, the butcher's wife (Kathleen Boutall). He takes her away from this job and they move on to the fair. The other temptation, which really grows from Bert's sudden access of wealth, comes in the shapely French form of Camelia (Simone Simon), the 'Disappearing Mermaid' who performs in the carnival sideshow that Bert takes Betty to see. After the show, he intervenes to stop her crude boss (Charles Victor) from bullying her. She subsequently joins him in the pub where she tells her true story of having been abandoned by her sailor lover. 'I know what it is to be alone,' she says, and strikes a chord of loneliness in the widowed Bert. Camelia is actually a grasping little thing, as well as being sexually attractive, and, like many a *film noir* man

11   Robert Newton (Bert Mallinson) and Simone Simon (Camelia).

before him, Bert finds in her another reason for not handing in the case
of banknotes. The double prospect of giving Betty a happier life and
of setting up house with Camelia clinches things for Bert. But this is
not intended to make the film sound conventional or schematic. Bert's
temptations are put before us with a quiet naturalism that makes them
and his responses utterly believable and touching.

Crime – but what sort?

Temptation Harbour would probably be – in fact, *was* – routinely
described as a thriller, as a crime story. And yet how inadequate that
sort of tagging seems for this complex film. Yes, it is the story of
a crime but unlike most films of the crime genre it is not a drama
with much external action. There is the initial quayside fight between
Brown (William Hartnell) and Teddy (boxer-actor Dave Crowley) over
possession of the case of money, leading to Teddy's drowning and Bert's
involvement. Then, in the film's third-last episode, there is the vicious
fight between Brown and Bert that ends with Bert killing Brown. The
tragic irony of this latter sequence is that it is Bert's innate goodness

that has led him to this: knowing that the runaway Brown is hiding in Bert's boatshed, his concern for the man has led him to bring him food and drink. Into the dark recesses of the shed, he calls 'Mr Brown', and the address seems oddly revealing of his decency. When Brown attacks him, Bert retaliates with an iron bar that comes to hand and kills him.

Between these two bursts of violent action, what has held our attention is essentially an inner drama, as we watch Bert juggling the claims of conscience and the understandable wish for a somewhat better life for him and his daughter. His wishes in this way are modest. The outcome of this inner drama is an ending that is both bleak and morally apt, as Bert walks to the police station to give himself up, having arranged for Betty to be looked after by friendly neighbours. Margaret Barton recalled spending two days on the final scene, and especially how Betty's final moments with her father were heightened by Mischa Spoliansky's musical score. He had actually played his music on the set for the sake of getting the actors attuned to it, and this was apparently a rare occurrence.[3]

Robert Newton's portrayal of Bert's inner conflicts is really eloquent enough not to need the nudging of the voice-over, though it is actually not as intrusive as several of the more captious critics suggested. Newton, noted for his somewhat over-the-top response to acting challenges, in such films as Lance Comfort's *Hatter's Castle*, here gives one of his most restrained performances and is finally very moving. It says much for Comfort's direction that he was able to get Newton to behave himself to such subtle effect in *Temptation Harbour*. While on the matter of the film's acting, the other performance that everyone noted was that of Margaret Barton as Betty. Rarely has a teenager been played with such naturalness and sympathy, and though Barton was twenty at the time she looks no more than fifteen.

Simenon and the man from London

Though the film transposes Simenon's *L'Homme de Londres* (aka *Newhaven-Dieppe*) from the French end of the ferry-run to the English, it both maintains the essentially interior nature of the action and proves to be perhaps the most French-*looking* film ever made in Britain. This was the first of Simenon's novels to be filmed in Britain. As *Picturegoer* magazine wrote at the time: 'Simenon specializes in retribution, building up with mounting excitement from the original crime to the inevitable

12   Robert Newton (Bert Mallinson) and Simone Simon (Camelia).

punishment.'[4] Lance Comfort's film retains this over-all plot trajectory, while in a very provocative way suggesting some utterly English ways of thinking and acting in a physical setting that keeps echoes of the original Frenchness. In fact the film was largely shot in the Associated British Studios, in sets recreating an old-fashioned street of houses with overhanging first floors, and an elaborate pub interior. As well, the producer Victor Skutesky hired a complete fair, installing it for a week at Welwyn Studios.[5]

The 'French' look is the more surprising since the location-shooting took place in the south-coast English resorts, Folkestone (mainly at the cross-Channel embarkation jetty at St Margaret's Bay) and Rye. Sole surviving cast-member Margaret Barton recalls being stationed in Folkestone for about three weeks and that all the beach shots were taken there.[6] But the look of the film is more than just the sum of its settings. Several of the key collaborators brought their European sensibilities to work on the film, including producer Skutesky, who also had a hand in the screenplay, along with Frederick Gotfurt, in adapting a French novel, Polish-born composer Spoliansky (who lived in Germany until fleeing the Nazi scourge), and Newton's co-star is the then-famous French actress Simone Simon, star of many French and Hollywood films. Above all though, Czech-born Otto Heller's black-and-white cinematography, with its heavy shadows and faces highlighted to catch the inner tensions, recalls powerfully such pre-war French classic films as *La Bête humaine* and *Quai des brumes*. Margaret Barton remembered his skill in lighting the violent fight between Bert and Brown and the highlighting of Brown's eyes.

Contending with comfort

In my view, only the very top names of the 1940s British cinema – Powell, Asquith, Reed and Lean – could marshal two such contrasting and memorable films as Lance Comfort offers in *Great Day* and *Temptation Harbour*. The former is an intelligent paean to Englishness of a kind perhaps only matched by Powell's *A Canterbury Tale*. The latter takes its place among the moody masterpieces of *film noir* and in doing so resonates well beyond its native English shores. Respected contemporary critic Campbell Dixon ended his review by declaring Comfort 'one of the British screen's white hopes'.[7] His career finished in 'B' movies, but they were some of the best of their kind, and Comfort remains perhaps the most undervalued director in the British film annals.

Notes

1 Sue Harper, *Mad, Bad and Dangerous to Know: Women in British Cinema* (London: Continuum International Publishing Group, 2000).

2 Georges Simenon, *Newhaven-Dieppe* (1942), trans. Stuart Gilbert (Harmondsworth: Penguin, 1952).

3 Interview with author, 22 May 2012.

4 Hubert Cole, 'Round the British Studios', *Picturegoer*, 12 October 1946, 10.

5 Production Guide, *Temptation Harbour* (Associated British Picture Corporation, 1947).

6 Interview with author, 22 May 2012.

7 'Good Thriller and Two Comedies', *Daily Telegraph*, March 1947.

6   *It Always Rains on Sunday* (1947)
– and other things go wrong too

Mention the word 'Ealing' now and people of a certain age (that is, older people) will tend to say nostalgically, 'Oh, I loved those Ealing comedies' and will go on to recall *Passport to Pimlico* (1948) and *The Lavender Hill Mob* (1951). Not so commonly, the tougher-minded pieces like *Whisky Galore!* (1948) or *The Ladykillers* (1955) – or *Kind Hearts and Coronets* (1949), Robert Hamer's black comedy masterpiece.

Mention of Hamer brings to mind other aspects of the Ealing output, and not just its realist strand. He could do this certainly, but there's also a vein of sophisticated but ferocious melodrama at work in some of his Ealing films, and melodrama and realism are expertly knitted together in *It Always Rains on Sunday*. It's realist all right in its surface recreation of post-war London streets and the lives lived on and around them, but it is so memorable, for me at least, for the way this underpins a tightly melodramatic framework that involves a convict on the run and family relationships under pressure. There's also more than a touch of the contemporary *film noir* in how it registers night streets and dark interiors, as well as an inner life torn with conflict. All up, it is one of Ealing's most complex achievements.

Sunday bloody Sunday

At the heart of the film's 'story' is the idea that Rose and George Sandigate's Sunday is about to be disrupted by the sudden reappearance of Rose's ex-lover, Tommy Swan, now a criminal on the run. Before Tommy (John McCallum) erupts on the scene, Hamer and the shrewd mosaic of the screenplay (by Henry Cornelius, Angus McPhail and Hamer himself) have set the scene of the Sandigates' marriage with brilliant economy. The film has opened on the deserted street at night, with George (Edward Chapman) observing from the upstairs window the late arrival home of daughter Vi (Susan Shaw). The fleeing figure of a man running along a railway cutting dissolves into a news-stand where a boy is reading a paper with the headline, DARTMOOR ESCAPE. Rose (Googie Withers), considerably younger than George, is still in bed, comes to and bangs on the wall behind her, shouting to Doris (Patricia Plunkett), 'Your father wants a cup of tea.' Sister Vi, who has gone to bed in her evening dress, says charmingly, 'Greedy old bag. She means she wants one.' Doris calls Rose 'Mum'; she is the pliable stepdaughter, whereas Vi has perhaps too much in common with Rose to treat her with any deference.

The link between Rose and Vi is reinforced by the way each is given a 'memory sequence' in this early part of the film. While Doris has gone off dutifully to make tea for George, Vi drifts into a reverie about her night out of dancing and dining with bandleader Morry Hyams (Sydney Tafler), who has led her on by talking of her chances of making it as a singer. That is, he has, however mendaciously, given her a glimpse of another kind of life. A little later, in a wonderful moment, the camera moves in on Rose's face as George reads from the paper about Tommy's escape, and the film dissolves to Tommy coming into the pub where Rose had worked. This in turn gives way, via another dissolve, to their brief idyll on a hillside, where Tommy offers her a ring. 'A present for a bad girl,' he half-jokes, and we return to Rose in close-up, looking in a mirror as Vi has been doing. The film's strength and subtlety lie in the way such parallels aren't overstressed but are registered as threads in a complex pattern: however snappish Rose is with Vi, we, if not she at any conscious level, must recognise that each has had glimpses of something more exciting, more potentially romantic than their everyday lives, of which this wet Sunday is typical.

Some questions

These opening sequences set up a lot of questions. Why has Rose married kindly, middle-aged George with his two grown-up daughters? What is this marriage like? How secure is it? They share a bed but do we ever see them embrace or kiss? Rose seems too young and sexy to have surrendered to the somewhat shabby confinement of this house on this wet street in this drab post-war East End. When she hears of Tommy

13   John McCallum (Tommy Swann), Patricia Plunkett (Doris Sandigate)
and Googie Withers (Rose Sandigate).

Swann's escape, there is something about her opaque stare, revealing as much as it conceals, that suggests to us that he has been in some way responsible for where she now is. The fact that he is now at large – we assume he is the fleeing figure we saw just after the credits – seems likely to be a threat to whatever stability, such as it is, that Rose has achieved. The fact that he is played by handsome John McCallum, albeit looking scruffy and unshaven, as contrasted with rather pudgy, plain George, calls up echoes and sets alarm bells ringing for Rose – and anticipations of conflict for us.

More generally, I think the film raises questions about the nature of marriages, of what holds them together and what can threaten them. From the outset, there is a look of discontent about Rose: it's pretty clear from the outset that her and George's marriage is not one of great passion, and Rose is probably not tolerant enough to be the stepmother of a couple of young women, certainly not of the stroppy Vi. She goes about her daily round with a more or less contained grudgingness, but when Tommy Swann bursts into her life again it's as though some long-repressed fires are reignited. The other marriage under threat in the film is that of Morry and Sadie Hyams, this time the result of Morry's philandering ways and, in particular, his attentions to Vi. Sadie (Betty Ann Davies) not unreasonably objects to Morry's bringing his latest girlfriend, Vi, into the house, and, as if to confirm the parallelism, the film cuts to a shot of Tommy asleep in George's bed.

The two sets of deception are linked when Rose and George's young son Alfie (David Lines) spots Morry and Vi kissing and 'blackmails' Morry into giving him a mouth organ in return for not telling anyone. A little later, there is a dissolve from Morry's nightclub, where Sadie has warned Vi about Morry, to the Sandigate kitchen where George is playing the mouth organ with his son, unaware of Tommy upstairs. The only relationship to offset these two marriages under outside pressures is that between the biddable daughter Doris and her nice young man, Ted (Nigel Stock). But even this seemingly more conventional relationship runs a momentary risk when Morry's on-the-make brother Lou (John Slater) chats her up, and gives Doris a fleeting glimpse of something more exciting. Some sharp words ensue between Doris and Ted. When she later goes to Ted's lodgings to make peace again, his suspicious and prudish landlady won't let her in out of the rain to wait for Ted, and the couple make up outside in the wet street. The film, in its richly textured way, seems to keep questioning the nature of marriages and other relationships and the precarious nature of their survival. But this is only part of the fascination of this multi-layered film.

Where and when

The film's opening shot is of a deserted street, an urban cul-de-sac, in the early hours of the morning while it is still dark and with rain falling. Arthur La Bern's novel,[1] the film's source, was set in 1939, but as John W. Collier wrote in his book about the film's making: 'the film represents a vague present. The practical consideration was that a bomb-blasted East End represented insuperable difficulties for location shots out of the post-war period.'[2] This is London's East End, Bethnal Green to be exact (we learn this later from Rose who has longed to leave it), and what follows is not a cosy picture of a community pulling together in the way made famous in British wartime mythology. This is a shabby, drab place, still very much feeling the aftermath of war in ways the film unobtrusively makes plain. For instance, the garden shed in which the fleeing Tommy Swann takes refuge looks as if it has also done service as an air-raid shelter; there's talk of ration coupons for cheese; and there's an undercurrent – not all that 'under', actually – of black-market trade and petty crime, with luxury goods like roller skates and nylons being displayed as items beyond everyday needs.

A very early episode has three petty criminals, Whitey (Jimmy Hanley), Freddie (John Carol) and Dicey (Alfie Bass), talking about how they can get and dispose of some illicitly obtained nylon stockings, and Whitey remarks that 'Tommy Swann's got his skates on'. You don't have to remember the reference to 'skates' later on when the three try to persuade their fence, the hypocritical Neesley (John Salew), to buy a consignment of skates they've got their hands on, but the echo is there. And their mention of Tommy is just another marker of how endemic crime is, at one level or other, in this place at this time. It's a matter of degree: Tommy has been inside for 'robbery with violence' (he later tells Rose he'd have been all right if he'd 'stuck to smash and grab'), while the trio are minor operators by comparison, but both contribute to the prevailing sense of a community in which crime is an everyday business.

In the thronging market street, respectable shoppers rub shoulders with spivs touting their wares. In this community, 'respectable' seems to have a hard time of it with the likes of the Hyam brothers making a good thing out of chances for excitement. Morry, billed as 'The Man with Sax Appeal', seems to be offering the disgruntled Vi a future as a singer, but is in reality cheating on his wife Sadie and merely using Vi for sexual ends. Sadie, who's had enough of Morry's slippery ways, leaves him, in a small victory for respectability. We feel the rightness of her stance but the film isn't being simplistic about this because the negative side of 'respectable' is found twice in other quarters. In the case of slatternly Mrs Spry (Hermione Baddeley), on bantering terms with the police, who insists she runs a respectable house, even if most of her dubious lodgers are apt to be called 'Smith', it's clear that the idea is simply meant as a cover for whatever game she is up to; and Ted's 'respectable' landlady (Grace Arnold) is simply seen to be censorious and mean-spirited.

The other Hyam brother, Lou, has set up a crooked boxing-match in the street. Like Morry, he is better dressed than the others in the community, and the implication is that he has access to means that mightn't stand up to scrutiny. And just as Morry works his sleazy charms on Vi, Lou tries to proposition Doris with a bunch of flowers and the offer of a job 'up West' in a beauty parlour. His sister Bessie (Jane Hylton) will later warn Doris against this, and Ted (perhaps suggesting a potential for male bossiness?) is displeased at what he sees as Lou's interest in Doris, but this film is again too intelligent just to write these attentions off as no more than a shifty infiltration of working-class lives. As Lou talks to Doris, we remember Rose's memory of the hillside idyll with Tommy and Vi's glimpse of other possibilities in Morry's nightclub. However shoddy the motives of the men are in such matters, in each instance the woman has been briefly allowed the vision of something beyond the drabness of post-war Bethnal Green. However transient this may have been, having recognised it gives the women a sort of yardstick for measuring – and for Rose and Doris, *valuing* – what they have in George and Ted. And, in a tiny culturally-dating detail, even the crooks wear ties! Has it been downhill for criminal dressing ever since? At least they *looked* respectable, even flamboyantly so in Tommy's case, before the law caught up with him.

So, from Tommy, violent and on the run, to young David doing a bit of juvenile blackmail, with the three small-time crooks and the Hyam brothers in between, Hamer establishes a world in which crime in various degrees is a fact of everyday life. Much of this derives from Arthur La Bern's novel, which has been out of print for decades and is hard to track down. It is a lively enough piece of work, but lacks the emotional and thematic texture of the film. Several of his books are still in print, but not this one nor *Night Darkens the Street*, filmed in 1948 as *Good-Time Girl*, another film in the post-war mode of gritty urban realism. Hamer's film retains most of the characters and incidents of the novel, subtly integrating them into a complex whole.

Shabbiness and crime are not all there is to *It Always Rains on Sunday*, and there's more to it than is commonly understood by 'realism'. Several of the key talents involved ensure this.

Three names to conjure with

Robert Hamer

Along with Alexander Mackendrick who made *Whisky Galore!* and *The Ladykillers*, Robert Hamer is probably the most sophisticated, the most hard-edged of the Ealing directors of its great period of the 40s and early 50s. He destroyed himself with drink, driven by demons that may have included closeted homosexuality, and was dead at 52.[3] His decade with Ealing – from his uncredited direction of sequences of *San Demetrio, London* (1943) when director Charles Frend fell ill – contains all his best work. This includes his three with Googie Withers – 'The

Haunted Mirror' sequence in the portmanteau film, *Dead of Night* (1945), *Pink String and Sealing Wax* (1945) and *It Always Rains on Sunday* (1947), as well as further uncredited work on *The Loves of Joanna Godden* (1947) when director Frend again took ill – and the brilliant *Kind Hearts and Coronets* (1949).

Of the last-named, it is possible that its success has tended to overshadow the rest of Hamer's career, but those earlier films can stand beside it as works of comparable subtlety and complexity. What interests me about *Kind Hearts* at present is the theme of aspiration, of a sense of wanting more than the confined life seems to be offering, of taking steps (elegant serial-killing in the case of Louis Mazzini, its protagonist) to secure this 'more', and of not quite making it. Mazzini, indeed, seems certain to head for the gallows, having left his tell-tale memoirs in his cell; it has been his aim to escape lower-middle-class gentility by getting rid of all the d'Ascoyne family members who stand between him and the dukedom which he believes is rightfully his. In *Pink String*, set in Victorian England, Withers plays the brazen wife of a slobbish publican, constantly frustrated at the confines of her life and taking desperate – and fatal – measures to change it. In *Joanna Godden*, in the annals of British cinema a proto-feminist piece, she holds out for her aim to run her farm and her own life. Even if she ultimately accepts marriage, one feels it will be on her own terms. Poor Rose in *It Always Rains on Sunday*, who has earlier had a glimpse of what passion might be with Tommy, seeming 'an oasis in an arid world',[4] settles for decency and kindness with George, having also felt the limits of passion when Tommy knocks her down as he tries to escape. For all these 1940s Hamer films, there are choices to be made about whether to accept what life has handed out or, with no certainty of outcome, do something about changing it. These are tonally very different films – potent melodrama, rural romance, urban realism, black comedy – but the lethal intelligence of Hamer's direction can be felt at work across the genre range. At Ealing, he clashed with studio head, Michael Balcon, because his vision was always darker than Balcon liked, but his individual stamp is on all the work he did for the studio.

Googie Withers
The 1940s now seems like a golden age for actresses in British films. There were the very (and to me, inexplicably) popular Anna Neagle, Margaret Lockwood flaring her nostrils, baring her cleavage and taking to wickedness as if to a profession, clever Phyllis Calvert somehow

14   John McCallum (Tommy Swann) and Googie Withers (Rose Sandigate).

contriving to make goodness interesting, elegant Valerie Hobson wittily doing her best work for Hamer in *Kind Hearts*, sexy bad-girl Jean Kent, heart-breaking Celia Johnson, blondely ambiguous Ann Todd, provocative Joan Greenwood and lovely, eloquent Sally Gray, among others. But Googie Withers, described recently in a brief *New Yorker* notice of the film's screening as 'strikingly intelligent',[5] was something else. There was no one like her in this heyday of the 1940s in British film (or perhaps ever): she was bold, sensual and confronting, brazenly refusing to let men boss her around. In her obituary I wrote: 'She predated feminism's later twentieth-century rallying, never needing theory to help her establish her credentials as a woman who knew what was what.'[6]

In her thirty–odd films of the 1930s, Googie Withers played any number of sassy blondes, more than able to hold their own with duplicitous chaps – and with comics such as George Formby, with whom she memorably fell into a vat of beer at the end of *Trouble Brewing* (1939). Her real film fame derives from the 1940s. Michael Powell used her beauty and authority in *...one of our aircraft is missing* (1942), as a leader of the Dutch resistance, and she was undaunted by

Clive Brook and the formidable Beatrice Lillie in the high comedy
of *On Approval* (1944). But it is four consecutive films she made for
Ealing in the latter 40s that, for my money, confirmed her as the most
exciting female presence in British film of the day. She sorts out a
vacillating husband in the horror compendium, *Dead of Night*; poisons
her husband in *Pink String and Sealing Wax*, prior to hurling herself over
a Brighton cliff; and convincingly runs a farm in *Joanna Godden* before
accepting, but not succumbing to, the embrace of a neighbouring
farmer played by real-life husband-to-be John McCallum. Best of all,
though, is *It Always Rains on Sunday*, as the unromantically married
working-class woman who unwisely shelters her former lover, now a
convict on the run. This quartet of roles gave her brilliant chances
which she seized with both hands.

When we first see Rose, she is grumpy, barely suppressing irritation
with those around her. She clashes with step-daughter Vi whose blonde
youth perhaps reminds her of her own, and her then-determination to
make the most of opportunities to break away from the down-at-heel
mundane life that confines her. The young Rose we glimpse in flashback
as she remembers her fling with Tommy is also blonde, the film's way
of suggesting the parallel with the discontented Vi, while the more
amenable Doris's brunette attractiveness links her to the older Rose.
And like the older Rose, she may end up in a comfortable if not very
exciting marriage. As Charles Barr has written of these girls, 'They are
blonde and brunette respectively, like Rose's past and present.'[7] This is
too subtle a film to make such points in obvious ways, but they come to
mind as one thinks about the film and tries to account for its richness.

It is Googie Withers' Rose which is at the heart of this richness.
Hamer clearly knew how capable she was of registering conflicting
urges from the magisterial performance he drew from her in *Pink String*.
Certainly her Pearl suicides in the remarkable final sequence, but,
whatever moral aptness there is in this ending, nothing can suppress
the fact that Pearl has more energy and intelligence, more forcefulness
frustrated of the means of expression, than anyone else in the film.
Withers was not backward about playing strong, seriously flawed
women, and does so without losing our sympathy for them, though she
never plays for this. Hence, in the last sequence of *It Always Rains*, when
she is lying in a hospital bed recovering from having tried to gas herself,
she can move us with the sense of having come to terms with what her
life is going to be. Tommy has clearly used her, *and* hit her on the jaw;
he has roused her sexuality again ('Why do you think I'm doing all this

15   John McCallum (Tommy Swann) and Googie Withers (Rose Sandigate).

for you? Because I *used* to love you?,' she asks him); and she is now left
with George, and grateful for it.

One critic has written: 'The film ends with George forgiving Rose,
condemning her to a life lacking in passion or excitement in the East
End, a place she has been trying to escape since puberty.'[8] Yes, true
enough up to a point, but this ending is also moving because she has
seen the value of a steady, kindly affection, even if it doesn't do away
with those other longings – any more than it did for Celia Johnson's
Laura in *Brief Encounter*. The film has not just arrived arbitrarily at this
conclusion. It has shown Rose pulled this way and that by claims of
memory and of decency. Withers' face as she reacts to the first news
of Tommy's escape may reveal nothing to George as he reads from
the paper but it is transparent enough for us to guess that something
serious is going on behind it. And, as if to intensify the sense of the
inner conflict, the reaction is recorded as she is looking into the mirror
and returns to this after the memory sequence that recalls her fling with
Tommy. Rose is looking not just *at* but also *into* herself in this telling
episode. Later, the camera catches her physically between her everyday
life with George inside the house and Tommy lurking in the shelter in
the yard, or on the stairs while George is in the kitchen and Tommy is
in their bedroom upstairs.

Rose is neither stupid nor heartless; she is simply – or not so simply – torn. About George, she has explained to reckless Tommy, 'He's decent to me', and the film's muted ending supports this 'decency' in Edward Chapman's touchingly understated performance. It is George who has the film's last moments as he walks home from the hospital and the rain is clearing.

Douglas Slocombe

There are plenty of distinguished collaborators at work on *It Always Rains on Sunday*, including composer Georges Auric, Hamer's co-screenwriters Angus McPhail and Henry Cornelius, and others, but I want briefly to draw attention to his great cinematographer. Oscar-winning Douglas Slocombe, nearing one hundred years old as I write, who makes a major contribution to the mood and drama of the film. For much of its length his camera establishes a powerfully realist look as it picks out bustling, rain-sodden streets, smoky pub and shabby housing, but this is not just another piece of British realism. There are key elements of *film noir* in Slocombe's work, particularly as the camera responds to the invasive presence of Tommy Swann on the run. Very early we see him running in the dark along a railway cutting; later, in the air-raid shelter the lighting creates him a threatening figure whose face is highlighted in the dark interior; and finally there is a full-scale menacingly atmospheric chase through the railway yards. (This, by the way, was not in the novel but an invention for the film). This chase, leading to Tommy's capture by Det. Sgt Fothergill (Jack Warner), could have been merely a conventional plot strategy, but Slocombe's cinematography, making the most of shadows and shafts of light, renders it a dangerous finale to a disruptive element in the story. John McCallum as Tommy recalled forty-odd years later: 'Bob [Hamer] was a perfectionist: he took five weeks to shoot that end sequence in the railway yard. We took awful risks – going under moving trains and running on top of them', and had praise for Slocombe who 'didn't interfere in the direction... but, by God, he was good.'[9] Slocombe worked with Hamer on several Ealing films, including *Dead of Night*, *Joanna Godden* and *Kind Hearts and Coronets*, and his visual dexterity ensures Hamer's morally complex vision finds appropriate visual style.

Conclusion

There is a great deal more one might say about this film: for instance, its skill in handling several sub-plots, all of them acted by a great cast of British character actors. These include the contrasting figures of Sidney Tafler, the archetypal 'spiv' of post-war British cinema, always looking immaculate as he pursues his sleazy way, and Jack Warner, everyone's idea of quietly authoritative police sergeant, a role he would confirm in *The Blue Lamp* a few years later. But the great thing about the way Hamer deals with these side stories (for example, of Morry Hyams, his wife and Vi) is actually two-fold. First, they help to create a rich texture of community; and, more important still, they are integrated so as to highlight the strong and humanly moving central story of Rose, her runaway lover and her loving, patient husband.

Notes

1 A. J. La Bern, *It Always Rains on Sunday* (London: Nicholson and Watson, 1945; 'Book of the Film' edition, 1947).

2 John W. Collier, *A Film in the Making* (London: World Film Productions Ltd, 1947), p. 10.

3 Referred to only as 'Robert', he figures largely in Pamela Wilcox's *Between Heaven and Charing Cross* (London: Allen & Unwin, 1977), the memoir which charts the decline into alcoholism during the period of Hamer's relationship with the author.

4 Collier, *A Film in the Making*, p. 19.

5 *New Yorker*, 2 April 2012.

6 'Assured leading lady of the screen took no nonsense: Googie Withers', Obituary, *The Age*, 19 July 2011.

7 Charles Barr, *Ealing Studios*, second edition (London: Studio Vista, 1993), p. 70.

8 Geoff Mayer, *Guide to British Cinema* (Westport, Connecticut, and London: Greenwood Press, 2003), p. 211.

9 John McCallum, in Brian McFarlane, *An Autobiography of British Cinema* (London: Methuen, 1997), p. 610.

7   *The Third Man* (1949) and several more

Has there ever been a more seductive opening to a film? A voice-over tells us, 'I never knew the old Vienna before the war with its Strauss waltzes and its easy charm. I really got to know it in the classic days of the black market'. While this is heard on the soundtrack, the camera takes in a long-shot of Vienna, with its snow-covered statues, before cutting to close-ups of watches and stockings changing hands – and a body floating by in the river. There are then rapid glimpses of the four occupying powers – British, American, French and Russian – with more long shots of the beautiful, ravaged city, with Ferris wheel and marching soldiers. This is accompanied by the voice-over which continues: 'I was going to tell you about Holly Martins who came here to visit a friend, Harry Lime...' I can't be sure how many times I've seen *The Third Man*, but I doubt if I could watch this opening sequence, with its friendly, intimate tone and shocking image, without staying for the rest. For me, it has become one of the most irresistible and poignant mementos of the post-war era that gave it birth.

The first man: Greene and the screen

Arguably, no other novelist has had so close and varied a connection with the screen than Graham Greene. He'd been a critic in the 1930s for the journal, *The Spectator*, and briefly a reviewer for a short-lived magazine, *Night and Day*, which collapsed when Greene was sued for writing an allegedly offensive piece about child star Shirley Temple. But it was as an author much adapted to film that his place in screen history is secured. By 1984, it was possible for an entire book to be written about film versions of his work.[1] Since then a further sixteen film or television productions have been made from his fictions. Most recently, both *The Quiet American* (2002) and *Brighton Rock* (2010) have been filmed for the second time.

However, it is probably his 1940s dealings with cinema for which he is most famous. His novels were filmed in the US as well as the UK, but the highlights are the classic *film noir* version of *Brighton Rock* (1947, made by the Boulting brothers, Roy and John) and the two films he made with director Carol Reed, *The Fallen Idol* (1948) and *The Third Man* (1949). Whereas *The Fallen Idol*, with a screenplay by Greene, was based on his novella, 'The Basement Room', *The Third Man* was written expressly for the screen, and, as Greene has said, it 'was never written to be read but only to be seen', because, 'To me it is almost impossible to write a film play without first writing a story... *The Third Man* was never intended to be more than the raw material for a picture'.[2]

Whatever its genesis, the film's bleak romanticism, crossed with the realities of the post-war world, seems utterly in line with what Greene the novelist had led us to expect. The story was subsequently published (as was the screenplay), but not with the opening paragraph that Greene claimed he'd once scribbled on the back of an envelope: 'I had paid my last farewell to Harry a week ago, when his coffin was lowered into the frozen February ground, so that it was with incredulity that I saw him pass by, without a sign of recognition, among the host of strangers in the Strand.' He had jotted this down when producer Alexander Korda invited him to write another film for director Carol Reed following Reed and Greene's successful collaboration on *The Fallen Idol*. Well, 'the Strand' got lost on the way from envelope to story to screen, but the essential notion of the apparent death of Harry Lime and the subsequent discovery that he is still very much alive underpins the plot of *The Third Man*.

The second man: Reed in the 40s

No one rode higher in British cinema of the 1940s than Carol Reed. He had been filming, and with some distinction, in the previous decade – *Bank Holiday* (1938) and *The Stars Look Down* (1940) were two notable titles – but it was with *The Way Ahead* and the two films with Greene that his reputation was assured. Sixty-odd years on, the post-war decade still seems the most richly productive in British film history, its prestige resting on such crucial strands as the literary adaptation (such as David Lean's Dickens films), the realist mode in the wake of wartime successes (the likes of *It Always Rains on Sunday*), and the legendary Ealing comedies. In *The Third Man*, Reed draws on the literary influence of Greene's story-telling capacity and the sort of realism that enables him to give such a potent sense of post-war decadence, tensions and attempts at imposing order. It's hard to imagine the film as deriving from any other period, or from a setting other than that in which a gaggle of authorities deals warily with each other and with the corruption that grows out of attempts to profit by human misery.

Reed would have other successes – or semi-successes – in later decades, as with the Oscar-winning *Oliver!* (1968), but very few films so successfully raise entertainment to the level of art or so hugely succeed in making art so entertaining as *The Third Man* does. Not merely does it belong in a period of such high achievement in British film history, when a remarkable range of talents at every level of production was to be found, but as well it is tempting to see the film as drawing on a mixture of British and American resources. The film's opening credit reads: 'Presented by Alexander Korda and David O. Selznick'. Korda, Hungarian but long resident in Britain and reputedly more British than the British, and Selznick, most famous as producer of *Gone with the Wind*, may be seen as pooling the expertise of two continents, and this impression is reinforced by the casting. Somehow, the clarity and purposefulness of classical Hollywood story-telling seems to meet the restraint of British realism with brilliant effect. Yet the US apparently couldn't cope with the opening voice-over comments as spoken by Carol Reed and replaced this for American viewers with Joseph Cotten's more casual but less enticing tones.

The third man himself

The other name that hovers over this film from the start is that of Orson Welles who plays Harry Lime. The film is nearly two-thirds over before he appears but when he does it is almost as though he picks it up and runs with it. The idea of Harry Lime has haunted the film since its opening and he is behind virtually its entire narrative line. Naive, tippling American, Holly Martins (Joseph Cotten), has come to Vienna to find him; English Major Calloway (Trevor Howard) believes him

16   Joseph Cotten (Holly Martins) on the set of *The Third Man*.

dead, and a good thing too; Harry's girlfriend Anna (Valli) still grieves
for him. When Holly arrives in Vienna, he is just in time for what he
takes to be Harry's funeral. By the time Harry does appear, it will take
a very charismatic performer to live up to our expectations, and that
is exactly what Welles does. At night, a tipsy Holly sees a shadowy
figure standing in a doorway when a cat runs over the cobbled street
and stops at the feet of this figure. A sudden flash of light from an
apartment opposite reveals Harry's face in one of the screen's great
close-ups, and he disappears in a city square when Holly tries to chase
him. Few characters in films are given such a build-up, even if it is only
in hindsight one recognises this, and it is easy to come away thinking
that *The Third Man* is really Welles's film – he is of course 'the third
man' who was said to be involved in Harry's 'death' – instead of the
remarkable collaborative effort it actually represents.

If that first close-up of Harry is so memorable, it is echoed in his
last when he is trapped in the sewer which 'runs right into the Blue
Danube'. There is no escape for him. His fingers helplessly seeking the
upper world through a fixed grille express his plight. (For lovers of

trivia, they are actually director Carol Reed's own fingers, and filmed in London because Vienna had no such grilles). In a final close-up he seems almost to beg his old friend Holly to shoot him, a just discernible nod of the head emphasising what the eyes have already indicated. It is not just a matter of camera angle and distance that fixes Harry so firmly in the mind and the memory of the viewer. These are crucial, but so is the musical score. At key moments, what we came to know as 'the Harry Lime theme' focuses our attention on the character who both was and was not the 'third man'.

An innocent abroad

When Holly Martins steps off the train at the end of the film's opening sequence, he seems to exude a certain breezy transatlantic confidence, but, as he makes to leave the platform without showing his passport to the Military Policeman at the control gate, we wonder if he has any real grasp of the situation he is getting into. We've already seen shots of the devastated city and of the four occupying armies, and can't help feeling Martins will be in for some shocks. Especially when he tells the MP that he's surprised that his friend, Harry Lime, who's offered him a job, isn't there to meet him. The Greene-Reed combination that had worked so well on *The Fallen Idol* the previous year was centrally concerned with the threats to a child's innocence by the adults who make up his world. Now, the 'innocent' – Holly – is a pulp fiction writer of Westerns who is about to face some sobering facts about the Old World he has stumbled into. The rest of the film will be taken up with how Martins deals with a series of crucial encounters.

Calloway

Holly's faintly garrulous, easily tipsy approach first has to deal with the English major, Calloway (Trevor Howard), who exhibits a no-nonsense reserve in his demeanour that contrasts with Martins' initially more relaxed behaviour. The very coats they wear seem to hint at this disparity: Holly wears a flowing tweed, often carelessly draped over his shoulders, while Calloway, first glimpsed in full-length belted leather, which seems to announce authority, later favours the functional duffel-coat of a man with work to do. They meet at what Holly takes to be Harry Lime's graveside and a prickly relationship gets underway when Calloway says that Lime's death was 'the best thing that ever happened to him', claiming that Lime was a dangerous racketeer and that 'murder was part of his racket'. By this stage, Holly has drunk a good deal and he tries to hit Calloway, but is knocked down by Sergeant Paine (Bernard Lee), who works with Calloway and is a fan of Holly's books. This detail will have repercussions in the rest of the narrative: it is Harry's killing of Paine in the final chase in the sewers that prompts Holly into shooting his old friend whom he now knows to have been criminally corrupt. By then Holly is cooperating with Calloway's attempt to bring Harry to justice.

Whereas Holly has to overcome the feelings of long friendship with Harry, the austere Calloway has only to pursue the facts. He can't afford sentiment but when he takes Holly to the hospital to observe the effects of Lime's criminal activities in the selling of watered-down penicillin it is made clear that his reserved manner is not an alternative to genuine feeling. From the opposite direction, Holly has learnt to respect Calloway's probity. In an effect of narrative balance, Calloway has initially driven Holly away from what he believed to be Harry's grave and, in the film's penultimate moments, drives him off from Harry's grave to catch his plane out of Vienna – before setting him down to wait for Anna.

Anna
Anna is still hopelessly in love with Harry, and even when she learns the extent of his crimes she cannot simply stop being so. Certainly she is unable to respond to Holly's increasing attraction to her. The beautiful Italian actress, Valli (under contract to Selznick), makes her devotion true and touching: in roughly mid-film, Holly calls at her apartment with flowers, saying he has come to say goodbye, and finds she also knows what Harry has done. 'He's better dead,' she says at this point, still believing he is dead, and Holly accepts that he has no chance against the image she retains of the Harry she loved. 'I'm just a hack writer who drinks too much and falls in love with girls,' Holly tells her, and this bit of self-knowledge makes us think more of Holly, who knows he 'wouldn't stand a chance' with her.

As if to accentuate this, in the immediately following episode Holly has his first glimpse of the still very much alive Harry. Holly wants Anna to be safe and tries to intercede on her behalf with Calloway, giving him a further moral edge over Harry who later refuses to help keep her from being handed over to the Russians. But whatever Holly does, he can't displace Harry in her affections. Just as she is in the train about to leave Vienna, thinking Calloway has been kind to her about her forged passport, she sees Holly sitting in the station café and realises he is in on Calloway's plans. They are trying to get Anna out of the way before they 'take' Lime, and she leaves the train and deliberately lets it depart without her. She will a little later accuse Holly of being a 'police informer', just as Harry enters the café, draws a revolver then runs away. It is in matters such as the quality of Anna's feeling for Harry *and* in Holly's throwing in his lot with Calloway when he learns the full extent of Harry's crime, and its effect, that *The Third Man* becomes much more than a mere thriller. It certainly *is* a thriller, and a brilliant one too, but it acquires in these matters a moral complexity that goes well beyond our normal expectations of 'thriller'.

Mr Crabbin

Unlike Holly's other encounters, his meeting with Mr Crabbin (Wilfrid Hyde-White) is almost wholly comic. I say 'almost' only because an element of suspense also plays its part. Crabbin, representing the CRS (Cultural Re-education Sector), mistakes Holly for a serious author and invites him to address his institution on the modern novel, and agrees to pay his hotel expenses. A wild and nicely anti-climactic ride through the night streets precedes Holly's arrival at this cultural event where he nonplusses the audience by naming Grey – that's Zane Grey (not Thomas Gray of the churchyard 'Elegy') – as his chief literary influence and even more so when he doesn't know whom they mean when someone asks him about Joyce – that's James Joyce. As the audience gradually leaves, Holly becomes aware that the sinister Romanian, Popescu (Siegfried Beuer), has entered. He asks a question about Holly's next book, which he says is to be called 'The Third Man'. Popescu warns him against mixing fact and fiction and advises dropping this idea. Into this comic sequence, a whiff of real threat has intruded. Holly senses danger and flees, with Popescu and two thugs in hot pursuit.

Assorted foreigners

Popescu's is just one of the vividly sketched 'foreigners' that Holly comes up against. The first is the porter (Paul Hoerbiger) of Harry's apartment building, who gives Holly an account of the car accident in which Harry has supposedly been killed and which he says he has watched from his first-floor window. In post-war Europe anyone with a foreign accent will always be suspect (in English-speaking films, that is), but the porter is actually telling the truth as far as he could have observed it. 'Three men helped to carry your friend to the statue [Holly names Kurtz and the Romanian]... Yes, there was a third man.' The porter, wisely enough, has not told this to the police, not wanting to get 'mixed up' in this, and in one of the film's most memorable close-ups he finds out just how wisely. He later offers to give Holly some information and as he turns away from the window from which he has been watching Holly in the street below, a look of fear crosses his face and he is shortly after found murdered.

There are three other importantly involved foreigners. Popescu and 'Baron' Kurtz (Ernst Deutsch) have first been glimpsed observing Holly as he stands by Anna in the cemetery at the start of the film. We know we shouldn't trust them, partly because this is a British film and they *are* foreigners, but in Kurtz's case also because his dress sense suggests European decadence – what can we expect of a man in a dark coat with luxuriant fur collar, a showy, spotted bow-tie, and carrying a tiny dog? – as compared with the more manly gear worn by Holly or Calloway. Kurtz meets Holly later in the Café Mozart and warns him that everyone is involved in rackets of one kind or other in Vienna, and that it will be dangerous to start 'digging up' information about Lime. By now Holly has determined not to leave and to meet Anna (against Kurtz's advice) and Popescu, who repeats the same story about Harry's death, and denies what the porter has said about a 'third man'. A few moments later the porter will be dead.

Regarding the porter, Kurtz, Popescu and Harry's doctor Winkel (Eric Ponto), I am reminded of actor Herbert Lom's comment about his career in England: 'I was a foreigner and in English eyes all foreigners are villains'.[3] These four key characters, connected in various ways with Lime, are each put vividly before us in the sort of scrutinising close-up that ensures their being remembered and suggests more may be going on than meets the viewer's eye. They are all characterised by an ambiguity that hinders Holly's attempts to find out what really happened to his old friend, as he begins to find it strange that only those who knew him were present at his 'death'. If there's any doubt about the likes of Kurtz and Popescu, the brisk sequence of shots after Holly's meeting with Popescu intensifies our suspicions. Popescu is glimpsed on the phone arranging a rendezvous on the 'bridge'. Kurtz is seen leaving his apartment on a bicycle. Both then arrive at the bridge and a wonderful overhead shot confirms the sense of their being involved in some kind of conspiracy that requires them to talk where they can't be heard. This sort of shot, together with the many

17   Joseph Cotten (Holly Martins) and Orson Welles (Harry Lime).

watching faces, creates a perpetually unnerving atmosphere. The war may be over but the potential for danger is still there.

Harry

The encounter that the film has been heading towards, of course, is that between Holly and Harry. We've seen how Holly first glimpses Harry in the shadowy doorway, then loses him as Harry races off into the night and disappears, inexplicably to Holly, in a deserted city square. Inexplicable, that is, until Calloway points to the advertising kiosk that gives entrée to the sewers. Holly's next meeting with Lime is at the Prater, the fairground, described in the screenplay as, 'A wrecked pleasure palace'.[4] As such it is an apt microcosm of the post-war Vienna depicted in the film. Holly and Lime take seats on the Great Wheel, and Lime refuses to intercede to help Anna who is to be sent to the Russian sector. He warns Holly that, 'There's no proof against me – besides you'. Harry's amorality is epitomised in his refusal to take seriously any idea of the 'victims' of his criminal trade and referring to the people moving down below the Wheel as 'dots': 'If I said you could have twenty thousand pounds for every dot that stops, would you really, old man, tell me to keep my money?' The famous line about what Italy achieved under the Borgias – the culture of the Renaissance – as compared with the Swiss who have only the cuckoo clock to show for five hundred years of industrious peace and democracy further emphasises Harry's jaunty approach to moral matters.

The line, as is well known, was Welles' own invention and doesn't appear in the novel. Though he is in the film for only about twenty minutes, he somehow almost hijacks it in the memory. The fact that Holly is played by Joseph Cotten who had played Jed Leland to Welles's Kane in the epoch-making *Citizen Kane* (1941) gives this meeting an extra piquancy. We never come to films in a state of virgin ignorance; we tend to carry recollections of past viewings, images and performances with us, and the subdued persona of Cotten up against the dazzling charisma of Welles again can't help informing our response, if we are familiar with *Kane*, as many people no doubt were in 1949. Their last encounter, in the sewers, where Lime seems to be giving Holly the nod to shoot him, pulls together all of the complexities of the Holly-Lime interactions we've seen, made more resonant because of what we recall about their relationship in the earlier film.

The 'Fourth' and fifth men: the sound and look of the film

If those images of Harry Lime in the doorway, or at the end in the sewer, stay tenaciously in the mind's eye, this is at least as much due to music director Anton Karas and cinematographer Robert Krasker as to the actor. The first thing shown on screen is the strings of the zither and we hear the 'Harry Lime Theme' (as it became known) played on the soundtrack as the credits come up. As Charles Drazin tells it in his fascinating book-length study of the film,[5] 'When the film opened, the music was a sensation, and the unknown zither player was hailed as the 'Fourth Man'. Carol Reed was 'entranced' when, at a welcome party for the crew in Vienna, 'suddenly a little man in the corner started plucking on a funny little instrument that looked like a cross between a harp and a guitar'. At some of the film's tensest moments, the 'Harry Lime Theme' pushes the tension to the ultimate outcome, perhaps most memorably in the sewer as Holly goes to confront Lime after the killing of Sergeant Paine, and then again at the graveside, before giving way to the zither's plangent chords in the unforgettable ending.

Australian-born Krasker won a richly deserved Oscar for the haunting chiaroscuro of his lighting of war-torn Vienna and for the way in which he lights faces to fix them and their ambiguities in our minds. Not just Harry Lime but all those devious Europeans – Kurtz, Popescu, Winkel and the last terrified close-up of the porter in Harry's apartment – and the serene beauty of Valli's Anna, caught so as to suggest that the apparent serenity is at odds with an inner anxiety. These along with Vincent Korda's production design account for some of the most memorable-*looking* moments in British film history. It's not just a matter of lighting, but often it's the way the camera is tilted to suggest a confused state of mind and to unsettle the viewer, or how it mixes close-ups with the long shots that take in vistas of the war-torn beauty of the city, or the desolate avenue of the film's ending.

Last moments

Perhaps if the Hollywood influence had held sway, *The Third Man* might have ended differently, with Holly and Anna providing the sort of 'closure' so endemic in classic American cinema. The fact that it was not altered in the American version suggests that Selznick was persuaded of its appropriateness. Calloway is driving Holly from the cemetery to catch his plane out of Vienna. Holly asks him to look after Anna; 'I will if she'll let me', says Calloway. As they drive down the wintry avenue, Holly tells Calloway to let him out. He goes to stand by a tree and waits for Anna who is walking down the avenue – and who moves straight past Holly without so much as a glance. The end of Holly's dealings with Anna rings with poignant precision.

Graham Greene wrote: 'One of the very few major disputes between Carol Reed and myself concerned the ending, and he has been proved triumphantly right. I held the view that an entertainment of this kind was too light an affair to carry the weight of an unhappy ending'.[6] He paid tribute to 'the mastery of Reed's direction' and the 'brilliant discovery of Mr Karas, the zither player'.

Watching the film for the umpteenth time, engrossed as ever, I can only say that this ending seems to me as perfectly judged as any I've ever seen. As a sign of how besotted I am, when my wife and I were in Vienna for a wintry week in 1992, we tracked down as many of the film's locations as possible, finally coming upon a bleakly leafless avenue at Schönbrunn Palace. I persuaded her to go to the far end of the avenue while I leant against a tree, and she was then to walk straight past me without giving me so much as a glance. Such a confession can do nothing for me as a critic, but as an addicted fan of this irresistible film it may seem forgivable.

Notes

1 Quentin Falk, *Travels in Greeneland: The Cinema of Graham Greene* (London: Quartet Books, 1984).
2 Graham Greene, 'Preface', *The Third Man* and *The Fallen Idol* (London: Penguin, 1971), pp. 9, 10.
3 'Herbert Lom' in Brian McFarlane, *An Autobiography of British Cinema* (London: Methuen, 1997), p. 377.
4 Graham Greene, *The Third Man* (London: Faber and Faber, 1973), p. 95.
5 Charles Drazin, *In Search of The Third Man* (London: Methuen, 1999), pp. 99–100.
6 Greene, 'Preface', *The Third Man*, p. 11.

8   *Genevieve* (1953):
old cars and 'the other thing'

There are two wonderful moments in this sunniest of comedies, moments that temporarily lift the film to new heights, but coming back to it after perhaps a dozen years I'm delighted to find how well the *whole* film works. Those whose notions of British film comedy are bookended by, say, Ealing and the 'Carry On' series, should be aware of a slender strand of romantic comedy that wears its sexuality lightly and perceptively but neither ignores it (as much of the Ealing comedy output does) nor caricatures it as 'Carry On' does.

London to Brighton

In 2006, Philip French reviewed a film with the title, *London to Brighton*, a powerful drama of drugs and youthful prostitution, writing: 'Paul Andrew Williams's highly promising debut, *London to Brighton,* is not, as the title suggests, a remake of the gentle 1953 comedy *Genevieve* but a violent gangster movie.'[1] My point in quoting this is merely to suggest the long life this affectionately-regarded comedy has had, so that a reference to it might still resonate with readers half a century later. Why is it so remembered?

The 'London to Brighton', as presumably most people would know, refers to the annual veteran car run that was first staged in 1896. It is a rally, not a race, and this is a distinction that enters into the film's plot. The film's male protagonists, Alan McKim (John Gregson) and Ambrose Claverhouse (Kenneth More), are obsessive about their crocks, but, as one whose interest in vintage automobiles is roughly on a level with that in, say, the history of bow-ties, I should in fairness add that this doesn't affect enjoyment of the film for a moment. I'd add that some of these unreliable vehicles even have a certain charm. The *Wikipedia* entry on the Veteran Car Run makes reference to *Genevieve*, perhaps another small marker of the film's place in popular memory.

The film opens with a post-credits title thanking the officers and members of the Veteran Car Club of Great Britain, and this is followed by a disclaimer which sets the tone of the film: 'Any resemblance between the deportment of our characters and any Club members is emphatically denied – by the Club.' As Alan and Ambrose later engage in a violent verbal exchange that looks as if it might degenerate to incompetent fisticuffs, Alan's exasperated wife Wendy (Dinah Sheridan) accuses them of 'hawling like brooligans', to which he replies, 'Don't you call me a brooligan'. At such a moment the opening disclaimer comes happily to mind again.

By this time, the 'London to Brighton' has, in defiance of the rules of the Club, become a race between these two obsessives, whose women are more than a little fed up. On the return journey to London. Ambrose's latest London-to-Brighton accessory, the glamorous Rosalind, announces tartly that, 'Ambrose only thinks about that silly old car – and the other thing'. To this, Wendy, by now a veteran of the run, replies resignedly, 'Alan only thinks about the car.' This exchange, and the men behaving like 'brooligans', coming near the end of the rally and the film, make their full comic impact because of the way they resonate with what has gone before. If the 'run' – and the race it turns into for Alan and Ambrose – is a treated as a male obsession, the women make their presences felt in their reactions and in the ways in which they establish themselves as persons to be reckoned with.

A 'road movie' – sort of

With the 'London to Brighton' as its starting-point, *Genevieve* can be thought of as a sort of cheerful road movie in which the two main couples run into a variety of idiosyncrats along the way. Certainly in Christopher Challis's luminous Technicolor cinematography, few road movies have ever looked so good. If, however, it looks a wonderfully sunny piece, Dinah Sheridan remembered otherwise the conditions of its making, recalling that, 'It was so cold on those locations in Buckinghamshire that every day before we started work we had a glass of brandy'.[2]

18   Kay Kendall (Rosalind Peters) and Kenneth More
(Ambrose Claverhouse).

'It's childish and a bore. I simply don't see what's so wonderful about getting into a fifty-year-old car and taking two days to drive to Brighton and back,' Wendy complains early on, having just torn up an invitation to a 'Cocktail party'. (Does anyone still throw or go to these? In lots of ways, *Genevieve* evokes a more or less vanished world). In these two days, one strand of the narrative will depend on the mishaps and machinations along the way. Ambrose, to avoid losing time to a flock of sheep that is blocking the road, takes a detour, only to find when he re-joins the road that the sheep have made more progress than he has and his way is still blocked. When Alan's car, the 'Genevieve' indeed, breaks down, Ambrose hurtles past braying superiority, but shortly afterwards Alan turns the tables when he passes Ambrose having similar engine problems. And so on.

Mishaps proliferate, such as when Alan, trying to start Genevieve again with a crank handle, causes Wendy to spill a thermos of coffee all over her clothes; or when the elegant Rosalind is ordered by Ambrose to get out and push when his car is stuck in a ford, with disastrous results for her *haute couture*. And there are meetings with an expectant father who begs Ambrose to get him to the district nurse in a hurry, with the pompous owner of a flashy red roadster that Alan literally runs into, and with a traffic policeman who has the two drivers in his sights when they turn the run into a race. What I would add is that, though none of these 'road-movie' episodes sounds very sparkling in cold print, in fact they are treated with an irresistible comic flair and a persistent good-nature that doesn't preclude some sharp perceptions about over-grown schoolboys and their toys.

'and the other thing'

This remark of Rosalind's focuses attention on the film's treatment of the relations between men and women. Alan and Wendy have been married for three years and in the pre-run sequences in their cramped London mews-flat, director Cornelius and his actors create a very attractive sense of an easy, sexy rapport, of a young married couple getting on with being just that. 'Proper lunch or proper dinner?,' she asks Alan, as Ambrose, unannounced, comes bounding in, opening a bottle of wine and, in a tiny revealing touch, they have it in unmatching glasses, suggesting the not-quite-secure financial status of the McKims, a matter which will be echoed later. So will the fact that Wendy, before meeting Alan, had gone on the Brighton to London with Ambrose, though 'nothing happened', as she will later assure Alan.

Rosalind's comment and Wendy's wry reply distil quite a lot of the film's attractive sexiness. In the opening sequences in which Wendy and Alan are squabbling about the rally ('It's childish and a bore,' she has said) there is a lovely moment when she finds the surprise he has planned for her. They've quarrelled about Ambrose, about the party and the rally; she is cross and he sulks. Just before going to bed she opens a cupboard and comes back into the bedroom wearing the new hat he has bought her as a surprise, and, with her forgiving him, they embrace.

What has been established is a real couple who love each other and are getting over a quarrel, and at this point one of the film's smartest bits of editing occurs. As they embrace there is a slow dissolve accompanied by a voice-over intoning: 'What is taking place here is an old story but it was quite illegal till 1896 [the camera moves in on a magazine photo of an early car].' By then, the commentator (real-life news commentator Leslie Mitchell) has appeared and continues with, 'Until then no self-propelled vehicle could take the road unless it was preceded by a man on foot, carrying a red flag.' The witty double entendre nimbly unites the film's two chief concerns – cars and 'the other thing'.

We've seen the McKims' domestic life and the easy intimacy that can move between bickering and affection and we've been led to expect a more raffish approach from Ambrose who believes he's found just the person for a 'beautiful experience' in Rosalind. There's always a danger in writing about comedy, especially one as airy and graceful as this, of being heavy-handed, but the fact is that patterns do emerge here. Wendy, reluctant as she is about the run, does try to make the best of it, spilt coffee, bungled hotel bookings and all. However, when she throws herself on the bed in the terrible bedroom they've ended up in at Brighton, with an abandoned cry of, 'Make love to me' (a bit surprising for 1952), Alan is too preoccupied with Genevieve's engine problems to oblige and spends the rest of the hours of dark tinkering with the third entity in their marriage. Matching Wendy's frustration is, not Rosalind, but Ambrose. Rosalind has passed out from an excess of wine and next morning it is clear that Ambrose's beautiful experience has been placed on hold.

In fact, of the two women, the more unlikely of the two – Wendy – is presented as the sexier one, notwithstanding the domestic scene she emerges from. Rosalind persuades us that *haute couture* is no reliable guide to sex instinct or anything else. As to the men, even Ambrose's routinely lubricious approach in the end gives way before the inane competitive element of the race. He may be interested in 'the other thing' as he keeps suggesting but it's touch and go whether it's more important to him than the old car, the rally, the race. Alan, a somewhat more sober character, clearly loves Wendy, but this weekend the car is his prime concern. Which brings me to focus on…

Two wonderful moments

The two all-but magical moments that have stayed with me down the decades actually give weight to our impression of the two couples. The first takes place in the dining-room of the smart hotel where Ambrose and Rosalind are staying but Alan and Wendy are not. Rosalind, as elegant as ever, chats to Alan about Ambrose's amorous attentions to Wendy, while the latter two are dancing. Rosalind recalls, somewhat to our surprise, that she was once a member of an all-girls orchestra.

19   Kay Kendall (Rosalind Peters).

Meanwhile Ambrose is confiding to Wendy that his ambition has been to 'combine the London to Brighton with a really beautiful emotional experience', but that 'every single year something has gone wrong'.

Ambrose may not recognise it as such, but this 'experience', if not perhaps what he had in mind, is about to happen. Rosalind leaves the table, approaches the orchestra, picks up a trumpet and takes to the stage, with a heart-stopping rendition of 'Genevieve'. She is given a glorious close-up, then Christopher Challis's camera homes in on the back of Ambrose's head, which registers something magical as it slowly turns to observe Rosalind in full flight. A jazzed-up version of the old song follows, with close-ups of Rosalind's lips and fingers as they do their stuff. After this exhilarating moment (for us as well as for those in the film), Rosalind passes out, and Wendy starts to laugh hysterically as Ambrose tries in vain to revive her, the prospect of 'the other thing' receding apace. It's hard to say why the vision and sound of Rosalind with the trumpet should be so memorable: perhaps it's just because it's the last thing we might expect of the *soignée* Rosalind; perhaps it's the sheer sense of release about it; or maybe Kay Kendall, having played her tall, willowy, and cynical, just shows something real lurking behind Rosalind's glamorous façade. Whatever explanation fits, Ambrose is forced – and charmed – to acknowledge that there's an individuality at work there that he hasn't expected.

The other great 'moment' occurs very near the end of the film. The cars have reached suburban London; the competition between the two men has now taken on the aspect of a race to the death, with some very funny obstacles encountered along the way as they make their way towards their Westminster goal. Alan is now betting not the £100 he could ill afford, but Genevieve itself, and even the women have entered into the spirit of the thing by this time. While a little ahead of Ambrose at one point, Alan is paused as a policeman directs traffic, when a dignified old man (Arthur Wontner) approaches and says, 'Good gracious! A Darracq. The first car I ever owned.' He takes enormous pleasure in seeing 'this wonderful car, so beautifully kept', telling the McKims that he proposed to his wife in his Darracq.

This intervention, likely to cost Alan the race, induces in him a touching display of good manners. He's given up his chance of winning to gratify this old man's nostalgia, and offers to visit the old man to give him and his wife a drive in the Darracq. We look at Alan with new eyes, and Wendy looks on with tears as he speaks. She knows what he's given up (or thinks he has) and it reminds her of why she has married this man. That is, there's more to him than an obsession with old cars. On the matter of Darracqs, the highly successful film sparked a huge increase in vintage automobile collecting and restoration. I wonder if the film's great moment had something to do with this.

Two pairs and a few others

The film distinguishes neatly between and within each of the two pairs. As we have seen, Alan and Wendy have been married long enough to have slipped into certain routines, while the debonair Ambrose (of course he's debonair, he wears a yellow waistcoat with his tweeds) is still playing the field and not finding it altogether satisfying. It's hard to apportion the praise for a film that works as happily as this does, but certainly the casting of the leading quartet carries a major load. Equally, William Rose's screenplay gives them some sharply observed material to work on. But the differences between the two couples are announced in the casting of Dinah Sheridan and John Gregson as Wendy and Alan, and Kenneth More and Kay Kendall as Ambrose and Rosalind.

Dinah Sheridan, after years of mainly 'B' films, was riding high in 1953 with several well-regarded films behind her, including *Where No Vultures Fly* (a Royal Command Performance film, no less), *The Sound*

Barrier (for David Lean), *The Story of Gilbert and Sullivan* and, opposite box-office idol Dirk Bogarde, *Appointment in London*. Though she was not the first choice for the role of Wendy, she emerges from *Genevieve* with all the attributes of a leading lady. Her English-rose beauty was allied to a crispness of delivery and a charming sexiness that makes Wendy the most fully realised of this attractive quartet. She might have gone on to become a major star if she had not then married Rank executive, John Davis, and retired from the screen for fifteen years. She and John Gregson make a couple one can utterly believe in. He is obsessive about his old car but Gregson's rueful, faintly scruffy charm makes us credit other possibilities about him. He knows that there are limits to how selfish you can be in a marriage, and when selfishness has to give way. Gregson had been busy in British films since 1948, in increasingly substantial roles, but *Genevieve* launched him into a new kind of stardom.

As for Kay Kendall, *Genevieve* made her career. After appearing in small parts since the mid-forties, she went on to a series of starring roles until her tragically early death in 1959 at age 33. She brought a touch of real glamour into British films, along with a smart sense of comedy, which makes her Rosalind such a memorable figure, which Hollywood was quick to notice. Kenneth More had also been busy since the mid forties, in some quite noticeable supporting roles, but *Genevieve* was his jumping-off ground for bigger things, and he became a major star of British films for the next couple of decades. His raffish persona is ideally suited to the role of Ambrose, the raffishness stopping this side of caricature, and it would be held up to a different sort of scrutiny as Vivien Leigh's lover, the perennially immature Freddie, in *The Deep Blue Sea* (1955).

These four play with and off each other with what seems effortless ease but this is not to underestimate the practised skill with which each one finds veins of truth in these lightly but acutely drawn figures, suggesting both types and individuals at the same time. And they are surrounded by one of those British supporting casts each of whom has a moment to remember – or, rather, *provides* a moment to remember. Along the road, they meet Michael Medwin as the anxious expectant father, Reginald Beckwith as the fusspot owner of the red roadster, Arthur Wontner's Darracq-fancier, Geoffrey Keen as an obsessive traffic policeman, among others. At Brighton, Alan having bungled their accommodation booking, the McKims fetch up at a shabby-genteel private hotel presided over by the ineffably toothy Joyce Grenfell, who tells them about the limited bath times and the like. When they express some concern at what looks like an uncomfortable stay, little old Edie Martin pops out of her room to enquire, 'Are they Americans?', as if to imply that no self-respecting English couple would be so concerned about such trivialities as lack of hot water. 'No one's ever complained before,' Grenfell intones wonderingly – and we believe her.

A British romantic comedy

So, with two pairs of comely leads, each engaging in its own way and meshing productively, and a cast studded with character cameos that stay just on the right side of reality, *Genevieve* is off to a flying start as a romantic comedy. It doesn't depend on one-liners, though it has its share of these. There's plenty of verbal wit in William Rose's screenplay, but, as well, visual comedy is allowed to grow out of the action rather than just seeming to be imposed on it. The possibilities for things going wrong with the ancient cars are properly exploited but not at the expense of our engagement with the characters. When Ambrose's car breaks down, a group of hikers (in excruciating 1950s leisure-wear) lends its weight, until only one woman is left pushing, leading Ambrose to exhort her crossly with 'Harder, madam'. When Alan's crock misfires, he enlists a pub-keeper in a ruse to detain Ambrose.

But it is the four at the centre of the film who maintain the crucial romantic comedy element. And the wonder is that none of them was the producer's first choice. Thirty-odd years later, Dinah Sheridan recalled:

> They [the filmmakers] didn't want Kenneth More, they wanted Guy Middleton; they wanted Dirk [Bogarde] instead of John Gregson, Claire Bloom instead of me and I can't remember who they wanted instead of Kay Kendall. But we got on so well together and it worked. Ninety per cent of the credit must go to Bill Rose, a wonderful writer.[3]

It is now hard to imagine any but the four we have, they play together with such accomplishment, but Dinah Sheridan was right to draw attention to Rose's screenplay. It is a key element in the romantic-comedy mix, as are the contributions of two other key collaborators: cinematographer Challis and composer Larry Adler. Challis captures the sheer sunniness of the film, both physically (for much of the time) and stylistically. Sixty years later, one of his obituaries claimed that *Genevieve* 'marked him out as a cinematographer who was at ease capturing vehicles on the move', citing several subsequent films, such as *Chitty Chitty Bang Bang* (1968) that drew on this talent.[4] Adler, an American refugee from the vileness of the McCarthy witch-hunts of the late 40s and early 50s, and long resident in the UK, received an Oscar nomination for his equally sunny, jaunty harmonica score, but because of the blacklisting the nomination was in fact passed to Muir Matheson, the music director. It took over thirty years for the Academy to send him his certificate of nomination.

Behind and orchestrating all these diverse talents is director Henry Cornelius. Like Kay Kendall, he did not outlive the decade, and neither of his succeeding films – *I Am a Camera* (1955) and *Next to No Time* (1958) – saw him in such perfect tonal control as he shows in *Genevieve*. Someone (I forget who) once described it as the most Ealing comedy not made at Ealing, and perhaps this comment was prompted by the fact that Cornelius, a South African, had made his name at Ealing by directing the very popular *Passport to Pimlico* (1948). In fact, Cornelius, after leaving Ealing on fractious terms with its managing director Michael Balcon, later offered the *Genevieve* project to Balcon, who declined the offer, and, as a result, 'the most Ealing comedy not made by Ealing' was produced by the Rank Organisation.

But is it really so like Ealing as to deserve that comment? There is plenty of British film comedy, but it is apt to be whimsical, like much of Ealing's output and those that aspire to the Ealing touch; or broad, possibly inheriting the mantle of the music hall; or with the black streak that peaked with *Kind Hearts and Coronets*. But British romantic comedy hasn't had much of an innings, compared with, say, Hollywood's command of the genre. There are a few feebly pretty jobs in the 50s with titles like *For Better, For Worse* (1954) and *Upstairs and Downstairs* (1959), but it probably isn't much of an exaggeration to say that *Genevieve* is the only one that anyone remembers. Its editor Clive Donner (later a director) claimed with some justice that, 'It was a very true story about four young people, their fights, their break-ups and so on. Almost nothing like this film had been made before in Britain.'[5]

Since then, romantic comedy has scarcely been a continuing strand in British cinema. There was the odd title such as *The Grass is Greener* (1960), *Georgy Girl* (1966) and *A Fish Called Wanda* (1988), but not until the 1990s does anything like a *genre* emerge. During this decade there was a series of popular films featuring star names and aimed at international box-offices, films such as *Four Weddings and a Funeral* (1994), *Shakespeare in Love* (1998) and *Notting Hill* (1999). These are all accomplished films, but personally I'd swap any one of them for *Genevieve*, which seems to me almost the quintessential *English* romantic comedy, about more or less grown-up people not always acting sensibly but never losing their hold on our liking, even at their silliest. Adding to this the look and sound of the film, the immensely attractive casting and a screenplay that knows how to be witty without descent to mechanical wisecracks, and we have an almost ideally put-together piece of good-tempered entertainment. It doesn't aspire to be more than that – and it doesn't need to.

Notes

1 Philip French, *Observer*, 3 December 2006.
2 Dinah Sheridan, Carlton DVD of *Genevieve*.
3 'Dinah Sheridan' in Brian McFarlane, *An Autobiography of British Cinema* (London: Methuen, 1997), p. 538.
4 Obituary, *Times*, 13 June 2012, 48.
5 Clive Donner, Carlton DVD of *Genevieve*.

9   Double bill:
Private Information (1952)
and Cash on Demand (1963)

These two are linked as my tribute to the pleasures to be had from the often maligned British 'B' film. As they are both so short, I am treating them as an entity. First of all, let me be clear about what a 'B' movie is – or was. It was a film made cheaply and quickly, intended for the bottom half of a double bill at the cinema, in the days when programmes most often consisted of two features separated by an interval: the main feature came after the interval and the 'B' movie, or 'second feature', preceded it. At their best, these 'supporting films' as they were sometimes called, had an unpretentious paciness and a narrative drive and economy that could put more prestigious 'A' features to shame.

American 'B' films had a champion in James Agee back in the 40s and 50s, and some have acquired cult status since then by serious-minded film academics and others, but the British 'B' was largely unseen by reviewers and mostly went in one eye and out the other with filmgoers. Perhaps their poor reputation was a hangover from the 'quota quickies' of the 30s, films made in satisfaction of legislation about the making and exhibiting of British films – and in the expectation of instant oblivion. And indeed many of them were unquestionably very bad, though filmmakers such as Michael Powell and Bernard Vorhaus did their bit in lifting the average.

Over-all, though, they were made swiftly and cheaply and received scant attention at any level. During the war there was little 'B'-filmmaking as studio space and personnel were commandeered for other purposes, and, when production of second features got going again post-war, there was a backlog of bad memories to contend with. The 50s and early 60s saw a resurgence of often perfectly respectable British 'B' films, but they had to wait until the later 90s to attract any serious attention. Having watched several hundred of them over the last decade I must say that I found viewing no hardship and was often rewarded with trim thrillers and some lively comedies, with other genres – costume pieces, musicals, sci-fi, etc. – less likely to appear, presumably because their production costs would have been beyond modest budgets.

I'm aware of cheating a little by squeezing two short 'B's into one chapter, but that seemed to me to strike the right note of appreciation without making huge claims for either. *Cash on Demand* is a taut thriller, set almost entirely in a provincial bank whose unbending manager comes under threat from a suave criminal and undergoes a humanising change as he deals with the crisis. *Private Information* is a rare social drama to be found in the ranks of the 'B' movies. It concerns a protest against slapdash post-war housing when a middle-aged widow takes up cudgels against the local council authorities. Both films offer more than the often perfunctorily-met demands of the second feature; both offer surprisingly sympathetic human insights; and both are held together by central performances that would command respect in much loftier circumstances.

Private Information

In its modest way this sixty-six-minute second feature recalls other better-known enterprises. Its real ancestor is probably Ibsen's *An Enemy of the People*, in which a protest is mounted against corrupt municipal authorities who refuse to take action about polluted swimming baths. There have been other films in which authorities come up against a threat to their power and/or prosperity, including such big prestige jobs as *Jaws* (1975), *Silkwood* (1983) and *Erin Brockovich* (2000), and there was an engaging British 'B' film, *Time Gentlemen Please* (1952), released in the same year as *Private Information*, which made comic capital out of its dealings with the pomposities of a local council, faced not so much with corruption as with eccentricity.

A 'B' with a bee in its bonnet

What is unusual about *Private Information* is the notion of a 'B' movie, in 1950s Britain, taking up a matter of public controversy and treating it in the mode of social realism. The latter was no stranger to mainstream

'A'-feature filmmaking in post-war Britain, but at the semi-submerged level of the supporting feature crime or, if not, feather-light comedy mostly prevailed. What is at issue in *Private Information* is the matter of post-war housing, and in 1952 Britain was still far from having repaired all the ravages of the war. The housing estate in which the widowed Charlotte Carson (Jill Esmond) and her family live has been shoddily conceived and executed. Very early on, in a nicely restrained touch, her daughter Georgie (Carol Marsh) finds the window stuck again as she tries opening it to release the burnt-toast smells. A budding writer, she quips that she could use her rejection slips to paper over the cracks in the house. In these small moments the film's theme is ushered in.

The film is adapted from Gordon Glennon's play *Garden City*, first performed in Wolverhampton in July 1951 with Peggy Mount in the lead, and Glennon co-wrote the screenplay with John Baines and Ronald Kinnoch. I mention these three because I think the film bears the signs of having been carefully adapted to the screen, so that it is not merely 'opened out' in the sense of moving among a number of different locations but that in other ways it has been given some real cinematic life. Baines and Kinnoch both had considerable experience in writing for films and would later work on larger-scale productions in various capacities. As to locations, it moves around the various rooms of Charlotte's house, into the Council chambers, the street with its market stalls, the hospital and exteriors of these several buildings. Merely shifting the settings with a freedom less easy to achieve on stage is no guarantee of a film's fluidity, but the film is well enough directed (by Fergus McDonell) and shot by famous cinematographer Eric Cross to make one reviewer's claim that it is 'thoroughly stagey in treatment'[1] seem unduly severe.

A woman with a cause
The central notion of a strong-minded individual taking on the system has often enough provided the basis for compelling drama, on stage and screen. The Mayor (Lloyd Pearson) and surveyor Freemantle (Norman Shelley) of the small town of Hamington have taken bribes from the contractor responsible for the faulty construction of the Turners Hill Estate, where the widowed Charlotte lives with daughter Georgie and architect son Hugh (Jack Watling). Hugh works in the surveyor's department and has prepared a confidential report which is critical of the graft at work in the municipal chambers. We have been prepared for this in the opening scene when the Mayor and Freemantle talk on

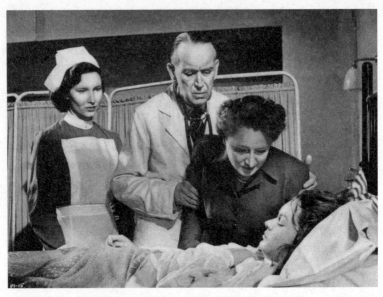

20   Jill Esmond (Charlotte Carson), Carol Marsh (Georgie Carson), doctor
and nurse uncredited.

the phone about someone who 'is a regular nuisance, always asking questions', ushering in the possibility of bureaucratic cover-up.

Hugh's situation is complicated by the fact that he is in love with Freemantle's daughter Iris (Mercy Haystead) and, of course, because his family lives in the estate. Charlotte has become incensed with the Council for not heeding complaints about bad drainage and leaking roofs. When she looks at the report which Hugh has left at the house, where sister Georgie reads it in mistake for a returned manuscript, she descends on a meeting of the Council at the Town Hall. She accuses the Council of ignoring the estate's deficiencies, and of accepting bribes. The matter is reported in the press, and Charlotte finds an ally in journalist Alex Hartman (Gerard Heinz) – and also finds that the town is on her side.

This is the film's essential situation. Pressure will be brought to bear on Charlotte. An attempt is made to silence her, when the Mayor, brother of her late husband, sends his snobbish and overbearing wife Dolly (Brenda De Banzie) to try to extract a letter of apology from Charlotte. An outbreak of typhoid in Hamington, introduced in a photographic montage of ambulances, newspaper headings and hospital, brings the matter to a crisis. Charlotte has refused to be bullied or to apologise, and her second appearance in the Council chambers is well built up with the Mayor and cronies expecting a retraction. The camera cuts to their faces as they react to the fact that she is not going to sign the letter of apology, which she then tears up, saying, 'I demand a public enquiry'.

It could be said that the film overdoes the connecting links between the characters: Charlotte is the Mayor's sister-in-law; Hugh wants to marry the corrupt surveyor's daughter; Georgie becomes a typhoid victim; Alex, the refugee newspaperman, detects talent in Georgie's stories; and so on. Nevertheless, at the time of viewing, these links, which may seem schematic when written about, serve to tighten the film's tension. Hugh, caught between Iris and a mother who now has the bit between her teeth, bursts out to Charlotte: 'You've lost me my exam [he's had to come back early from London]. You've lost me my job. Now, Iris. I hope you're satisfied.' Yes, the link can seem contrived; on the other hand, it also intensifies Charlotte's conflict, and, precipitated by Georgie's illness, and the market shoppers' telling her how 'grateful' they are to her for speaking out, she now has the courage to make her stand against the corrupt municipal officials.

What the papers said

As was customary, the major newspaper reviewers had nothing to say about this, or 'B' films in general. *Private Information* was received with modified enthusiasm by the trade press. For instance, *Kinematograph Weekly* claimed that, though the film 'leans slightly to the Left and contains more talk than action' and 'means well', 'its epidemic climax, resulting from bad drainage, can be smelt some time before the end' – while still allowing that 'it definitely has its moments'.[2] *The Daily Film Renter* found that, 'Sincerity and simplicity are the essence of this appealing British picture', despite its 'rather overdrawn climax',[3] while the fan magazine, *Picturegoer*, praised it as a 'Sincere and forthright British small-town melodrama', adding 'this "B" picture aims a straight left at corrupt officials and building contractors'.[4] Several reviewers drew attention to its theatrical origins, but there was also a suggestion that the British 'B' film was at least focusing on matters more serious than usual.

This is one of my two main reasons for including the film here. The first reason is that it *was* uncommon for a British 'B' to address a subject of contemporary concern and controversy, and to do so with some firmness of purpose and dramatic tightness. As well, what all the reviewers, most of them in the trade papers, singled out was the performance of Jill Esmond in the central role of Charlotte. Linking these two reasons, *Picturegoer*'s opinion was that 'her performance prevents propaganda from getting the better of straight drama'.

I sought this film out at the time of its release because I'd always felt indebted to Jill Esmond for having made me aware at an early age of the difference between art and life. She'd played a mean governess to a little girl in an American 'B' film called *My Pal Wolf* (1945) and I was puzzled by how much more interesting this character was, whom I'd have disliked in real life, than all the tedious good people she was giving a bad time to. Checking out her career, I found she'd had a busy time in the US in the early 30s, returned to England with husband Laurence Olivier, then her own career had lost a lot of momentum. However, every time she appeared in supporting roles in film, she stamped her often-brief scenes with an authority and naturalness that was always impressive. *Private Information* was meant to kick-start a mid-life spurt of filmmaking but, in the event, it was little seen and was followed by only two more film roles – in *Night People* (1954) and *A Man Called Peter* (1955) – and as Queen Eleanor in TV's *The Adventures of Robin Hood* (1955–6).

As the crusading Charlotte Carson she brings strength and dignity to a role that needs both, and her scenes with each of the main characters have appropriate warmth (with son and daughter), or forcefulness (with mayoral brother-in-law) or burgeoning friendship (with newspaperman, Adam). She makes the woman's underlying generosity apparent in dealings with her son's girlfriend, and she persuades us that this woman, essentially private in everyday matters, has the moral firmness and sense of justice necessary to take on the grafting councillors. The limited critical response the film received nevertheless uniformly praised Esmond's work: 'thanks to the skill with which Jill Esmond covers provocative ground as the middle-aged heroine, it's pretty certain of popular and mass appeal,' said *Kinematograph Weekly*. 'Jill Esmond as the gallant housewife works hard to inject some vitality into the proceedings and is, in fact, very successful despite the handicaps of the script,' claimed *Today's Cinema*, while *The Daily Film Renter* praised her 'excellent portrayal'.

The rest of the cast is adequate to the demands placed on it, especially Mercy Haystead as the very attractive Iris who proves to be a woman of character, and Lloyd Pearson and Norman Shelley as the corrupt Mayor and surveyor, but Esmond carries the weight of the film.

The director, McDonell, was better known as an editor and the film's brisk cutting among settings and characters in conflict probably reflects this. He directed only two other films, *The Small Voice* (1948) and *Prelude to Fame* (1950), and subsequently returned to a long career as editor, but each of the three features he directed is marked by sensitive performances and a seriousness of purpose.

Cash on Demand

Unlike *Private Information*, my second choice, *Cash on Demand* (1961), is in line with the British 'B' movies' preoccupation with crime, though it is a very superior example of the thriller genre, putting to shame many a more ambitious venture. But it has several parallels with the other film. Both films are set in small provincial towns. Like *Private Information*, *Cash on Demand* also has echoes of a famous work, in this case Dickens's *A Christmas Carol*, in the way that its austere protagonist undergoes a change of heart, because, like Charlotte Carson, he will be put under unusual pressures. His are admittedly more immediately dangerous than hers. There is real interest in how each responds to these pressures as these two films go well beyond the perfunctory plot demands of so many second features. As a piece of trivia, the film runs for sixty-six minutes, as did *Private Information*, and the trimness of their running-time is no doubt a factor in the tensions they develop.

Both films had their origins in plays. In the case of *Cash on Demand*, this was a television play called *The Gold Inside*, first aired on 24 September 1960, as an entry in ATV's 'Theatre 70' series, so-called because these plays filled a 70–minute time slot. The play is by Jacques Gillies, described as 'British author of superior television thrillers in the sixties, mostly for ATV and directed by Quentin Lawrence'.[5] Lawrence also directed *Cash on Demand*, and the film reveals a real intimacy with its confined setting and the working lives lived in it.

The bank and the staff
The small-town setting is suggested in the opening moments. Santa Claus is in the street urging people to 'Give this Christmas to Haversham charities', the camera pulling in on the plaque announcing the 'City and Colonial Bank. Haversham Branch'. It then tracks into the empty bank, coming to rest on the Manager's door before prowling into his

office, checking out his desk and safe, with some ominous music on the soundtrack. What is established, neatly and wordlessly, is a small, provincial bank, awaiting the arrival of its staff. Production designer Bernard Robinson and cameraman Arthur Grant have served well the director's apparent intentions in creating this setting: a series of empty spaces awaiting occupants.

There are brief identifying sketches of the staff as they arrive. Sanderson (a lugubrious-looking Norman Bird) alters the calendar to the 23rd and corrects the clock's time to 9.45, carrying out what is clearly his daily routine. He is followed by cheery middle-aged Miss Pringle (Edith Sharpe), sympathetically tolerant of the mildly flirty young pair, Sally (Lois Dane) and Harvill (Barry Lowe). Pearson (Richard Vernon), austere and middle-aged, is the bank's second-in-command, a role that will matter in the ensuing drama. There is talk about arrangements for the bank's Christmas party that evening, but generally the film establishes neatly a sense of these people working more or less harmoniously with only a minimal suggestion of knowing each other personally.

As they go about settling in for the day's work, we get our first glimpse of 'His lordship', the manager Fordyce (Peter Cushing), a blurred reflection of his face in the bank's plaque which he fastidiously polishes before entering. Everything about his demeanour signifies a man lacking in human warmth, from the way he folds his scarf to reproving Miss Pringle for the array of Christmas cards on her desk and to the even more severe reprimand of Pearson for a corroded nib on the pen provided for customers' use. There is further chill between Fordyce and Pearson about a minor discrepancy in the books: a mistake is something Fordyce cannot tolerate, and the brief scene between these two in Fordyce's office makes clearer still that Fordyce 'is not interested in personalities', and why Pearson wants to be recommended for a transfer to the city.

With the situation of the bank and its staff economically but vividly in place and the doors due to open at 10am, the scene is now set for the arrival of…

The intruder

For a man who is not interested in personalities, Fordyce will receive a shock to his system with the entry into the bank of a well-dressed man who has arrived in a posh car and, with grating self-assurance, asks for the manager. This is 'someone of consequence,' says Pearson as he tells

Fordyce of the arrival of Colonel Gore Hepburn (André Morell). Even before his real purpose is revealed – that of robbing the bank's vault – Hepburn's jocose assumption of superior authority grates on Fordyce: 'You people in the provinces...,' he reproves Pearson for letting him in to Fordyce's office without first checking his credentials.

The phone rings and it's apparently Fordyce's wife begging him to, 'Do what he says'. Hepburn claims that there are two men at Fordyce's home, with electrodes attached to his wife's head, and she and their son will be killed if Fordyce doesn't obey orders. Lawrence directs the ensuing moments with a tense alternation of close-ups between the two men, and in doing so signals what will be the film's main interest: that is, the interplay between the two men is more compelling than whether or not Hepburn will get away with the bank's holdings. (These, by the way, add up to a mere £90,000, which, even in 1961, is a way of stressing the small-time provincial bank we're dealing with, and it is a rare 'B' thriller that takes provincial life at all seriously. There are also glimpses of a few customers quietly coming and going in the bank, just enough for realism.)

There is a very smart opposition set up between these two men. Fordyce's cold rectitude and his provincialism contrast with Hepburn's amiable criminality and metropolitan suavity. When he's not delivering steely instructions, such as ordering Fordyce to behave with 'absolute naturalness', he seems a much warmer figure, one who 'can't help interesting [him]self in people'. He even reveals a touch of wit: 'I detest brutality. I want bank robberies to be smoother, more sociable', which contrasts with Fordyce's austere claim: 'I am not in the habit of ingratiating myself with my subordinates'. And indeed we've seen evidence of this. Hepburn, however nefarious his purposes, is right when he accuses Fordyce of being 'not a very charitable man, let alone a sporting one.'

The build-up

A thriller in which the one moment of overt violence occurs when the criminal slaps the bank manager on the face clearly has other things on its mind than the usual sorts of action expected of 'B'-movie crime. This led one writer to claim that the film is 'told entirely without violence [give or take the slap] yet thick with the atmosphere of menace'.[6] That is absolutely true: few films exercise a more gut-twisting tension than this unpretentious but gripping thriller. It is told in 'real time' so that we are aware of the minutes ticking by as the intruder works his psychological pressure on Fordyce until he bursts out of his defensive armour to threaten, 'If anything happens to my family I swear I'll kill you.' And this means something to us when he later appeals to Pearson for help, explaining why he has had to follow the intruder's orders: that he is a man who has no friends and that his family is 'all I've got'.

As the time moves on inexorably to the moment when Fordyce will be forced to open the bank vault, what has really been compelling our attention is the clash of wills between two utterly opposed types, let alone agendas. There are more conventional tensions created by, for example, the window-cleaner outside Fordyce's office, which acts as an obstacle when they are about to fill Hepburn's cases with banknotes, or when Fordyce momentarily 'loses' the combination to the safe in the vault. These moments are skilfully directed and edited for suspense, but at least as riveting is the changing perception of Fordyce. Whereas Hepburn's passing himself off as a representative of the bank's London insurance firm and as 'Colonel' is nothing but convincing fraud, Fordyce's chilly exterior has been a fair indicator of the inner man.

What happens to Fordyce is that long-submerged or suppressed human warmth and spontaneity make their way to the surface. The threat to kill the intruder is only the most extreme example. When Hepburn says his plan is to 'kidnap [Fordyce's] wife and child if anything goes wrong' and to release them at the end of the hour he needs to escape, Fordyce collapses at his desk and offers himself as hostage. We now begin to see why the film opens with Santa in the street and 'The First Noël' on the soundtrack. Fordyce is a modern version of Dickens's Scrooge and by the film's end he will have learnt to value something more than mere efficiency in the exercise of his job. When the police arrive, his fate is in the hands of his staff who tacitly rally, and as he leaves the bank he asks them, 'What is the usual sentence... for completely failing in my duty towards my staff?', and exits saying, 'I'll see you tonight at the staff party'.

Assessment

It's easy to make this sound schematic. Stiff, cold man finds regeneration and human warmth when his life and family and work-place are threatened, and when he has been subjected to the sort of persecution that is a variant on how he has treated his staff. However, it is done with such skill and precision that it avoids seeming predictable. Made in 1961, it was only released in late 1963 as support to the US musical, *Bye Bye Birdie*, when it received notices well above the usual critical fate of the British 'B'. The *Monthly Film Bulletin*, no friend to British second features, praised the story as 'watertight, terse and gripping', finding that 'the menace is more pronounced than in many films relying on physical brutality'.[7] A more recent writer praised it as 'an intelligent melodrama [which], with minimal resources, maintains tension with its tale of regeneration'.[8]

Above all, the immaculate performances of Peter Cushing as the increasingly tormented Fordyce and André Morell as the cruelly jocular Hepburn maintain a real interest in character and character interaction. How each responds to the challenge of the other is essentially what grips us and raises the film well above the usual level of the 'B's. The rest of the cast does its stuff unobtrusively, especially the staff members getting on with their work under the chilly cloud of Fordyce's disapproval and maintaining a level of humanity that he will finally recognise.

The whole film is set in the bank, apart from the opening and closing glimpse of the street outside, and its veteran cameraman, Grant, gives it a look of authenticity. There is an element of unlikely contrivance involving the wife's voice and a tape-recorder, but this is to quibble about a film that gets everything else so exactly right. It was a product of Hammer Film Productions, famous for its horror output in the 50s and 60s, and this trim thriller, scarcely noticed at the time, was described in 1997 as 'one of Hammer's lost films'.[9]

Notes

Cash on Demand is now available on DVD and now that it has been found it deserves a serious audience. I could wish for a similar fate for that other, still-lost 'B', *Private Information*.

1 *Monthly Film Bulletin*, August 1952, 112.
2 *Kinematograph Weekly*, 12 June 1952, 23.
3 *The Daily Film Renter*, 9 June 1952, 21.
4 R. H. B., *Picturegoer*, 13 September 1952, 18.
5 *Halliwell's Television Companion*, third edition (London: Grafton Books, 1982), p. 311.
6 Allen Eyles, R. V. Adkinson and Nicholas Fry, *The House of Horror* (London: Lorrimer Publishing Ltd, 1973), p. 71.
7 *Monthly Film Bulletin*, December 1963, 171.

8 Geoff Mayer, *Guide to British Cinema* (Westport, Connecticut, and London: Greenwood Press, 2003), p. 59.

9 *The House That Hammer Built*, No. 3, June 1997, 155.

10   A *Kind of Loving* (1962)
– and of living

The 'New Wave'

In May 1956, a new play opened at London's Royal Court Theatre and changed the face of British theatre, forever as was supposed. This was John Osborne's *Look Back in Anger*. Enthusiastic critics such as Kenneth Tynan fell upon it, and there was a suggestion that it had ousted Coward and Rattigan and Priestley and all those tired old-timers in one fell swoop. As it has turned out, this wasn't quite the case, and these days we are probably more likely to see theatre revivals and film adaptations of, say, Rattigan than we are of *Look Back in Anger* which so remorselessly hit out at the British middle- and upper-middle classes. For a decade or more, the transformative effect of Osborne's windy polemic and its protagonist, angry young Jimmy Porter, spawned a lot of similarly 'angry young' plays. Those around at the time would have found it hard to believe that, fifty years on, we have just had a fine new film version of Rattigan's *The Deep Blue Sea*, ironically released at the same time that *Look Back in Anger* was playing on Broadway. There was always, of course, room for more than one way of confronting the world in the theatre – and film.

When the 'New Wave' (the Anglo version of the French '*nouvelle vague*' which had got in first) broke on English film shores, those shores were more likely to be bleakly northern than at more fashionable southern locations, Sunderland rather than Eastbourne perhaps. British film, at least as much as the London theatre, desperately needed a shot in the arm by the end of the 1950s. This decade had been too much taken up with the rehearsing of wartime exploits or romantic comedies set in the Technicoloured purlieus of the Home Counties, with a nice young professional couple whose serenity might be disturbed by a Swedish *au pair*. Film lagged behind the theatre in taking up the challenge so vigorously adopted by *Look Back*, but in early 1959 the film version of John Braine's novel *Room at the Top* did something like the same service for a cinema in serious danger of doldrums. This film about a young man on the make brought a new openness about sexual matters and a challenge to existing class structures.

What were these films like?

The films in the wake of *Room at the Top* over the next few years were all set in the less glamorous areas of England's north, as if in a determined effort to break new ground. Ken Loach would say in 1995 that the directors of these films 'used the north of England and the working class as a location for four or five or six years, then they all left'.[1] He implied that they made a film or two, then hurried back to the south which they really found more congenial for their work. This is perhaps a jaundiced view from one who has persistently taken on the marginalised lives of people, often in discouraging circumstances. Nevertheless, the New Wave films – as well as *Room at the Top*, the titles include *The Loneliness of the Long-Distance Runner*, *A Taste of Honey* through to *A Sporting Life* – did open up new ground and that was partly a matter of going north, giving audiences vistas of bleak rows of terraces and even bleaker shots of the skyline dominated by factory chimneys belching smoke. These panoramic moments were often the result of sending young people up on a hillside out of town on a liberating excursion, frequently sexual in nature. There is too a generally smoky, grey look about the exteriors in these films.

I don't mean to make these films sound merely depressing. In fact, they were an exciting break with so much of earlier 1950s British cinema which tended to offer a middle-class view of life as if that was the norm with no questioning required. The New Wave films took working-class lives seriously almost for the first time in British cinema. Too often it had relegated working-class characters to comic relief, implying that emotional life was really the preserve of their social betters (even the great *Brief Encounter* is guilty of this), or if not for comic relief then as objects of social concern. It was rare for a film to treat them, as *It Always Rains on Sunday* did, as individuals with inner lives as complex as any. In

Room at the Top and *A Kind of Loving* there is an aspirational element: their working-class protagonists aren't about to be constrained by the class boundaries accepted by previous generations. They are aware of other possibilities and want to try them.

'Working-class *men*': yes, these films are essentially masculinist in their narratives. Only in *A Taste of Honey* is there a central female figure, and even she, like several other of the women in these films, has got herself pregnant. The difference is that she, Jo, is the creation of a woman playwright, Shelagh Delaney, and the rest of the cast take secondary places in relation to her. Elsewhere, getting the girl pregnant hinders the chap's attempts to find a more exciting life. All right, in some ways these films no longer seem like the breakthrough they did back then. They are all, too, based either on novels or plays, like so much British filmmaking. But they certainly did constitute a change of direction, both literally in the sense of going north and metaphorically in the ways in which they took on a class most often intended to be funny or pathetic in the past and now treated as real, as deserving and getting perceptive attention. If, as Loach suggested, those filmmakers went north, made their films and scuttled south again, they did in fact perform a real service.

Why choose A Kind of Loving?

A great deal has been written about *A Room at the Top*, and rightly so. Its 'hero', Joe Lampton, in a way did for cinema what Osborne's Jimmy Porter had done for theatre. Joe's upward mobility from working-class roots to marrying the boss's daughter he has made pregnant hasn't left him unscarred. The explicit observation of class was pretty much new in British cinema, and so was sexual candour. Matters such as these (and the film's subsequent dealings with censorship) have ensured a lot of critical coverage. Similarly, the film version of *Look Back in Anger* and the big commercial success of *Saturday Night and Sunday Morning* attracted a lot of attention. In some ways, *A Kind of Loving* is less venturesome than these, or *The Loneliness of the Long-Distance Runner* and *A Sporting Life*, but in its less clamorous, less polemical way it still seems absolutely typical of its period and the New Wave. Much less seems to have been written about it.

Perhaps its virtues are less striking; it is less 'plotty' than some of the others, but it still has a great deal in common with them. There are still the archetypal 'Long Shots of Our Town from That Hill'[2] and all that these imply about the life of the towns and the need for some escape. There are the familiar rows of terraced housing, the drab factory sites, and the popular-culture resorts of cinema and dance hall and café. It's still the man who calls the shots that get the narrative moving, and of course we're steeped in the working-class and lower-middle-class aspects of the life lived in this clearly northern town. Above all, though, the film deserves attention for the insight and compassion with which it considers and represents a kind of living, as well as of loving. As director John Schlesinger observed: 'It was about love in a general sense: it had no particular political axe to grind, and I think it was a film about human difficulties and the illusions of love, and the compromise that he [the film's protagonist, Vic] felt he finally had to make.'[3]

Where does it come from?

Like all the New Wave films, *A Kind of Loving* has a literary source. (How strange that in their urge to be different none of these filmmakers sought out original screenplays. It could be argued that the essential 'newness' was a matter of physical and social setting, as much as, or more than, of style.) It is based on Stan Barstow's 1960 novel which is the first in a trilogy which embraces the life, with its vicissitudes and frustrations and small triumphs, of one Vic Brown. The other two in the trilogy, *The Watchers on the Shore* (1966) and *The Right True End* (1976), not only trace Vic's marriage and its failure and its aftermath, but also register unobtrusively some of the shifts in English society over the relevant decade or so. It's a substantial piece of work that was used as the basis for a 1982 television miniseries.[4]

A *Kind of Loving* as novel (and as film) grew out of an exceptionally lively period for English fiction, ushered in by the likes of Kingsley Amis's *Lucky Jim* (1954) and John Braine's *Room at the Top* (1957). As with them, in *A Kind of Loving* you can feel the protagonist straining at the bit. Barstow's control over narrative and tone seems to me entirely assured, as he gets absolutely inside Vic's longing for something more in life or at least for making the best that can be made from what's available. From a working-class background (father's an engine-driver), he has seen sister Chris become a teacher and marry a nice bloke from a rung or two further up the social ladder, and he wants a married life as rewarding as hers.

Equally, though, Barstow has insight into what makes girlfriend Ingrid tick. Ingrid works in the same firm as Vic, who fancies her but fairly soon realises that his attraction to her is almost wholly sexual. Whereas he has had the advantage of Chris's intelligent sympathy to offset the narrower worldview of his mother, the 'Old Lady', Ingrid's engineer father is mainly absent and she has been shaped intellectually by her snobbish and viciously self-centred and self-righteous mother. Barstow can find real poignancy in Vic's wish that he could love Ingrid more, but even as he allows Vic to note that 'She sips her coffee, dainty like, with her little finger sticking out' and that she has 'all sorts of little ways that set [him] on edge',[5] he knows she can't be held wholly responsible for such genteel affectations. We are told all this in Vic's voice but are aware that Barstow also wants us to spare some feeling for her.

What's it all about then?

Marriage

Much of the film, like Barstow's novel, is about marriage and class, and Schlesinger's film version keeps closely to its main narrative movement. After panning a wintry urban landscape behind the credits, the film, like the novel, opens on a marriage – Chris's (Pat Keen) to the quietly amiable teacher David (David Mahlowe) – and the bridal party emerges from the church to be observed and chatted about by the crowd of gossiping neighbours. By starting with these images of the clearly happy couple surrounded by their approving families, the film establishes the sort of life Vic (Alan Bates) will want. As he makes clear later, much as he fancies Ingrid (June Ritchie) sexually, he can't really find any common ground with her on other matters. He will later describe Chris as 'dead lucky' when he's talking to his draughtsman workmates. But the film doesn't sentimentalise Chris. When Vic has left Ingrid near the end of the film, Chris isn't about to offer him a shoulder to cry on. He's married Ingrid because he made her pregnant, and he tells Chris he wishes he'd married someone like her. But Chris, for all that she says he can stay on their couch for a few nights, does for a moment sound like her mother when she tells Vic, 'You've only yourself to blame.' Marriage has worked well for Chris but, just as Ingrid reflects her mother's ways of thinking, so too Chris hasn't shaken off all her traces of *her* mother's firmly held opinions. And perhaps, too, Chris's touch of astringency

21   Alan Bates (Vic Brown) and June Ritchie (Ingrid Rothwell).

influences Vic in returning to his own marriage and the possibility of 'a kind of loving'.

The other marriages in the film don't offer especially attractive models. Vic's parents (Gwen Nelson and Bert Palmer) have been together for several decades without much suggestion that they ever have anything significant to say to each other. The 'Old Lady' is prone to be close-lipped and judgmental, pretty much wrapped in a culture of working-class respectability. When Vic goes to see her after he's left Ingrid, she's cleaning the front windows and she tells him she doesn't want to talk to him till he's back with Ingrid. 'Your Ingrid cares a lot about you, but you've never cared a tuppeny damn about anyone but yourself,' she says, and, though he has always had an ideal of marriage to which Ingrid doesn't conform, he might perhaps have expected a shade more sympathy from his mum. His engine-driver dad advises Vic (they are on the more neutral site of the allotment) to 'get a flat, get a tent, but get Ingrid away from her mother'.

Ingrid's mother in the film is a widow – and a monster, but, as brilliantly played by Thora Hird in a rare major role, wholly believable.

It's hard to be sure what John Schlesinger had in mind in omitting Ingrid's father from the film. In the novel, he is an engineer whose work keeps him away from home for long stretches of time and, in view of his wife's rigid, censorious and snobbish attitudes to everything and everyone, it is easy to imagine his extending these work-related absences. When seen briefly, he seems a reasonable, amiable character, so that it is likely that Ingrid's narrow views are more or less the result of constant exposure to her mother's smothering, meanly snobbish opinions. Deleting Ingrid's dad from the film (he's dead, we're told) makes the mother's influence seem even more monstrous. For her, Ingrid's marriage is a matter of letting her mother down when this should have been 'the proudest day of [her] life', instead of the hole-in-the-corner affair it is. The drab registry office marriage in which the registrar intones the idea of a 'lawful and binding unit', watched unhappily by Vic's parents and with bitter resentment by Ingrid's mother, contrasts tellingly with the joyous occasion with which the film opened.

Vic and Ingrid's marriage never stood much of a chance. Once sexual gratification has been achieved, he realises that he and Ingrid have almost nothing to talk about, nothing on which to build a life together. She tries to ward off sex when she is pregnant and, when she falls down the stairs and loses the baby, she refuses any sexual activity for the next three months. She is entirely under her mother's sway; they can't even quarrel without her overhearing; and he accuses her of using the miscarriage to prolong sexual abstaining. One of the strengths of the film is in the way it allows each of them access to the rights of the situation: Vic is not just after sex and Ingrid might not have seemed so limited if she'd been more fortunate in her choice of husband.

In several of the New Wave films, marriage comes to seem more like a trap, a closing down rather than an opening up of life's possibilities. At the end of A Room at the Top Joe Lampton (Laurence Harvey) has married the boss's daughter, Susan (Heather Sears), whom he has made pregnant (she has found the wedding 'super'), and their car makes its way to 'the top' where Susan's family lives. Along the way, though, Joe's social ambitions have been complicated by the fact of his falling seriously in love with another woman, Alice Aisgill (Simone Signoret), and marriage to Susan can now be no more than a sort of compromise. Something of the same fate befalls Arthur Seaton (Albert Finney) in Saturday Night and Sunday Morning. The very title hints at the contrasting relationships he has engaged in, with an older married woman (Rachel Roberts) and the younger one (Shirley Anne

22   Alan Bates (Vic Brown) and Thora Hird (Mrs Rothwell).

Field) he is set to marry. In the film's last moments he warns her he's
not done with stirring yet. In *Billy Liar*, Schlesigner's other film of the
New Wave period, Billy (Tom Courtenay) has several girlfriends before
seriously falling for the independently-minded Liz (Julie Christie), but
he finally opts out of the challenge she sets him. Now, all these films
are made by men, and it could be claimed that their point of view
is essentially male, but they and *A Kind of Loving* by no means let
men off the hook. If marriage looks like a trap, they have helped to
make it so.

   The only other marriage we hear about in *A Kind of Loving* is that
of Vic's friend Jeff (James Bolam) whom he meets by chance in a pub on
the evening when he's stormed out of the Rothwell home after a quarrel
with Ingrid, overheard of course by her mother. Jeff tells Vic how he
escaped from an unsatisfactory marriage ('You can always get out of it,'
he tells Vic), how it wasn't too complicated, and suggests a pub crawl as
an answer to Vic's problems. The very notion of marriage as a situation
you 'can always get out of' echoes the idea of marriage-as-trap. What
follows Vic's meeting up with Jeff is a lot of stupid false camaraderie,
increasingly quarrelsome, in several bars, with some oafish behaviour
involving a revolving door and the drunken singing of 'Down by the
riverside', before Vic staggers home. Well, it's hardly 'home' to him since

he doesn't even have a door-key, and is confronted by Mrs Rothwell, blazing with anger, waiting up for him, Ingrid having gone to bed. Mrs Rothwell accuses him of having seduced Ingrid, to which he replies coarsely that he didn't actually have to tie her down, and as he throws up on her carpet she denounces him as a 'filthy upstart'. The term conveys all kinds of disapproval but also has the thrust of class snobbery – the lower-middle sneering at the working class. Vic's behaviour is reprehensible on this occasion but the attitudes of Ma Rothwell (as Vic calls her) are mainly repellent.

Class
Vic's is an entirely working-class background, and from the start he doesn't want to be confined by this. It's not that he is as socially ambitious as, say, Joe Lampton, but he has an instinctive sense that there is more to life than the securities of routine work and 'settling down'. His draughtsman's job is a step away from the life of his parents, and Chris has moved up a sub-class in marrying the teacher, David. 'I love weddings,' Ingrid yearns vacuously. Whereas her aspirations are bounded by, 'When I find the right chap', Vic wants to travel. 'Sometimes I feel I'll never see anything if I stick at home'. Unlike Ingrid he is a reader, whereas she says, 'I haven't got much time for reading'. They are both products of their homes and of the class culture these embody, but they react differently to the limits of their respective backgrounds.

The urban streetscapes which are so endemic in these films make an immediate comment on the class differences between the Browns and the Rothwells. Vic's family lives in a row of terrace housing with no claim to variety or individuality. It is absolutely in line with the characteristically drab streets over which the camera pans at the very start of the film, made to look even bleaker by the faintly foggy atmosphere. When Vic takes Ingrid to her home after scraping acquaintance with her on the bus, it's clear that he's in a slightly posher neighbourhood, where more substantial semi-detached houses make their point about the status of the owners. The Rothwells are clearly established as a step up the social ladder but this hasn't had any liberating effect on Ingrid's mind or imagination. Inside the houses, the purely functional comforts of the Browns' rooms has given way to furniture-store-window gentilities as the expression of Mrs Rothwell's taste. Aspiration means different things to each. To Vic's family it is a matter of steady employment and decent, if limited, values. In the Rothwell house, comfort takes second place to having everything immaculate. Even so, she doesn't deserve to have Vic throw up on her nice carpet.

The film's distinctions between working- and lower-middle-class are felt in all sorts of ways. In clothes for instance. Mrs Rothwell's fur-collared coat and white-winged spectacles announce her as being at a remove from Mrs Brown's characteristic turban and overall; as are Vic's workmates in the draughtsmen's office (his father jokes about 'white-collar workers') from his father's working dress. Ingrid's aspirations run to clothes and one of her quarrels with Vic arises over what he considers an unnecessary coat she's bought (in collusion with her mother) when they should be saving to get a place of their own. It comes down to a matter of aspiration: in this case, the working class aspires to something solid, life having perhaps been more precarious for it, while the lower-middle has its eye on appearances, on what will make its higher status more apparent. When it comes to the cultural life of the classes, the film makes a nice discrimination between Mrs Rothwell's incessant telly-watching (quiz shows in particular, which may help to account for Ingrid's vacuity of mind) and the brass-band concert in which Vic's dad plays the trombone. The brass band is seen as a symbol of a culture that is remade every time it performs, as it will be in the 1996 film, *Brassed Off*, whereas the TV programmes are dismissed as inane and vulgar rubbish endlessly replicated. This doesn't do justice to TV but it serves to make Schlesinger's point, as it did Barstow's before him.

The film is spot-on in nailing the sorts of class distinctions that are part of the problem for Vic and Ingrid. When, early in their relationship, she has entered enthusiastically into an embrace, she quickly follows this with, 'You don't think I'm common, do you?', as she adjusts her make-up, unaware of how such a remark pins her to both class and cast of mind. But this is a generous-spirited film which also allows her a moment of real feeling, cut free from gossip and gentility, when she says: 'It's rotten being a girl sometimes,' as Vic hedges about his commitment to her.

What is now perhaps hard to recall is the sheer strangeness of hearing lower-middle and working-class accents in central roles in serious films. Actors such as Alan Bates, Albert Finney, Tom Courtenay, Rachel Roberts all came to prominence in the New Wave films, sporting regional and class-based accents that would have been highly unusual, almost unthinkable, in earlier decades, except for Cockney cameos. When Mrs Rothwell speaks scathingly of 'some of these people' and, after abusing the window-cleaner, announces, 'You can't rely on anyone these days', she is talking of the class that was being taken seriously for the first time. 'They're holding the country to ransom,' she claims; in preceding decades, 'they' might have done well to hold British filmmakers to ransom.

Schlesinger and a kind of filmmaking

Like many people in British cinema, Schlesinger had had the help of the Boulting brothers in getting his career launched. He had small acting roles in about twenty film or television programmes, including a couple of the Boultings' films, before directing *A Kind of Loving*, his first feature. Prior to this, he'd made something of a name for himself directing the award-winning documentary, *Terminus* (1961), which chronicled a day in the life of a great railway station. These two matters are significant in Schlesinger's later work. He would prove to be a very sympathetic director of actors, and this is apparent in *A Kind of Loving*, and his documentary background no doubt influenced the kind of life he was able to capture so vividly in this film and in his other New Wave job, *Billy Liar*. There is a sense of his getting at the reality of these lives through close observation of their surface details. His social sympathies, as suggested in these films, seem to be with those whose horizons are limited, and his admiration is for those who try to break away from whatever constricts them. He knows, though, that this can be hard and doesn't dismiss those whose courage fails them or who haven't the imagination to make the break. Even the appalling Mrs Rothwell is *understood* if not endorsed.

Schlesinger would go on to have a long and uneven career. He later disparaged *Darling* (1965) but it remains an incisive critique of a different social class and of celebrity culture; he took on literary adaptations, such as *Far From the Madding Crowd* (1967); and made a significant splash in Hollywood with such films as *Midnight Cowboy* (1969). It is at least arguable that he never did anything more affecting than *A Kind of Loving* or his 1971 British film, *Sunday Bloody Sunday*, and the eloquent television movie *An Englishman Abroad* (1986). All the New Wave directors – Karel Reisz, Lindsay Anderson, Tony Richardson – had distinguished enough careers, but, like Schlesinger, they might be said to have done their best work 'up north'.

A kind of ending

Vic, sick of the lack of privacy of life in the Rothwell house, has found scant sympathy from sister Chris and none from his mother. Taking his father's advice about getting Ingrid away from her mother and finding a flat, they go looking at places to let. Ingrid's not enthusiastic about what they see, but Vic says, 'I reckon we ought to give it a fair try', talking to her about the need to 'stand up to' her mother. They walk away from the flat in silence towards the park shelter where they used to cuddle. It is a very tentative ending, but one that may allow for 'a kind of loving' to survive, even if it's not what they originally wanted. It is honest enough not to end with a clinch we wouldn't believe in.

Notes

1 'Ken Loach' in Brian McFarlane, *An Autobiography of British Cinema* (London: Methuen, 1997), p. 372.
2 J. Krish, 'The New Realism and British Film', *Society of Film and Television Arts Journal* (Spring 1963), 14.
3 'John Schlesinger', McFarlane, *An Autobiography*, p. 510.
4 Stan Barstow, *The Watchers on the Shore* (London: Michael Joseph, 1966) and *The Right True End* (London: Michael Joseph, 1976).
5 Stan Barstow, *A Kind of Loving* [1960] (London: Robert Hale, 2001), p. 193.

11   *The Servant* (1963):
things fall apart

This may well be one of the least cosy British films ever made. There is ultimately nowhere for our sympathies to go in a fable of masters and servants as grimly witty as an Ivy Compton-Burnett novel about the balance of power in a house, and it utterly eschews any redeeming warmth. It's not just the house and its occupants that are so unsettling; *The Servant* gives off the sense of a corrupt – or, at least, corruptible – society.

A film of its time

Scandals

Its director Joseph Losey had been summoned to appear before the House Un-American Activities Committee (HUAC) to answer charges relating to alleged communist affiliations. He got this news while he was filming in Italy in 1951 and decided then to exile himself to Britain rather than return to deal with the notorious Committee. Appearing before this Committee had cost quite a few filmmakers their careers, and several had sought refuge in the more liberal political climate of England. It is probably true that none eventually produced so many remarkable films in this context as Losey. He worked initially under the pseudonym, Victor Hanbury,[1] then as Joseph Walton (his middle name), but by the mid 50s he was credited as Joseph Losey and went on to make a half-dozen films of varying quality before hitting his great period with *The Servant* in 1963. With his political background, it is not surprising that he should make films more contentious than the general run of mid-50s British cinema: he knew what it was to be a member of a difficult society, which is how the US must have seemed to him and to others placed as he was. What he brought above all to British cinema was the freshness and acuteness of an outsider's point of view. In 1976, he said: 'In a way my being blacklisted was one of the best things that ever happened to me because it forced me to go to Europe to continue my career as a filmmaker. Otherwise I might have stayed on in Hollywood merely making money instead of making pictures I wanted to make.'[2]

It is not just Losey's personal situation that places the film so precisely in its time. If the scandal of the HUAC was still hovering in the cultural air, closer to home in Britain was what came to be known as 'the Profumo affair'. Of this, it is enough to say that John Profumo, the Secretary of State for War, having denied any impropriety in his relationship with Christine Keeler, girl-about-town whom he met at Cliveden, Lord Astor's mansion, later recanted in Parliament. He said that he'd misled the House. Also involved was the society osteopath Stephen Ward, who may have been responsible for putting Keeler in the way of notable conquests. There was a question of the leaking of government secrets because Keeler was simultaneously involved with Yevgeny Ivanov, attached to the Soviet Embassy in London, so that the scandal became a matter of national security. The public latched on to the affair, perhaps because it seemed to undermine several key pillars of the British social structure, and the atmosphere it created makes itself felt in *The Servant*.

Neither this nor that

In British film-making, *The Servant* occupies a place between those other British film phenomena of the 60s – the New Wave realists and the 'swinging London' excesses of the latter half of the decade. The last of the New Wave pieces, Lindsay Anderson's *This Sporting Life*, was released in January 1963, and the films that preceded it had brought a fresh impulse into British cinema. From *Room at the Top* in early 1959, through such titles as *Saturday Night and Sunday Morning*, *The Loneliness of the Long-Distance Runner* and *A Kind of Loving* in the early 60s, these films had exhibited a rougher authenticity about the life of the country. They were focused on working lives, so often marginalised in earlier decades, and were franker about matters of class and sexuality. In the latter half of the 60s, London was supposedly the swinging centre of the universe, attracting a cover story in *Time* magazine, which claimed that, 'Ancient elegance and new opulence are all tangled up in a dazzling blur of op and pop.'[3] This mythology, happily endorsed by British media, produced a run of films barely watchable today, with titles like *The Knack* (1965), *Georgy Girl* (1966) and *Duffy* (1968), all complete with built-in obsolescence. Whereas the social realist batch still seem to be about matters of continuing relevance, the 'swinging London' numbers, with rare exceptions, come over as vapid bandwagon passengers.

The Servant emerges as tougher-minded than most of the New Wave films. These tend to find in the end some reconciliation of working-class aspiration and achievement, or at least encourage sympathetic alignment with those for whom this fails. More simply, for these films one might say: their hearts are in the right place. *The Servant*, looked at in this way, is a comfortless film. It compels attention because it rigorously *refuses* comfort or easy alignment. If it goes beyond the sorts of realism espoused by the New Wave, it also utterly resists any of the flashy distractions of 'swinging London'. There is a scene set in and around a public telephone box where the central character Barrett (Dirk Bogarde) is making a call while a gaggle of mini-skirted dolly-birds giggle on the outside. This is the nearest it comes to suggesting what lies ahead when girls like these may be the protagonists of films.

Losey and *The Servant*

Given his back story, it is probably not surprising that Losey should be interested in offering some kind of critique of the ambience in which he found himself filming. His career in 1960s British film is prolific and distinguished, but it could be argued that its crowning achievement is contained in *The Servant*, *Accident* (1967) and *The Go-Between* (1971), and that these offer a trilogy that submits British – or, more exactly, English – attitudes to class and sexuality to abrasive scrutiny. All three tell riveting 'stories' but they all have much more on their minds than that implies. Class can be brutal and sex can be destructive: these are not new perceptions but they rarely come in for such unsparing, darkly poetic treatment in British cinema.

Part of the reason for the success of Losey's 1960s films, especially of the three just named, no doubt derives from his collaboration with playwright Harold Pinter, who wrote the screenplays for all three. Each of these was derived in turn from a novel by a well-known author and each is wrought into a brilliantly shaped screenplay. In adapting Robin Maugham's prescient 1948 novella, *The Servant*, Pinter and Losey have dispensed with its narrator figure Richard Merton to focus from the beginning on the servant-master relationship at its heart. Whether it was Losey's or Pinter's idea to open the film as it does, it was clearly impressive enough for Maugham's publishers when they reprinted the book in 1989 to use the first shot of servant and master together for cover illustration.

The class notions at the heart of the Losey-Pinter collaboration also surface in *King and Country* (1965), set in World War One, and again starring Dirk Bogarde, who is the other key figure in Losey's work in 1960s Britain. In 1990, Bogarde recalled that, in *The Servant*, 'it was originally planned that I should play Tony, the nice young man, but... I was too old by that time... so I said to Joe we should get Ralph Richardson for the servant. Joe said we couldn't afford it so that's how I came to play the servant'.[4] Bogarde was entering what he would later call the 'European' phase of his long career, having pretty much put behind him his 'idol of the Odeon' days, and as well as *The Servant* and *King and Country*, he made two further films with Losey, *Modesty Blaise* (1966) and *Accident*. His subtly ambiguous playing of Barrett accounts for much of the tension of *The Servant*.

Putting it together

How it all begins

The film opens on a wintry London square. This is a different kind of terrace from those so common in the social realist films of the preceding years. We are clearly in upper-middle-class terrain from the word go, but it is not a simple message the overhead shot gives us. The over-all impression is bleak, with leafless trees and haunting music on the soundtrack, as the camera tracks over house fronts, the empty square, the arrival of Bogarde's Barrett, and the small black joke of the business facade announcing 'Thomas Crapper, Sanitary Engineers'. This opening shot creates a sense of faint unease from the start, and this is not dispelled when Barrett, severely dressed in black hat, coat and gloves, enters one of the houses without knocking. Is he merely an intruder? Why is the front door unlocked? The camera now tracks Barrett through the empty house until it settles on the prone figure

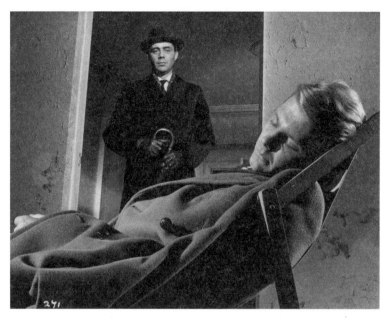

23   Dirk Bogarde (Hugo Barrett) and James Fox (Tony).

of a young man, Tony (James Fox) asleep on a chair. His fair thatch of hair and light-coloured coat contrast at once with Barrett and the camera comes to rest on the low-angle shot used for the book's cover: Barrett stands looking down on Tony, in a way that anticipates the later reversal of roles which is at the heart of the film. Tony is established from the outset as supine, 'too many beers at lunch' having drained him of the authority an interview with his potential manservant might have needed.

These opening shots prefigure a great deal of what is to come. The dismal look of the street appears to be making a comment about upper-class lifelessness, and this is of course reinforced when the camera (and Barrett) enters the house. The image of Tony reclining and his failure to have locked the door before dozing off, or to think out in advance what he really wants Barrett to do, seem to indicate an upper-class lassitude. This contrasts with the clamped-down sycophancy of Barrett, whose carefully simulated modesty gives nothing away – certainly not to the slothful Tony. When Barrett, not unreasonably, asks what sort of services Tony wants, Tony can only answer: 'Apart from the cooking [pause] well... everything. General looking after, you know.'

To which Barrett replies: 'Yes I do sir', and the rest of the film does indeed show that he 'knows'.

Barrett ascendant

In a long series of alternating day-and-night sequences, both vividly and economically conceived, Barrett inserts himself into the house. 'You might bring me a lager,' says Tony. 'I was just about to, sir,' counters Barrett, implying that he can anticipate – and will pander to – Tony's every need. While renovations are going on in the house, the essentially lazy Tony leaves supervision of the tradesmen entirely to Barrett, who checks prissily on their progress, his manner here much different from the deference he flatters Tony with.

Tony's girlfriend, Susan (Wendy Craig), giggles at the idea of a manservant, but she will soon be forced to take Barrett more seriously. With upper-class insolence, she all but ignores Barrett, snaps out commands such as 'Vodka on the rocks' with no hint of please or thank-you. A little later, she and Tony are lying together in front of the fire when Barrett, deliberately not knocking, interrupts them, just after Tony has proposed marriage to her. From this point, Susan begins her campaign against Barrett. 'For God's sake restrict him to quarters!' On her next visit, this time to see Tony who has been in bed with a cold, she moves the flowers she has sent from a hallway table into Tony's room. Barrett has observed the move from below, comes into Tony's bedroom, and goes to take the vase out again. 'Put that down,' Susan barks at him. When Barrett later opens the door to show her out he smiles to himself, as if he knows he is winning.

When Susan and Tony are dining in a restaurant, she states her lack of trust in Barrett and tells Tony to 'Stop making him so bloody important'. She even urges Tony to tell him to go, but he merely finds it 'hurtful' that she doesn't trust his judgment. That prone figure we saw in the opening sequence is only too ready to have someone to wait on him. Barrett has recognised weakness when he sees it, and knows how to make it work for him.

More infiltration

In the period leading up to Tony's dismissing Barrett, the film inserts another strand into its complex narrative. We have seen Barrett talking to someone in the public phone box and heard him say, 'Are you being a good girl?' The girl is Vera (Sarah Miles) whom he will introduce into the Chelsea house as his sister and who, in a scene of remarkable tension, will seduce Tony. Vera waits on Tony in bed, recalling the earlier scene in which Susan had busied herself around his sickroom. She smiles with secret knowledge as she observes Tony's taking Barrett's services for granted, as if she knows who is really in charge here.

'That's bloody inconvenient,' Tony replies crossly when Barrett says he and Vera must go to Manchester where their 'mother' is ill. Barrett is lying, and we may wonder why, but Tony's snappish response typifies a pampered aristocracy, used to having its way and certainly not used to having its way cluttered by the affairs of the lower orders. In the event, Barrett goes away so as to leave the coast clear for Vera to go to work on Tony. Prior to this, Tony finds Vera has invaded his bathroom. Barrett had told her to. In other words, he is acting as a pimp in a way that perhaps recalls how Stephen Ward undermined the upper classes by introducing Christine Keeler into their lives and houses.

The seduction scene is one of the most brilliantly wrought in the film. When Tony returns to the house late one night, after a lonely drink in a bar and a phone call from Susan, whose conventional attractions he is finding less urgent, he is surprised to find lights on. The camera frames Vera's bare legs in the kitchen doorway. She hasn't gone to Manchester, because, she lies, she was unwell, and she now launches a concerted attack on upper-class sensibilities and nerves. Losey directs this sequence for brilliantly sustained tension. He admittedly draws closely on Robin Maugham's novella here:

> He [Tony] felt he had lost control of reality. The plates on the dresser and the two cups on the sideboard seemed part of another world. A tap was dripping into the sink. Each drop fell at regular intervals like the beat of a metronome. He was breathing heavily. It worried him that his breath did not keep time with the drips.[5]

The idea is certainly there in Maugham, but Losey makes the sequence entirely his own, the long take executed with wonderful eloquence by cinematographer Douglas Slocombe. Notice how the camera settles on objects such as the dripping tap and, at the end, on the kitchen light made to suggest the third-degree lamp of a police procedural. Such observations are heightened by spare dialogue, such as Vera's disingenuous, 'Can I get you anything sir?', and by the phone's ringing. It is Susan on the phone and neither Tony nor Vera makes a move to answer it. There is silent challenge from her and weak succumbing from him. Again, she smiles the secret smile that suggests she knows where things are heading.

When Barrett returns, he asks Tony, 'Has she been able to do anything for you? She hasn't done the washing-up, I notice.' 'Been under the weather I suppose,' Tony tries. 'Under what?,' asks Barrett. An exchange like this offers evidence for Bogarde's describing the film as a black comedy.[6] But like the best comedy it is intensely serious. This is a drama about corruption and corruptibility. Barrett may be using Vera to corrupt Tony, perhaps even to undermine a class that always treats him with patronage, but equally Tony is eminently corruptible. He is so used to taking his privileged position for granted that he is quite without moral defences when that position comes under threat.

Crisis

When Tony and Susan return to the house after a weekend in the country, in which she has tried to provoke him into sexual commitment, they find that Barrett has invaded Tony's bedroom. On the simplest level, this reinforces the idea of one of the lower orders not knowing his place. More crucially though, the episode reveals Tony's lack of authority at a moment when it would have been appropriate to exercise it. He doesn't know how to respond when the shadow of Barrett's naked figure appears above. He rests his head on the stair banister as if defeated by the knowledge of what Barrett has done. Susan urges him to act, but he has lost the capacity to do so, and instead gives way to screaming.

His initial shock is caused by believing Barrett and Vera are engaging in incestuous sex. Then Vera tells him that she and Barrett are to be married, and Tony in his dim way realises he has been victim of their deception all along. Incidentally, though, the film may also be suggesting the lower classes are franker in sexual matters than their so-called betters. There is something inhibited in Tony and Susan's relationship: there is a real sensuality in the scene between Tony and Vera, she having taken the initiative, that is lacking in his scenes with Susan. Susan will later refuse his invitation to bed with a shudder of distaste about which we can only wonder.

On Barrett's departure, Tony's life is in a state of collapse. He can't bring himself to speak to Susan on the phone. The camera picks out dead flowers (which Susan had brought) and unopened mail on the hall floor, and a glimpse of Tony curled up on Vera's bed, looking like a child in a cot as he is seen through the rails of the stair's banister. This shot becomes almost a metaphor for the way Tony has been infantilised as a result of Barrett's ministrations.

24   Dirk Bogarde (Hugo Barrett) and James Fox (Tony).

Role reversal

Tony is not the only one whose life has fallen apart. Drinking morosely in a pub, he finds and makes up with Barrett who tells a pathetic story of how he was 'besotted' with Vera. The camera cuts between the two men, with Tony palely twitchy and Barrett half-sobbing as he tells how, 'She's living with a bookie in Wandsworth. Wandsworth!' Even the servant is class-conscious in this film, and Wandsworth is beyond the pale for him.

Once back in the house, Barrett is no longer whinging but flounces about, showing no respect for Tony who feebly protests, 'Why don't you leave me alone?' Barrett has become like a bickering housewife, wittering on about 'making ends meet' while Tony stretches out on a couch. Barrett now resists Tony's orders, even hurls a sponge at him. 'You're supposed to be the bloody servant,' Tony yells, but Barrett's reply is, tartly, 'I'm a gentleman's gentleman, and you're no bloody gentleman.' The house is increasingly a mess as they play silly games in which ornaments get smashed. At one moment, Tony can say, 'Now Barrett, don't you forget your place. You're nothing but a servant here,' to which Barrett bellows, 'I run the whole bloody place and what do I get out of it? Nothing.' Eventually – and there may be a homoerotic element here – a feeling of their being 'pals' emerges, and Tony, now sucking up to Barrett, accepts the fact that, ' I don't know what I'd do without you.'

Barrett now has Tony where he wants him. With the collapse of Tony's 'manner', there's nothing left, his class and gender roles are overthrown. The insinuating camera now moves in on faces as if that's where the truth of the situation is to be found. When Susan calls, it is clear she can no longer compete with Barrett's power over Tony. The conflict is suggested in a shot in which they stand on either side of the hapless Tony, and Barrett, with increasing insolence and confidence in his ascendancy, blows smoke in her face. In the party sequence, in which the house is invaded by 60s swingers, Tony watches, giggling, as Barrett kisses Susan and a little later orders the guests out. Barrett now runs the house. Servant and master have swapped roles.

Class

In British cinema, perhaps in all British fiction, class is the ever-interesting topic, even more so than sex. In *The Servant*, the house becomes the symbolic representation of a crumbling class system. The film begins and ends there and the glimpses of life outside the house offer no grounds for confidence either. For a Britain shaken by recent scandals, Tony, in his dignified Chelsea terrace, stands for the upper classes caught out in dissipation, yielding to seduction from the lower orders, lacking in backbone. He is depicted from the outset as a ready prey for a predatory intruder. Barrett makes the house comfortable, reminding us that there is a long tradition of servants doing just this for the upper classes. Barrett subtly assumes control of Tony's life. It's as though Losey were making something darker of the situation involving dim Bertie Wooster and his much smarter valet, Jeeves, in the novels of P. G. Wodehouse.

But Barrett, whatever his class origins, is not like the working-class protagonists of the New Wave films. We are never meant to feel sorry for him or to align ourselves with his aspirations. Even Joe Lampton in *Room at the Top* goes through with marriage to the girl he has made pregnant despite his having fallen seriously in love elsewhere. Barrett, on the other hand, is motivated only by – what? Resentment? The urge to dominate? Absolute egoism? He and the sluttish Vera are on the make and the film requires of us only to understand, not to sympathise with, whatever they are up to. When Tony, in the exchange quoted above, ends by saying to Barrett, 'I don't know what I'd do without you', this seems no more than a spelling-out of an upper-class born-to-rule outlook supported by an increasingly resentful under-class. We don't feel sympathy for Barrett, who is too clearly opportunistic. There is undoubtedly a sense of the have-nots reacting against the haves, though not in the interests of a depressed class but of personal power. In the end, Barrett is freed from the sycophancy of service into mere vengefulness.

As a footnote to the film's commentary on class, note Sarah Miles's 1994 recollection of how her family would react to the film and her performance as Vera: 'I dreaded my parents seeing it. I was right about that because, when they'd seen a preview, they came to my home and said, "How dare you! The servants will leave!"'[7]

If Tony is made to sound merely fatuous in his early talk about creating cities in Brazil and peopling them with 'peasants from Asia Minor who're having a tough time', Susan's way of talking to inferiors brands her as stiffly snobbish and lacking in any sort of natural warmth. Dark comedy has its fling in the episodes set in the stately home of Tony's friends Lord and Lady Mounset (Richard Vernon and Catherine Lacey). After a long pan around the extensive grounds, the film cuts to a static indoor scene in which the stilted conversation reverberates around the grandiose room. As Lady Mounset maunders on about ponchos when she means gauchos, the image is of a mummified, ignorant aristocracy.

The other sequences set outside the house are similarly devoid of warmth or openness. From the yawning expanses of the Mounset mansion to the cramped confines of the telephone booth or the curiously unfriendly pub interior, there is little sense of place that might be an escape from the increasingly uncongenial spaces inside the house. The pub, for instance, is the site of people nattering away in the high-pitched snootiness of the society couple or the hectoring tones of an older woman quarrelling with a younger.

Gender
Regardless of how far a homosexual subtext is intended in either the film or Maugham's novella, there is a pervasively acrid aura of sexuality hanging over the film. This was the 60s when sexual matters were being

aired with much more freedom than before; the Wolfenden Report had been tabled in 1957 and debate was continuing; and Dirk Bogarde had memorably starred in *Victim*, the first mainstream feature dealing with homosexuality, in 1961. As well, the Women's Liberation Movement got under way in the 1960s. I quote this, not because *The Servant* is infused with feminist sympathies in any overt way but only to draw attention to the climate of the times in which matters of gender and sexuality were up for discussion. Women, in fact, are seen as secondary figures in the film's central master-servant drama, but their capacity to undermine male resolve, in Vera's case, or keep a man at bay sexually, as in Susan's, might be seen as offering some muted critique of women's roles in a moribund society.

And now...

In the end, the film's continuing power doesn't depend on its historical resonances and portents for today, but on such matters as the magisterial use of Douglas Slocombe's camera. Dirk Bogarde remembered Slocombe's saying on the last day of shooting that 'this was the first time he had been able to put into practice all the things he had learned'.[8] As the camera winds its way through the house, from room to room and up and downstairs, it colludes with Losey's determination to focus on the house, as a realist setting *and* as a symbol of a corruptible society. Our attention is also riveted by the interplay of the four leading actors – Bogarde, Fox, Miles and Craig – and the tense oppositions represented by Barrett and Tony, Susan and Vera, Susan and Barrett, Tony and Susan. It is in these tensions, in this house, that Losey and his team have created such a rich and unsettling film. It is certainly a film of its time, but equally it is a film which has lost none of its unnerving power in the intervening fifty years.

Notes

1 The real Hanbury had directed several films in the 30s and would produce and/or direct several more in the next two decades.
2 Gene D. Phillips, 'Hollywood exile: An interview with Joseph Losey', *Journal of Popular Film*, Vol. v, No. 1, 1976, 34.
3 Piri Halasz, *Time*, 1 April 1 1966.

4 'Dirk Bogarde' in Brian McFarlane, *An Autobiography of British Cinema* (London: Methuen, 1997), p. 71.

5 Robin Maugham, *The Servant* (London: Allison & Busby, 1989), p. 53.

6 'Dirk Bogarde', McFarlane, *An Autobiography*, p. 71.

7 'Sarah Miles', McFarlane, *An Autobiography*, p. 405.

8 'Dirk Bogarde', McFarlane, *An Autobiography*, p. 71

12   Sex, talk, men and
Women in Love (1969)

The redoubtable literary critic F. R. Leavis, a great admirer of D. H. Lawrence's novels, described the filming of *Women in Love* as 'an obscene undertaking'.[1] Sight unseen of course. I'm not sure how many now take Leavis seriously, but *Women in Love* has surely earned its place among the indispensable British films. Its director Ken Russell had made his name with a series of BBC films about composers, and in the 1970s he would tax admirers with the excesses of some of his films. The prospect of re-viewing, say, his *Lisztomania*, is about as attractive an idea as open-heart surgery, but on *Women in Love* his touch was sure, his approach to filming a literary masterpiece and making a film that is utterly his own beyond question. Everyone remembers the famous nude wrestling scene, but it is at least arguable that the film's most audacious aspect is the amount of talk, of sheer dialectic, that it is prepared to include – without for a moment descending into the aridity of mere polemics.

Lawrence and the Cinema

The screen was slow in coming to terms with Lawrence. He had been dead nearly twenty years before the elegant British film version of his short story *The Rocking-Horse Winner* (1949) appeared. Perhaps filmmakers had to wait for a more enlightened approach to censorship to do justice to Lawrence's preoccupation with the life of the body as well as, and in conjunction with, that of the mind. Since that first go, a black-and-white study of a destructive obsession, there have been fifty film or television adaptations of his novels and stories, and he has proved surprisingly amenable to screen treatment – or maybe he has just been lucky with his adaptors. Among those that leap to memory are Jack Cardiff's *Sons and Lovers* (1960), Christopher Miles's *The Virgin and the Gipsy* (1970), Tim Burstall's *Kangaroo* (1987) and, most recently, Pascale Ferran's *Lady Chatterley* (2006), the beautifully sensuous French version of Lawrence's most notorious work. All of these and others had a good deal to commend them.

There have also been numerous television miniseries derived from the novels, including *Sons and Lovers* (1981), *Lady Chatterley* (1993) and *Women in Love* (2011). The novellas and short stories have also been filmed often for both large and small screens. There is clearly something irresistible to filmmakers and, presumably, audiences about him, even if it's only the whiff of scandal. He has attracted some distinguished directors and other collaborators but, on the evidence of the 1969 version of *Women in Love*, I'd say he and Ken Russell in many ways seem made for each other.

Russell and Lawrence

These two were iconclasts in their day and in some ways it might be said that British cinema needed Russell as urgently as the English novel needed Lawrence. (I wonder why it's always 'British' cinema but the 'English' novel?) If the novel had reached some awe-inspiring peaks in the nineteenth century, it was going to need someone more robustly in touch with the post-war life of the new century than, say, some latter-day Henry James to make literary diagnoses of it. James had four years left when Lawrence's first novel, *The White Peacock*, appeared, and it is hard to imagine his being much drawn to *Sons and Lovers* (1913), even if Leavis saw Lawrence as somehow belonging to the 'Great Tradition', and devoutly admired both authors. Lawrence brought a new roughness, a new polemicist spirit to bear on crucial matters of human behaviour.

While Russell was acclaimed for his television documentaries on composers, including *Elgar* (1962), *Debussey* (1965), *Delius* (1968) and *Richard Strauss* (1970), his film career had stalled after the failure of *French Dressing* (1963), an amiable enough comedy set in a scruffy seaside resort, which made fun of film-festival machinations. He didn't film again until 1967 when he had more success with the Harry

Palmer thriller, *Billion Dollar Brain*, starring Michael Caine. But it was
undoubtedly *Women in Love*, two years later, which established him as a
force to be reckoned with in British cinema. Not since Michael Powell
had it produced so flamboyant a talent, a director prepared to be as
much a maverick as Powell had been – or as Lawrence has been in the
history of the English novel.

Russell went on to direct two further versions of Lawrence – *The
Rainbow* in 1989 and, for television, *Lady Chatterley* in 1993 – but,
though these had their merits, *Women in Love* represents the peak of
his dealings with Lawrence. It also represents a highpoint in British
cinema's dealings both with literature and with the erotic.

On reading *Women in Love*

When I first read this novel, I found it the most exasperating 'classic' I'd
ever addressed myself to. I tried to work out why. There seemed to me a
numbing insistence in the writing, a hammering away at points as if to
persuade us by force. The writing often seemed dreadfully overwrought,
especially in its dramatising of emotional responses. The novel's 'action'
seemed not to proceed from character, nor did character seem to be
forged and developed in the action. In other words, Lawrence was not
writing a nineteenth-century novel of the kind I was used to. Where was
that psychological realism in the creation of characters and the action
they gave rise to? Or the social realism that put before us particular
places at particular times?

Many, perhaps, most of these 'obstacles' disappeared on re-reading.
Even what I'd felt as a worrying insistence of the style came to be seen
dramatically as an attempt to come to grips with the elusiveness of
intricate emotional responses. Further, the motives for 'action' in life
are very often not the result of what is most easily observable in people.
In trying to present this, Lawrence may seem to be creating incoherent
bundles of impulse and will, creatures whose traits don't add up to
fully rounded characters. The whole notion of the stable character or
the clearly developing character, traditionally found in the nineteenth-
century novel, is challenged by Lawrence. It's almost as if he believes
that a human being is never at any two different moments the same
person. As he wrote:

> If the one I love remains unchanged and unchanging, I shall cease to
> love her. It is only because she changes and startles me into change

25   Jennie Linden (Ursula Brangwen) and Glenda Jackson
(Gudrun Brangwen).

and defies my inertia, and is herself staggered in her inertia by my changing, that I can continue to love her. If she stayed put, I might as well love the pepper-pot.[2]

Well, what is film to make of all this? In my view, something pretty remarkable. It takes on the central relationships of the novel: Birkin and Ursula's, which ends with marriage and an acceptance of compromise; Gerald and Gudrun's, which ends with his death and her going off alone to Dresden to follow up her art as a sculptor. As well, the novel wants us to understand the rapport between Birkin and Gerald and the essential differences between the sisters, Gudrun and Ursula, and there are two important secondary characters, the pretentious, upper-class, doggedly 'artistic' Hermione Roddice, influential early on in the Ursula-Birkin relationship, and the artist Loerke, whose presence helps to drive the final wedge between Gudrun and Gerald. And Lawrence is always concerned with the relation between people and the world they live in at that moment.

A British film about love and sex
and the whole damn thing

Glenda Jackson, who won an Oscar for her performance as Gudrun, was full of praise twenty-odd years later for Ken Russell's approach to the film. She said:

> I think it is entirely possible to interpret a book for the screen in a way that is absolutely truthful to the creative energy or the interior state of the writer. Ken took what is central to the book, which is life, energy, the sexual directives and imperatives of life, the confusions that come out of that... the central pulsing theme of the book is life and that is very much what he was on about.[3]

Jackson is making some large claims for the film here, but they are claims that can be well supported.

'Sexual directives' and related matters

Though Russell quickly gained a reputation as an unusually flamboyant filmmaker, especially in the ranks of British cinema, in *Women in Love* he fixes his eye on the key relationships of the novel and keeps them there. He has decided to explore their complexities and resists simplification. There are contrasts to be made between the Birkin/Ursula and the Gudrun/Gerald pairs but not at the expense of how they might also overlap in their intensities. As played by Oliver Reed (in his one indisputably great screen performance as Gerald) and Glenda Jackson, the Gerald/Gudrun pair has a combative edge which suggests they will never be able to relax into even the qualified domestic calm experienced by Birkin (Alan Bates) and Ursula (Jennie Linden).

Gudrun and Gerald

There is a withdrawn stiffness, a need to dominate, in Reed's Gerald that is often met with a taunting look and verbal challenge from Jackson's Gudrun. There are moments of sexual passion between them. From the first exchange of looks outside the church where Gerald's sister is being married, a suggestion of sexual attraction passes between them, but there is too much resistance to surrender in either of them to ensure anything permanently fulfilling between them. He comes to her for comfort on the night of his father's death ('I came because I must,' he says) and they make love for the first time. This episode, with Gerald creeping into the Brangwen house and upstairs into Gudrun's room without disturbing her father as he sleeps in a downstairs room, is no more probable in its logistics than it is in the novel – and this matters no more here than it does in the novel. What matters is a rare sense of emotional neediness in Gerald who as a rule is ready to take charge of situations.

When they, with Birkin and Ursula, are finally snowed up in Zermatt in the film's penultimate sequences, the scene between the two of them seems absolutely the outcome of the difficult nature of this relationship. Jackson makes Gudrun seriously confronting. 'How much do you love me?,' she asks provocatively, implying that no answer he can give will satisfy or convince her. There is something touching in Reed's sense of not being able to answer except with another question, 'How much do you think?', followed by her reply, 'Very little indeed', and his confession: 'I don't know what you mean by the word.' These two actors make something almost excruciatingly painful of this scene. She begs him to say 'I will love you always' and, when he does, she rebukes him with, 'Try to love me a little more and want me a little less.' I quote this exchange to suggest the unusual extent to which Russell has sought to explore the nature of sexual love rather than accepting it as a mere fact of life.

There is also something cruel in the way Gudrun persists in an extraordinary discussion to unravel what is and has been between them. Jackson does not shy away from presenting the element of bitchiness in the way she teases and taunts, then tries to seduce, Gerald. In the performances of these two actors, all the nuances of pain and confronting anger are felt in their physical beings, in the contest between his urge to dominate, coupled with an odd vulnerability, and her incessant need to argue the toss over every emotion that surfaces, her unwillingness to give in to love. In his direction of Jackson and Reed, Russell has achieved an amazing sense of the 'imperatives of life, the confusions that come out of that', and arrives at a moving denouement as Gerald, in a last act of will, trudges off into the snow to die.

There is a wonderful close-up earlier on in which Reed appears to imprison Gudrun against a tree: his tensely commanding look is matched by the mocking tilt of her chin and her half-closed appraising eyes. In hindsight, it seems to foreshadow the whole ensuing trajectory of their volatile connection.

Ursula and Birkin
In the event, it is Birkin who more openly mourns Gerald than Gudrun, though perhaps his having nearly strangled her before walking away

helps to account for this disparity. Birkin weeps over the body of Gerald, saying, 'I didn't want it to be like this. He should have loved me.' He is not speaking here of homosexual love, though there may be an element of this in Birkin's feeling for Gerald. In the film's last scene, as in the novel's, Birkin and Ursula appear to be comfortably and conjugally settled in front of their open fire, when Ursula asks 'Did you need Gerald?' Russell and screenwriter Larry Kramer hew very closely here to Lawrence's final moments between this pair. Bates subtly conveys a suppressed inadequacy in his life, when Birkin tries to articulate this to Ursula by explaining that she is 'enough for me, as far as a woman is concerned'. Bates makes us believe this and also feel what Gerald's death has meant to Birkin. 'I wanted a man friend, as eternal as you and I are eternal.' Ursula's relative simplicity is felt in her remark: 'You can't have two kinds of love', and his final words, 'I don't believe that', points to how far Russell's film is from the closure of classical Hollywood cinema.

Ursula and Birkin have reached this final episode via a series of finely differentiated sequences in which Russell's eye for detail and for what the camera can 'tell' is clear. (Presumably this is what Russell has 'told' his famous cinematographer Billy Williams to aim for). As with Gudrun's first glimpse of Gerald, we first catch Ursula's eye on Birkin at the Crich wedding. In this case, though, the film alternates between Ursula's obvious interest in Birkin and a later episode when he, as a schools inspector, appears in her classroom where, in some kind of botany lesson, she is teaching about catkins. As the Lawrentian mouthpiece in the novel, and his alter ego in the film, Birkin makes of these catkins a subject for discussion of male and female parts, and this kind of charged dialogue is pushed further when Hermione erupts into the classroom. What the pupils can have been making of all this is hard to imagine. Certainly Ursula quite soon has had enough and rings the class dismissal bell angrily and the film cuts back to the church bell ringing – as Gerald and Gudrun exchange looks. What Russell has established here is the potential for further relationship but also the idea that it will not be plain sailing.

The film astutely places the Birkin/Ursula relationship in a series of settings which help us to 'read' what is happening between them. As they push their way through the crowd at the war memorial (an invention for the film), Birkin expatiates wildly on what he believes in. He answers Ursula's query, 'What about individual love?', by insisting that he only believes in 'the end of the world and rabbits', that human beings and their ideas of love are unnecessary to the world's survival. It is a daring film that risks so much talk: we're so used to the notion that it is film's job to show rather than to tell that it takes a while to accept the view that people reveal themselves at least as much by what they think and say as by what they physically show us on the screen. With Birkin and Ursula, both matter. In Bates's easy, consciously iconoclastic rendering of Birkin and Linden's watchful but malleable Ursula, we are made to *see* the progress of their relationship, but their talk of love and how it may or may not be manifested makes us also concentrate on what is going on in their heads and how they are moving towards their final moments before the cottage fire.

There is a lyrically beautiful sequence in which, in a field of grain (and the natural setting is important here), he gives her a present of rings. They quarrel when he says he must go to farewell Hermione, who hovers challengingly over the early stages of their relationship. Ursula storms off shouting abuse, claiming it's not jealousy she feels but distaste for all that Hermione stands for. Bates and Linden capture here something of the bizarre intensity with which Lawrence endows such scenes, and it is touchingly followed by the close-up of a hand and Ursula's voice saying, 'See what a flower I've found for you.' In Birkin's secluded cottage, in a precursor of the film's final moments, he says to her, 'We'll get married right away. Then we'll wander a bit and we'll never go apart'. Then, Russell chooses, with what seems absolute rightness, to show them in a series of sideways shots, their naked torsos locked in joy and tenderness.

Whereas the Gerald/Gudrun affair never seems as if they could count on overcoming their temperamental differences to arrive at full or at least workable understanding, the film's resources work to persuade us that Birkin and Ursula might well. The looks they exchange, how they are placed in the frame, how they appear in such social settings as the memorial gathering or the water-party at the Crich house or in the marketplace: all such decisions of the director, as well as the skill of the actors, lead us to have different expectations of them from those we have of the other chief pair, who always seem more like combatants than prospective partners. And those important supporting roles of Hermione and the artist Loercke play their roles in defining the two chief pairs. Birkin has to grow past Hermione's egoistic pretension, qualities made plain in Eleanor Bron's entertaining if somewhat caricatured portrayal, and Gudrun has to realise that Loercke can offer her a freedom to work at her sculptor's art that Gerald would never have understood.

Censorship relaxes

A decade earlier it would have been difficult, almost impossible, for the film's relationships to have been depicted with the candour available to Ken Russell, who takes full advantage of this situation. The love scene between Birkin and Ursula is not just 'lyrical' but is sensuously – and sensually – potent as well. Sexuality is at the heart of the film's main relationships and Russell is now able to render this without being exploitative. Similarly when Gerald comes to Gudrun's bedroom on the night of his father's death, she is allowed to remove her nightdress without any sense of embarrassment and, because it seems so exactly right in tone, we accept it then as wholly natural.

The famous nude wrestling scene in which Oliver Reed and Alan Bates strip for action may well have been a first in British cinema. Breasts were one thing, but other things were another, as it were. Oliver Reed has written amusingly about how he and Bates approached the shooting, preparing themselves for the ordeal with vodka, 'polishing off a bottle apiece. We staggered out on to the set naked but were partly sobered by the cold. It was freezing...'[4] The scene is shot in the warm glow of a log fire and beautifully lit in the way it casts shadows and flickering beams of light on the lofty room. The wrestling is led into via a discussion between the two, including the comment that, 'Nothing matters except something to take the edge off being alone', followed by talk of how, 'We are mentally and spiritually close, therefore we should be physically close.' Birkin wants them to 'swear to love each other, you and I', but his spontaneous reaching out comes up against Gerald's guarded, 'Wait until I understand it better.' There may well be repressed homosexual longings in Birkin's appeal here, and this may also feed into the film's final scene between him and Ursula, but again what is really impressive is the amount of *talk* about matters of love and sexual responsiveness the film dares to include.

The nude wrestling scene *is* daring, though shot as it is in a montage of close-ups its intention seems not at all prurient. Perhaps the Bristol cinema-going lady who was reported at the end of the scene as 'saying to her neighbour in a strangled voice, "Nice carpet, Eth"' is witness to this. Reed quotes this with obvious satisfaction, along with the comment that, '*Women in Love* was banned in Italy. Russell and I were warned that if we ever set foot in the country, we would be arrested as pornographers the minute we stepped off the plane.'[5] Reed may not be wholly reliable in all his recollections but, if this is true, along with the fact that the wrestling scene was cut in the South American version, it does point to

LARRY KRAMER and MARTIN ROSEN present
ALAN BATES · OLIVER REED
GLENDA JACKSON · JENNIE LINDEN
in Ken Russell's Film · D. H. Lawrence's
"WOMEN IN LOVE" x
with ELEANOR BRON
Associate producer ROY BAIRD   Co-producer MARTIN ROSEN
Written for the Screen and Produced by LARRY KRAMER
Directed by KEN RUSSELL   Eastman Colour   United Artists

26   Oliver Reed (Gerald Crich) and Alan Bates (Rupert Birkin).

the fact that British censorship had become a good deal more liberal.
This in turn enabled a more honest adaptation of a great novel.

The pulse of social England

Lawrence tells us that, 'Gudrun had touched the whole pulse of social
England'.[6] How far does this interest Russell? Certainly, his production
designers, Ken Jones and Luciana Arrighi, create a broadly convincing
spectrum of 'social England'. The spacious grounds and lofty, even
grandiose rooms of the Crich house, 'Shortlands', and the even grander
setting of 'Breadalby', Hermione's 'country cottage', a huge mansion
in fact, work as markers of affluence and social status. These set them
apart from the Brangwens' modest home, let alone from the more or less
squalid streets and lanes of the miners' cottages.

The crowd gathered around the war memorial where the minister
(James Laurenson) discourses on love, which Birkin angrily and rhetor-
ically dismisses as 'the lie that kills'; the market square in which Ursula
and Birkin dispute noisily about the value of 'the past' and Birkin buys

a chair that he then gives away to a young couple; the colliery where Gerald dismisses an employee and then drives off with his father in their sleek white car as it weaves through smoke and dark-coated miners: in these three potent sets of images, the individual lives are shown in relief against the wider social canvass. Shirley Russell's attention to costume design similarly evokes a period and, in this context, also creates individual differences. For instance, our first glimpse of the sisters bears this out: Ursula looks freer in her multi-coloured jacket than Gudrun in a more severe costume of royal blue.

The period is also registered in other ways, sometimes in details, sometimes in the larger picture. In the film's second sequence, as the sisters walk through the streets to the church, they pass a girl holding a collection tray marked 'SOMME', at once placing the action as post-World War One, a reference picked up a little later at the war memorial with the minister's talk of 'no greater love'. We need to remember that the action of the film is taking place shortly after the huge and hideous disruption of the Great War. This is poignantly reinforced by the repeated use of the popular song of 1919, 'I'm Forever Blowing Bubbles', on the soundtrack. The evanescence of the 'pretty bubbles in the air', as 'like my dreams/they fade and die', serves as a comment and warning about the fragility of human aspirations – to love or anything else.

Talking things out

Not just through the music, the film *sounds* so good. It dares as films rarely do to insist on our attention to a great deal of talk. Critics often suggest that films shouldn't be too 'talky', that they should show rather than tell. Surely that depends on the quality of the talk and what it reveals about those who engage in it. In Russell's film, the key relationships are largely created through how Birkin and Ursula argue their way to a level of understanding, whereas the darker exchanges between Gudrun and Gerald move them inexorably to a different end. There is an amazing number of sequences devoted primarily to the thrashing out of ideas, with varying degrees of perception and pretension. Think of Hermione and Birkin lolling by her pool and pondering the inequalities of world organisation. Or the discussion between Gerald and Birkin that precedes the wrestling sequence, or their later talk of marriage and other relationships when the intensity of the exchange is caught in a series of intercut close-ups. Russell's decision to focus on the faces in this and other sequences may be seen as his determination to make his characters reveal themselves in what they say – and how they look while saying it.

There are some striking visual set-pieces as well: for instance, the episode in which Gerald brutally disciplines a horse terrified by a passing train. Or the entertainment 'in the manner of the Russian ballet' devised by Hermione for her house guests. Or the water-party at Shortlands, when Gudrun's improvised dance unsurprisingly terrifies some cattle and, tragically, the young newlyweds are drowned. And so on.

It is enough, though, to refute Leavis's typically mandarin dismiss-iveness by drawing attention to the remarkable complexity of intention and achievement of Russell's film. He has had the advantage of some brilliant collaborators certainly – actors, cinematographer, designers, editor – and the result is a film which honours its great antecedent and which is a major work in its own right.

Notes

1 Quoted in *Sight & Sound*, Winter 1969–70, 49; from a letter to screen-writer/producer Larry Kramer. See *Novel Images: Literature in Performance* (London: Routledge, 1993), p. 121.

2 D. H. Lawrence, 'Why the novel matters', in B. Steele (ed.), *A Study of Thomas Hardy and Other Essays* (Cambridge: Cambridge University Press, 1985), pp. 196–7.

3 'Glenda Jackson' in Brian McFarlane, *An Autobiography of British Cinema* (London: Methuen, 1997), pp. 315-16.

4 Oliver Reed, *Reed All About Me* (London: Coronet Books, 1979), p. 131.

5 Reed, *Reed All About Me*, p. 132.

6 D. H. Lawrence, *Women in Love* (1921), (London: Penguin, 1966), p. 470.

13   Hard men:
Get Carter (1971)

It may seem that Hollywood invented and subsequently collared the market in the gangster film, but actually British film gangsters have a long and honourable history from the 1930s to the present day. The 1940s spawned such major examples of the genre as *Brighton Rock* and *They Made Me a Fugitive* (both 1947), as well as the rough-and-ready attempt at US-style thuggery in the then-notorious *No Orchids for Miss Blandish* (1948). Gangsters figured prominently in the B-movie output of the 50s and early 60s, and again, in the late 90s through into the new century, films such as *Lock, Stock and Two Smoking Barrels* (1998) and the under-valued – and under-known – *Gangster No. 1* (2000), which showed that the tradition was alive and well. Poised almost half-way between these periods of prolific British gangster activity on-screen was Mike Hodges' *Get Carter* (1971), which on many counts is still one of the most memorable of them all.

British *noir*

Talk of the gangster genre almost automatically raises the matter of *film noir* which takes its name from the moody French stylistics of such 1930s pieces as *Quai des brumes* (1938) and *Le jour se lève* (1939). It was then made famous to English-speaking audiences in a series of remarkable 1940s Hollywood films, usually thrillers, such as *Double Indemnity* (1944) and *Out of the Past* (1947). The dark perceptions of *film noir* were typically expressed in black-and-white films of that period, but, in what has become known as neo-*noir*, the term encompassed colour while

27   Film poster for
Get Carter.

retaining many of the unsettling plot elements of the earlier films. *Noir* was perhaps always especially suited to the gangster world and, in a British gangster film such as *Get Carter,* it gives a distinctive flavour to the prevailing realism of setting that was familiar from the New Wave films of a decade earlier.

British *noir* at work in the gangster genre always seemed to bring out the seediness of the places in which the criminals conducted their affairs as well as the scruffiness and sheer brutality of those affairs. In general they lacked the patina of glamour we had got used to in Hollywood counterparts, in which improbably seductive women and suave chaps fetched up in apartments and nightclubs that testified to elaborate production design rather than, say, location-shooting in the more sordid circumstances in which actual gangster life seems, if the newspapers can be trusted, to be situated.

Newcastle

The look of *Get Carter* is very important to its bleak, almost nihilistic atmosphere, and that 'look' depends a great deal on how cinematographer Wolfgang Suschitzky has gone to work on Newcastle-on-Tyne. We're in roughly the same terrain explored by the New Wave directors a decade earlier, but this time it's in Metrocolor (as an MGM film). This should make things look less depressed than, say, *Room at the Top* or *A Kind of Loving*. It doesn't, though; instead it intensifies the aura of the run-down, the squalid and the sleazy. Director Mike Hodges has not gone in for great long-shots of the Tyne Bridge, for instance, but has concentrated instead on getting from his cameraman a muted, grubby ambience in which the gangland activities of the plot are convincingly located. There are odd excursions away from the drabness of docks and terraced streets and alleyways strung with laundry when the plot takes us to the country seat of local gangster Cyril Kinnear (John Osborne), but the over-all impression is of a city seething with barely legal activities in the fields of gambling and pornography. As well, there is an insistent feeling of characterless new building – of concrete tower blocks and huge car-parks – beginning to make the older terraced streets look strangely obsolete but without the new bringing anything much in the way of beauty.

There is probably not much about the film's setting to encourage tourism in this northern city. To my knowledge Newcastle hasn't figured in British film very often. It was the setting for Sidney Hayers' vengeance thriller, *Payroll* (1961), Mike Figgis's excellent feature debut, the thriller *Stormy Monday* (1988), and, in different vein, Stephen Daldry's first feature, *Billy Elliot* (2000), and it has been the setting for several television series. But in no other film does it emerge with the sort of *character* it acquires in *Get Carter*. Not all the film is shot in Newcastle, there are other locations from 'up north' too, but what is exciting is the way in which these locations seem to act as pressures on the action, to the point where one can hardly imagine it happening elsewhere, let alone in Seattle, scene of the greatly inferior American remake of the film in 2000.

What brings Carter to Newcastle?
The film opens in London with Jack Carter (Michael Caine) looking out from a penthouse apartment window, with a woman visible in the background. Inside, his gangster boss, Gerald Fletcher (Terence

Rigby), Gerald's wife Anna (Britt Ekland) – who we assume was the woman in the opening shot – his brother Sid (John Bindon, an actor who had real-life underworld connections) and Carter are watching a porn movie. Carter seems less engaged by the movie than the others and clearly has something else on his mind. 'The north', the setting for the porn film, is described by Gerald as Jack's 'old stamping ground'. Gerald says, 'We don't want you to go up the north, Jack'. But Jack is going, 'To find out what happened'.

In these clipped exchanges the essential plot manoeuvres are put in place. Jack's brother Frank has been killed in Newcastle and the complex network of dangerous connections and betrayals is set in motion by Jack's determination. The pornographic film business will also play a crucial role in the film's narrative, and the look that passes between Jack and Anna suggests another possibility for trouble in Jack's life. Heading north from London will propel him into a sort of moral darkness that is hinted at in the rapid tracking shots of the train passing into and out of tunnels. On the train he is reading Raymond Chandler's *Farewell My Lovely*, a cunning choice that resonates with other gangster films and films *noirs*, and on a very obvious level Carter has farewelled his lovely for the moment anyway. But unlike Chandler's hero, Carter's moral streak is less pronounced as we shall see when he makes his way about the mean streets of Newcastle – less pronounced but not entirely missing, in spite of his casual way of killing people who displease him or obstruct his purposes.

A revenger's tragedy?

'Tragedy' is probably an overwrought description of Jack's story, but in its pervasive bleakness *Get Carter* becomes a surprisingly moving tale. A thriller that ends with its protagonist dead on a grey northern beach as the tide gradually washes over him is some emotional distance from, say, Bogart and Bacall finding each other at the end of *The Big Sleep*. How has he arrived at this ending? The two narrative impulses that propel him to that beach both involve revenge.

He has gone north to find out how his brother Frank died. Arriving at night reinforces the sense of descent. Carter will discover that his brother was killed to prevent him from exposing the pornographic network run by local crime boss, Kinnear. When he goes into a bar on arrival, he is the object of a few furtive looks – are these anxious or

28   Bryan Mosley (Cliff Brumby) and Michael Caine (Jack Carter).

merely curious? – as the film cuts from face to face to establish a mixed clientele. He phones Frank's girlfriend, Margaret (Dorothy White) and in a move that is typical of the film's narrative habits we hear his brusque questions to her but not her answers, and then we hear the sound of her hanging up abruptly. Here's a connection we'll have to find out more about. And who is the 'Doreen' he asks her about? Though we don't know at this stage, 'Doreen' will, from about halfway through the film, provide Jack with the second basis for his revenge agenda.

Mid-film, Carter finds that Doreen has been involved in making porn films for Cyril Kinnear, and with Margaret's knowledge. There is also a suggestion that Doreen may be Jack Carter's own daughter. He now has two motives for some vengeful violence. Keith (Alun Armstrong), a barman who'd worked with Frank, tells Carter how shocked he was at Frank's death. Carter finds that Frank's death was not an accident as he picks his way through Newcastle criminal circles. These latter include the wealthy Kinnear, who has interests in the gambling and porn-film rackets, slot-machine tycoon Brumby (Bryan Mosley), Eric Paice (Ian Hendry), an ex-con now working as a chauffeur, and Albert Swift (Glyn Edwards), who's been involved in the blue movie with Margaret and Doreen.

Each of these four chaps will be very sorry about Carter's having come north. Kinnear's various criminal enterprises will come to a sudden halt as police raid his country house, having been tipped off by Carter. Three of them will be killed: Brumby is tipped over the edge of an upper-storey construction site; Swift is knifed in an alley behind a betting-shop, after which Carter casually leaves via the shop; Paice is dispatched near the seashore where Carter himself will be picked off by a hired assassin. Paice's death is Carter's revenge for his brother's death. He pursues Paice until the latter stumbles and falls exhausted, then forces him to drink a bottle of whisky which was the treatment meted out to Frank before pushing him into the car that led to his death. After whacking Paice round the head with his rifle, Carter loads him into a coal-bucket on a passing cable and watches as he is tipped out into the sea.

There are women casualties too. Kinnear's girlfriend, Glenda, who's told Carter that Kinnear had set up the porn film involving Doreen, ends up in the boot of Carter's car which is then pushed off a pier into the harbour. Margaret also reaches a watery end. She denies knowledge of Frank's murder but Carter doesn't believe her and calls her a 'bloody whore'. Later, at night, he grabs her in the street near her home, drives her to a deserted wood, forces her to strip, injects her, then tips her into the lake in Kinnear's grounds, where the police find her when they come to round up the inhabitants.

The telling of the tale

It is not possible to make the twists of plot sound anything other than complex, and it is not, at first viewing, always easy to keep all the connections in mind. However, the film repays repeated viewings in which the network of criminal affiliations does become clearer and an over-all sense of a dangerous underworld grips the imagination. *Get Carter* takes on the northern ambience of the New Wave films but adds an aura of menace to the mere drabness of the earlier films; though they of course were telling different kinds of stories. They were less interested in cryptic narrative procedures, involving bursts of violent action and unexpected revelations, than in the exploring of relationships in a shifting social climate. In some ways, the look of *Carter* does recall those films, but in its concern with how a gangster negotiates the criminal terrain it has a much stronger sense of 'plot' than most of the New Wave films, in which observation mattered more than action.

Certainly, there is often something cryptic about the film's story-telling habits, though these can be properly teasing. For instance, there are several phone conversations in which we are privy only to one of the speakers but are required later to grasp their significance. Apart from the call to Margaret who hangs up on Jack, we also see him phoning the police which is followed by a long line of police cars arriving at The Heights, Kinnear's country estate. Most cryptic of all is the moment with Kinnear speaking quietly into the phone while a party is going on behind him. He is saying: 'I want you to listen carefully. Jack Carter... You know what he looks like?' This doesn't sound like good news for Carter, and it isn't: Kinnear is actually ordering an assassin to finish Jack off. There is a brief shot of the man in bed listening on the phone; he doesn't speak and we note (and will remember in the scene early next morning on the cliff top) that he wears a ring with the letter 'J' engraved on it. Most enigmatic of all is the conversation between Carter and the bearded Kinnear, whose attention he catches with 'Listen carefully, you hairy-faced git', and whom he threatens with having 'enough evidence to put you away for a long time'. He suggests 'a simple deal' with Kinnear and the camera stays on the listening Kinnear who finally says, 'I see. I think that can be arranged.' The only information we are given in relation to this exchange is that, when Kinnear comes off the phone, Eric Paice comes into the room and Kinnear simply says, 'Yes, Eric. A word with you.' He's actually sealing Eric's fate, but neither we nor Eric quite grasp this at that moment.

Another unusual stylistic device is the film's variant on the classic shot-reverse-shot technique for dealing with conversations between two people. Instead of cutting from one to the other, John Trumper's razor-sharp editing offers instead a close-up of one speaker whose face is partly obscured by the back of the head of the other. In one example, Kinnear and a gambler, Harry (Kevin Brennan), playing for high stakes in Kinnear's house, are engaged in a very strikingly shot battle of wits. Neither face gets the screen to itself: when the taunting Kinnear is talking, the back of Harry's head is still in the frame, and vice-versa when nervous Harry is talking. We feel the pressure of Kinnear's holding him with the look we assume but can't see. These strange semi-close-ups create a tension that is in line with the film's enigmatic narrative procedures.

There is also a high incidence of people watching other people, sometimes at long range (most notably at the very end when the assassin has his sights literally set on Carter) and sometimes in tight exchanges. The editing and camera placement constantly put the viewer on guard. In another similarly opaque moment, soon after his arrival in Newcastle,

Carter is talking to Paice at the races and the camera is placed so that passing people and horses fleetingly obscure the two men, thereby increasing the viewer's tension about what is happening between the pair.

Despite ambiguities and moments when the plot manoeuvres may seem as misty as the landscape, the film's over-all trajectory is not muddied as a result. 'Who killed Frank?' is the key question that has brought Carter up north, and he finds a great deal of equivocation when he starts posing it to the Newcastle locals. His quest then inevitably becomes a matter of vengeance, which is reinforced by finding that Doreen has been procured by Paice to appear in the pornographic film. These two plot starters will become closely connected and lead to several killings and a number of other ugly encounters.

Getting Carter

A film that closes with its hero – if that's the word – lying dead on a desolate beach can only make us wonder what sort of protagonist we are dealing with. The glimpse of Carter reading *Farewell My Lovely* as he travels north can't help but set up expectations, though they are largely misleading. Of course Chandler's heroes are detectives, ostensibly on the side of the law, which, from time to time, they will take into their own hands, but they are also men with an irreducible moral core that inures them to further tarnishing by the corrupt lives they investigate. Carter is well and truly tarnished from the start. He is a gangster attached to a London-based mob which his boss Gerald tells him has 'connections' up north: 'Some hard nuts operate up there, Jack. They won't take kindly to someone from London poking his bugle in.' But Jack is not about to be deterred by this, because he's not 'satisfied' about how Frank died, even if 'the law' was. Gerald warns him to 'think again' before going. Jack says 'I will', and the film cuts sharply to a train plunging into a tunnel, then to a compartment where Jack is reading.

What's established from the outset is that Carter, however morally dubious he may be, is a man with a mission he is determined to carry out, and that he has no illusions about himself. When Margaret tries to suggest that Frank was up to no good, that she'd thought he might kill himself, Carter tells her, 'I don't believe you, Margaret. Frank wasn't like that... I'm the villain in the family, remember?' Carter can lie and cheat in the name of business, but not about himself. His determination to find how Frank died and later to exact some sort of justice for the corruption of Doreen evince a level of rectitude in Carter that is not on show in any of the other hard men with whom he does business, in either London or Newcastle. He finally laughs when Paice's body, loaded on to the coal bucket, is dropped into the sea with the coal slag. He has only moments to live, but he has achieved what he came north to do. He would repudiate anything so high-sounding but in fact a sort of honour has been served. He even looks peaceful when he is lying dead on the shore. In his autobiography, Michael Caine claims that *Get Carter* is not about vengeance, 'it's about honour, family honour. I understood all that, because there was a very strong code of honour round where I came from.'[1]

The raising of Caine

In 'getting' Carter, the crucial factor is no doubt Caine himself. There was no one quite like Caine in British cinema, and perhaps there has been none since to match that persona which could suggest either a vacancy of spirit or a taciturn concealment of feeling – or any number of other possibilities. He had nothing in common with that earlier generation of British male stars such as James Mason, Stewart Granger or the younger Dirk Bogarde. Unlike their generally middle-class resonances, Caine came from an impoverished working-class background, pottering around in small roles in films for half a dozen years before hitting his stride in the mid 1960s when three films confirmed his versatility and his standing with the public. These roles were in *Zulu* (1963), as an aristocratic officer, *The Ipcress File* (1965), as an un-Bond-like intelligence agent, and above all as the tireless womaniser, *Alfie* (1966), who begins to ask himself, 'What's it all about?' He impressed audiences as one of those actors who, like so many Hollywood stars, seemed to *behave* rather than act, exuding an aura of total immersion in the role and thus of total credibility.

As Jack Carter, he brings his laconic authority to bear on what is essentially an unsympathetic role. That first shot of him gazing out of the penthouse window seems to establish him at once as a man alone, at least detached from those around him, but also as one not likely to be much swayed by the opinions of his gangster colleagues. Caine suggests an affectlessness in Carter's usual gaze, so that it is hard to know what he is thinking. As a result, his bursts of violence, leading to several deaths, are the more shocking. Further, the moments of restrained feeling are equally memorable because their coming is so rare: for example, when he quietly takes his dead brother's hands as Frank lies in his coffin, then gently pulls the shroud over his face; or when he gives Doreen money and advises her, 'Be good – don't trust boys'. He virtually never laughs and rarely smiles, but at the end as Paice's body is making its way to the sea via the coal-bucket he laughs seriously for the first time, as though to suggest he has done what had to be done. There are echoes of John Wayne's implacable Western hero of *The Searchers*, Ethan Edwards, both in his quest for vengeance in relation to his brother's family (and especially his niece) and in the economy with which he renders his implacable intentions.

Forty years later, Caine was still mining this screen persona, this sense of doing nothing but meaning everything, in films such as *Harry Brown* (2010). This film's one incontestable virtue was Caine's magisterial performance in the title role of the elderly housing-estate vigilante who takes on the neighbouring thug population. Over all these decades, he has been honing a kind of screen acting that ends by his seeming to inhabit roles rather than perform them. As well as those mentioned above, think of such varied roles as those in *The Italian Job*, *The Honorary Consul*, *Mona Lisa* – the list seems endless. He is the least 'actorish' of actors. In his minimalist way, he reminds one of the great American stars, such as Wayne or Gary Cooper, drawing on aspects of a recognisable persona subtly adjusted to the demands of each role. In the softened, flattened, glossed-up American remake of 2000, Sylvester Stallone's Carter seems merely empty of meaning.

There are of course plenty of other creative talents involved in making *Get Carter* so memorable an experience.[2] Producer Michael Klinger, capitalising on recent gangster trials such as those of the Richardsons and the Krays, settled on Ted Lewis's crime novel, *Jack's Return Home*,[3] as the basis for a thriller about contemporary violence. To ensure the film's financial viability, he insisted on Caine for the title role, though it was a departure from his preceding parts. More adventurously, he chose for director Mike Hodges, who had done some superior television work but had not made a feature film. In view of the swift-moving, emotionally charged piece that resulted, Klinger's choice was triumphantly vindicated. As well as TV thrillers, Hodges had also directed some episodes in the documentary series *World in Action* (1964) and it is tempting to suppose that this experience fed into the look of seductive realism that characterises *Get Carter*, especially in the way it catches Newcastle as a city poised between the terraced streets of the past and the vast new concrete structures used for some of the film's most dangerous encounters. Hodges went on to direct another film for Klinger, the comedy-thriller, *Pulp* (1972), a sort of 'reply' to *Get Carter* in which he felt he'd created a sort of monster, albeit a compelling one. The rest of his career, though, was surprisingly sporadic. In his 1998 film, *Croupier*, he showed some of the same flair for drama in dubious places that had typified his work in *Get Carter*.

In a large supporting cast, not everyone gets the chance to establish a firm sense of character. Certainly not Britt Ekland who, as the wife of Carter's London boss, exchanges a charged look with Caine early on, but only appears once more when she engages him in an erotic phone call. Clad, only just, in black underwear, she teases him with her account of what she is doing as she undoes her bra. She is never seen again in the film, though we learn that her husband has had her carved somewhat when he learns of her affair with Carter. Of the rest, playwright John Osborne in an enjoyable turn as the smoothly corrupt Kinnear, Ian Hendry (Hodges' first choice for Jack) as the equivocal Paice who meets such a nasty end, and the young Alun Armstrong (Brian in TV's *New Tricks*) as Keith, a rare almost likable character, offer vivid sketches. As far as actors go, *Get Carter* is not exactly a one-man band, but it is inconceivable without Caine, even if the reviewer who asserted that 'no one else has time to establish character at all'[4] is overstating the case.

Forty years on...

Viewed today, *Get Carter* still carries a most potent sense of unease and threat. It has touches of wit (Jack recalls Paice's eyes as looking like 'piss holes in the snow') and enough underlying feeling in what motivates Jack to make the final effect something other than merely nihilistic. There's a certain nostalgia to be felt for the days when even gangsters wore jackets and ties, but there's no softening of the film's impact. Caine's Carter is a definitive creation and the world he moves in seems as real as ever.

Notes

1 Michael Caine, *The Elephant to Hollywood* (London: Hodder & Stoughton, 2010), p. 154.

2 For an illuminating account of the film's production history, see Andrew

Spicer and A. T. McKenna, *The Man Who Got Carter: Michael Klinger, Independent Production and the British Film Industry, 1960–1980* (London: I. B. Tauris, 2013), Chapter 4.

3 Ted Lewis, *Jack's Return Home* (London: Michael Joseph, 1970).

4 Nigel Andrews, *Monthly Film Bulletin*, April 1971, 73.

14   From life:

A Portrait of the Artist as a Young Man
(1977)

What is this film doing here?

There is undoubtedly an element of self-indulgence at work here, but this is simply a film I love. Someone to whom I mentioned its inclusion in this book said, 'Isn't it an Irish film?' As far as I can discover, it was made by the Ulysses Film Company, whose only feature it seems to have been and whose production quarters were, according to the end credits, located in London's Soho. The sound recording was completed at Elstree Studios, Boreham Wood, England. It was made in co-operation with Radio Telefís, Éireann, and some of it is clearly set in London. Its country of production is designated as 'Great Britain' by the *Monthly Film Bulletin*[1] and by the 'Film Index International'.[2] So, at very least, a UK/Irish co-production?

If that won't do, I repeat: this is a film I love. Based on one of my favourite novels, it is not only a hugely attractive piece of filmmaking in its own right, but it comes to the most eloquent terms with one of the most eloquent *Bildungsromans* ever written. And this is a mode that embraces such titles as *Great Expectations* and *Sons and Lovers*, from which notable *Bildungsfilms* (if the term is allowable) have also been made. The notion of the coming-of-age story, of the moral, spiritual and aesthetic growth of a young person as he or she strains or lurchs towards adulthood has often been a proving-ground for the ideas and ideals that shape our lives.

Further, Joseph Strick's film adaptation of James Joyce's *A Portrait of the Artist as a Young Man* is in one important way a very daring film. Like Ken Russell's version of *Women in Love* (1968), it doesn't subscribe to the conventional wisdom that it is film's primary job to show rather than to tell. Oh, it can show all right, as both Strick and Russell attest, but their real boldness is in requiring their audiences to listen to a great deal of talk. In this talk all sorts of ideas are thrashed out, and sometimes these will be teased into serious levels of awareness. Not many films risk so much talk but those that do so in ways that hold our attention and further our understanding deserve to be noticed.

Whose portrait?

Strictly speaking, Stephen Dedalus is the artist whose 'portrait' is indicated by the title of novel and film, but there is also clearly a strong element of James Joyce's own struggles towards adulthood and writerhood. But this shouldn't be over-stressed. A 1975 biographer[3] draws attention to some obvious inventions by Joyce, the artist behind *A Portrait of the Artist*, while allowing that 'there are parts... which are plainly accounts of what happened to James Joyce'. My concern is not with how closely it adheres to the facts of Joyce's life but what the film makes of the novel which offers not 'The' *Portrait* but 'A' *Portrait*. In some ways, the film mirrors Joyce's book devotedly, but some of the filmmakers' decisions show that they haven't been enslaved to the unproductive goal of 'fidelity'.

Actually, in both novel and film what we have is less a 'portrait' than a work in progress, a series of pictures which capture Stephen at various stages on his journey. From the small boy being told a story about a 'moo-cow', to the watchful child at the schism-rent Christmas dinner-table, the schoolboy bullied by a classmate and beaten by a priest-teacher – all these and more until the final image of the young adult Stephen bidding his parents farewell as he sets off to the Continent contribute to the 'portrait' in which details are always being filled in on a canvas which perhaps will never be complete. In its ninety-minute running time, the film makes some very judicious decisions about which 'pictures' need most dramatic weight if we are to understand the final portrait of the young man leaving Ireland, 'the old sow that eats her farrow'.

A film 'portrait' must necessarily come to terms with the visual as well as the verbal and Strick's film steers its course between the two with calm precision. The faces matter as much as the words issuing from them, and cinematographer Stuart Hetherington, whose only feature film it was, knows how to frame them and how long to leave the camera on them. How people relate to each other is again and again made clear in how they are placed in the frame: for instance, in the contained unease Stephen (Bosco Hogan) feels as he shares a train carriage with his father Simon (T. P. McKenna), who keeps his spirits up with those from a small flask. The space between the two men, the way they avoid looking at each other, tells us as much as what is said on this occasion.

Joyce and the cinema

So idiosyncratic a writer as Joyce was never likely to attract great numbers of film adaptations, but in general he has been well served by those that have emerged. His most ambitious adaptor is Joseph Strick, the American producer-director who had made a name for offbeat productions such as the *faux*-documentary *The Savage Eye* (1960) and his version of Jean Genet's *The Balcony* (1963), both with strongly erotic elements. Unusual as these both were, they were minor challenges compared to his next venture, an adaptation of Joyce's *Ulysses* (1967). It reminds one of what Samuel Johnson had to say, in his politically incorrect way, on another matter: 'Sir, a woman's preaching is like a dog's walking on his hind legs. It is not done well; but you are surprised to find it done at all.' To imagine you could make a coherent film, of a little over two hours, from that massive and daunting novel was surely an act of courage in the first place, and enough of it worked to warrant praise from all but the most entrenched purists. Indeed, Barbara Jefford's soliloquy, as Molly Bloom, has stayed in my mind over the decades since I saw it. Not the highest accolade but one that has something going for it.

Ten years later, Strick's beautiful film of *A Portrait*, admittedly not quite such a daunting encounter for the filmmaker, goes a long way to reminding one of the felicities of its source. He later claimed that though the film was 'well received, had good audiences, [he was] not sure it worked for a mass audience, as it was not so deeply about sex as *Ulysses*'.[4]

Joyce, a man who liked films, and decided that 'he could earn a little profit by providing [Dublin] with its first cinemas',[5] might well have been pleased to know that a half-dozen films were later made from his life and works. Apart from the Strick pair, there were: Mary Ellen Bute's *Passages from James Joyce's Finnegans Wake* (1966), a venture of almost lunatic daring; Sean Walsh's *Bloom* (2003), adapted from *Ulysses*; Pat Murphy's *Nora* (2000), a version of Joyce's romance with Nora Barnacle; and John Huston's *The Dead* (1987), as eloquent a swansong as a director ever had, and one which would surely have gratified Joyce. There are other TV and little-seen foreign adaptations of his novels and stories. An author who might have seemed intransigently tied to the page has inspired quite a lot of film attention, some of this surprisingly successful in film terms, and not merely reverential homage.

The portrait on the page

The novel is divided into five large sections, and the film deals unequally with these. The first evokes Stephen's infancy and early childhood, when he is already trying to make connections between his inner self and the world around him. It's not told in a first-person narrative but we still feel inside Stephen's mind, as he evinces a fascination with words and an acute response to physical sensations. The section doesn't proceed in conventional fashion, but instead sketches a series of seemingly discon-nected scenes – at school, at home, back at school – and ends with Stephen's first challenge to authority when he complains to the rector about an unjustified beating. He becomes the hero of the hour, but, while we may feel we are in Stephen's mind, aglow with his sense of the rightness of what he has done, we are also in Joyce's, as his ironic prose makes clear the limited nature of Stephen's achievement.

He is after all still only a small boy. In the subsequent sections, Stephen comes to question certain assumptions about his world, feels a growing awareness of his own identity and individuality. There are the beginnings of intellectual revolt; he is assailed by religious doubt, and his sexual awakening finds relief with a prostitute. The religious retreat at his school leads him to a violent, emotional swing away from physical indulgence, to an adolescent wallowing in the notion of his own sin. The emerging 'portrait' is constantly in a state of change, almost as if it is lying in wait for film to render the changes with a visual as well as a verbal precision. If the retreat represents one watershed in Stephen's emerging sense of self, his religious zeal, and the possibility of his having a priestly vocation, take an irreversible tumble at the end of Section 4 with the image of the wading girl he observes on the beach. '"Heavenly God!" cried Stephen's soul, in an outburst of profane joy.' Again we're invited to share in and respect an adolescent response *and* to keep seeing that that *is* indeed what it is.

The final and longest section, which the film, with some real daring, takes on almost in full, is largely a matter of discussion, as Stephen, with a succession of undergraduate friends, seeks to argue out what he believes and what he repudiates. He is not yet an artist at the end of the book, which creates and records the processes of his growth. Perhaps it is true to say that, as a prospective artist, he has nothing yet to express but his self, but he has begun to understand the paths he must follow if he is ever to fulfil his vocation. Neither book nor film is the portrait of the artist; it is the emerging portrait of the young man who may *become* an artist. The book's over-all movement is in the direction of striking out, away from an Ireland fraught with political and religious strife, and the film is shaped by this same over-arching narrative concern. Joyce's novel is also about the power of words and this represents a challenge for a filmmaker whose medium often subdues the verbal in favour of the visual. Not Joseph Strick, though.

The portrait on the screen

In view of the novel's complexity of structure – a real sense of achievement in each section followed by a series of let-downs and discouraging reappraisals – and the sensuous resonance of its prose, the film's accomplishment is pretty remarkable. Even more demanding is the business of rendering the book's dual vision – Stephen's and Joyce's. It would have been simpler to adopt a more conventional approach to the events of the narrative but Strick has chosen the more difficult course of both showing us Stephen in action and, at the same time, encouraging us to stand sufficiently apart to permit a more detached view of his development.

Visual cues

Our first glimpse of Stephen is of a small boy (Terrence Strick) on a beach behind the film's opening credits. We pass through an elegant Georgian façade to a room in which the boy's father, Simon Dedalus, is telling him the story about a 'moo-cow', with his mother (Rosaleen Linehan) at the piano, and 'Dante', Mrs Riordan (Maureen Potter) watching. This charming scene of domestic life is undercut in several ways. It is preceded by a caption that refers to an Ireland ruled by Britain but moving towards independence under the leadership of Charles Parnell, and is followed by one that states: '1891. Parnell has fallen from power. Named as the secret lover of Mrs Kitty O'Shea in a divorce suit, he was vilified and abandoned by most of his supporters and forced from politics in disgrace.' The apparent domestic harmony is thus placed in relation to an Ireland in turmoil, as if foreshadowing the world in which Stephen will have to make his way – or flee from it.

On a simpler level, school will replace the warmth and security of home, and this loss is presaged by the way he is delivered to the school steps. Simon practises an austere notion of how a father should behave, barely touching his small son and leaving him only with the limited wisdom of, 'Whatever you do, never peach on a fellow.' There is an embrace from his mother but as they drive away in their horse-drawn carriage there is no looking back to wave and the small boy is left solitary. School is called up in a few images: a boy quizzes Stephen about his father; he is kicked into a ditch by a bully; his glasses are broken; and he is beaten by a priest for whom flogging seems a substitute for some suppressed passion. While in bed, recovering from his soaking in the ditch, he hears priests talk of Parnell and Kitty O'Shea. In this way the film reminds us of the world outside, and prepares us for the dissensions of the Christmas dinner-table when he is home on holidays.

This latter sequence is brilliantly filmed. As early as this in the film, Strick (abetted by screenwriter Judith Rascoe) makes plain that he will not be shirking the dialectic that is so central to the novel and to Stephen's growth. With father Simon seated as the patriarchal head of the table, the scene offers a microcosm of the conflicts of religion and politics that were tearing at the heart of Ireland. The camera moves from face to face, resting on speakers in turn as if to ensure everyone gets a chance to put forward his or her view. The words matter, but so do the faces. Simon, over-jocose, flushed with drink, and given to profanity, expects to hold court and to air his views and prejudices uninter-rupted, albeit he is the host on this occasion. He refuses to heed Mrs Riordan's request for 'no political discussion on this day of the year.' She is obdurate in her disdain for Parnell's adultery and in her belief in the priests' absolute rights, while Simon, sounding more tolerant than he is, replies, 'No one's saying a word against them as long as they leave politics alone.' He declares that 'We are an unfortunate priest-ridden race' to which her answer is, 'The priests were always the true friends to Ireland', while a guest, Mr Casey, weeps for Parnell.

The camera rests several times on the face of the young Stephen who listens warily but says nothing. Mrs Riordan, truer than she knows, warns that, 'He'll remember all this when he grows up', and in fact he is beginning to identify some of those 'nets' he'll have to 'fly by' to become an artist. When she leaves the house, she charges him to become 'a good

Catholic boy', and this ideal is put to the test in the ensuing sequence at school when he is beaten for not doing his work, even though his glasses are broken. The film picks up the novel's anti-Catholic bias in this episode, following which the boys cheer him but Strick keeps the camera at a distance, echoing Joyce's ironic assessment of just how far Stephen's little moment of rebellion has taken him on the long road ahead.

The intense visual quality of these early episodes persists in the way the film registers the failing fortunes of Simon Dedalus. A removal van is stationed outside the graceful Georgian façade as the family's wares are loaded on board and the film cuts wordlessly to the shabby terrace which is to be their future home. A poignant note is struck when a woman's voice is heard singing 'Oft in the stilly night... Fond memory brings the light of other days around me.' Poignant but not sentimental, it proves to be Stephen's mother singing in the terrace where her domestic life will now have to rearrange itself, profitlessly but painfully recalling what she has lost. She is most touchingly played by Rosaleen Linehan, and T. P. McKenna is superb as the vainglorious, self-deceiving father who has brought them to this pass. A brief shot of an 'AUCTION' notice and a statement from the auctioneer makes clear that Simon has been declared a bankrupt. Simon gives Stephen phony advice about 'always mixing with gentlemen', and is embarrassingly boastful and loud in a pub, and Stephen's growing wariness with his father is caught in that image of the space between them as they sit in a railway carriage. Learning how to come to terms with his family is as crucial at this stage of Stephen's development as imbibing talk of politics and religion, and his face registers responses subtly and surely.

Fleshly images
The first women seen to stir Stephen's adolescent sexuality are nudes reclining in provocative poses on sepia postcards. Dimly aware that there is something forbidden about his growing preoccupation with these images, he keeps the postcards in a box which is hidden up the chimney of his room. When he wins an essay prize, the topic is 'Trust not to surfaces', which of course is exactly what he is doing, and, while the essay is being read out in an assembly, students pass around pictures of a naked girl. Sex has now definitively entered and complicated Stephen's life. When he is in a pub, there are close-ups of girls' faces, as seen from his point of view. The visual has no need of the verbal to make the meaning plain. Nor does it later in the street at night

when prostitutes are posed against the dark, as if suggesting nothing else competes for his attention at this point. The one who takes him to her room and unburdens him of his virginity is presented with some generosity, and the entire sex scene is both discreet and convincingly sensual.

The retreat and the wading girl

The contrasting female image is that of the wading girl. Unlike the prostitute who satisfies bodily urges, she is an ideal of the female, of the feminine, and, more than that, a symbol of secular beauty. She is crucial to Stephen's growth, not just aesthetically, let alone sexually, and this importance is partly due to her placement in the film. By this I mean that this glorious image and the scene with the prostitute are separated by the retreat sermon.

It always impresses me when an author or a filmmaker is prepared to take time to show a character going about his work and if his work is with words that is perhaps an even riskier undertaking. (Think of J. M. Coetzee's *Elizabeth Costello* in which the title character's lectures are daringly allowed many pages as they work to fill out the contours of her character.) Joyce allots about twenty-five pages to the sermons of the retreat, which address the students as 'my dear little brothers in Christ' and which paint terrifying pictures of the horrors of Hell which they can expect if they don't heed the priestly teachings. One of Strick's master strokes was to engage John Gielgud for the role of the preacher and to grant him enough running time to justify Stephen's violent emotional swing from sensual physical indulgence to religious commitment. Strick claimed that Gielgud, 'told me he was an atheist, and [the sermon] allowed him to express what he thought about the church. He took the part also because of the beauty of the writing… He was magnificent.'[6] Indeed, it's hard to imagine anyone doing this better. With his look of ascetic concentration and his astonishing vocal control, he makes the viewer believe that these mad but terrifying speeches might work to unnerve a susceptible adolescent. It is clear that both Strick and Gielgud fully understood their significance in the film's narrative arch (even if Gielgud did complain that, after learning the spiritual tirades by heart, his running time was 'cut to pieces'[7]), and most of the sermon is given in close-up.

As if to underline the wildly fanciful account of Hell's horrors, the film plays down the visual element in its handling of this episode. At first spellbound like the other boys, Stephen then lowers his gaze, suggesting that he will now look inward. He makes his confession (relating to his fleshly sins) and discusses the possibility that he may have a religious vocation with the Dean of Studies (David Kelly). None of this is caricatured in the film, and it would lose its potency if it were. As Stephen wanders off, pondering the likelihood of his having a vocation, he passes a church from which strains of the hymn 'O come, O come Emmanuel' can be heard on the soundtrack and the aural image is made quietly and subtly. Music director Stanley Myers heightens the emotional charge of many moments with his plangent score and discreetly chosen echoes of familiar tunes. Stephen's walk takes him to the beach where he sees the wading girl in the shallows, and he utters the novel's cry of 'Heavenly God!' as if in recognition of the beauty of the earth. But his face then lights up with a smile that indexes his commitment to the secular. The image could easily have been exaggerated but instead the girl is always seen in long shot, so that she seems to belong utterly to the natural world. She feeds Stephen's mind with a delight partly erotic, but also with a sense of the wonder of the world. Again, the film asks us to see this and respect it as an adolescent response *and* to be aware that it is indeed just that.

Going verbal
The preacher's sermon is a watershed in the film, not just because of its convulsive effect on Stephen's development, crucially propelling him into a youthful wallow in his own sin. It is also a stylistic turning-point because of its stress on the verbal. In Gielgud's transcendant performance, the verbal does the work of the visual, as the preacher works to make the boys *see* the horrors he evokes. In the last thirty-five minutes of the film, the verbal will be given a prominence unusual in film, as Strick bravely address the fifth and last section of the novel, allowing it almost forty percent of the film's running-time.

Recalling the film's opening titles about Parnell and Ireland's political and religious conflicts, this last movement of the film is essentially a matter of three long conversations with his university friends, in turn Davin, Lynch and Cranley. The peasant friend, Davin, announces himself as an Irish nationalist and tells Stephen, 'You're a born sneerer'. Stephen can only reply fiercely with, 'This race and this life and this country produced me'. With Lynch, he talks bitterly about Parnell's treatment and the nets that he 'shall try to fly by', and their conversation covers matters such as sexual imperatives and the lure of art, with Stephen's becoming rather slyly knowing, rather pleased with himself, as he utters his undergraduate pronouncements. 'Wholeness, harmony and radiance,' he claims, are the prerequisites for beauty and the enchantment of the heart. There is real camaraderie in his dealings with Cranley who is perhaps testing him when he asks him about love of parents, or whether he thought Jesus was a self-deceiver or whether he has lost his faith. He says, 'I have tried to love God. It seems now I've failed.' He will not be doing his Easter duties: he cannot receive Communion unless he is absolved in confession, and he can't be absolved unless he is repentant.

In many films, as much concentrated talk as Strick has ventured to include might risk a waning of the viewer's attention. His achievement is to keep it dramatic. That is, it all works in terms of distinguishing Stephen's relations with his various friends, who are each physically distinct types, and who each fulfil different needs in Stephen's arguments with himself, as well as with them. Above all, this long section enables us to witness, as they are happening, the processes by which he is arriving at the self-knowledge he will need.

Much credit for the holding power of these talk-laden sequences is due to Bosco Hogan's beautifully judged playing of Stephen. Physically, he has just the right look of someone waiting for experience to write the decisive character into the lines of his face, and he plays with a watchfulness in the earlier parts of the film that contrasts with the forcefulness of youthful conviction he expresses in the later sequences. The actors who play Stephen as a child (Terrence Strick and Luke Johnstone) have been skilfully directed to convince us that they might have grown into the young man who 'do[es] not fear to be alone' at film's end. Hogan's quiet, observant playing gives weight to such rhetorical flights as 'I will try to express myself... as wholly as I can, using for my defence the only arms I allow myself to use – silence, exile and cunning.'

At the end...

In the film's last moments, Stephen meets Emma (Susan Fitzgerald), for whom he had written the poem, 'Are you not weary of ardent ways?' This encounter reminds us that words are the medium through which he will seek to make his mark on the world. 'I'm going to Paris to find the freedom to write as I wish.' The film ends with a long shot of the steamer bearing him away from Ireland, from parents on the quay, and from the kinds of strife that have constrained him. It opened on a long shot of the Irish coastal countryside, with Stephen playing with Mrs Riordan, and there is a sense both of completeness and of a different future as the Irish coastline recedes at the end. Strick may have been right about his *Portrait*'s not finding a mass audience; I can only say that the mass audience was the loser.

Notes

1 *Monthly Film Bulletin*, November 1977, 238.
2 *Film Index International*, software copyright, Chadwyck-Healey Ltd, 1993.
3 Stan Gébler Davies, *James Joyce: A Portrait of the Artist* (London: Davis-Poynter, 1975), p. 29.
4 Joseph Strick in 2008 interview with Gielgud's biographer, Jonathan Croall, in Croall, *John Gielgud: Matinee Idol to Movie Star*, second edition (London: Bloomsbury, 2011), pp. 603–4.
5 Gébler Davies, *James Joyce*, p. 163.
6 Joseph Strick interview, Croall, *John Gielgud*, pp. 603–4.
7 'Sir John Gielgud' in Brian McFarlane, *An Autobiography of British Cinema* (London: Methuen, 1997), p. 218.

15   Alice in the real world: *Dreamchild* (1986)

This has always seemed to me one of the most overlooked of British films. Because it is neither a full-blown biopic nor a conventional adaptation of a famous novel, but has in fact elements of both and a great deal more, it has perhaps been hard to categorise. And perhaps a film 'about' *Alice in Wonderland*, but not a film for children, makes this even harder. Nevertheless, for those who take on board its hybrid nature, in terms of both content and style, it is a very rewarding and ultimately very moving experience. Those who knew screenwriter Dennis Potter's television work, especially *Pennies from Heaven* (1981), were less likely to have been surprised.

Three Alices

Alice 1
The Alice we all know is, of course, the heroine of Lewis Carroll's *Alice in Wonderland*, first published in 1865 and surely one of the most popular children's books in the language. A book written *for* children certainly, it is also one which gives immense pleasure to adults for its play with language and its turning conventional notions on their head. Alice, as an American reporter in *Dreamchild* says, 'fell down a rabbit hole and took tea with a rabbit'. Well, once in this strange world Alice does a great deal more than take tea but exercises her wits to come to terms with all manner of eccentricity, including a playing-card Queen whose only response to any situation is to shout, 'Off with his head'.

This first Alice is set before us in *Dreamchild* in four sequences which come nearest to our usual expectations of a film adapting a celebrated work of literature. But there's nothing *usual* about the ways in which these episodes are enacted. After the opening shot of an old woman flanked by two bizarre creatures, the Gryphon and the Turtle, she is replaced by a little girl who is much more at home with these. This imagined Alice will later be seen both conversing with the Caterpillar, who quizzes her with, 'Who are you?', and taking her place at the Mad Hatter's tea-party. Even in episodes such as these there is no suggestion of straightforward adaptation from Carroll's original. For one thing, Carroll's Alice and the older 'real' Alice replace each other at unexpected moments, so that we know that there is much more at stake than just the rendering of scenes from a well-loved book. The film only uses a handful of such sequences but they are sufficient to remind us of Carroll's creation of this little Victorian girl trying to cling to common sense in the bizarre world of her fantasy.

Alice 2

The second Alice (Amelia Shankley) is the lively little girl who lived in Oxford and was the inspiration for the Reverend Charles Dodgson's stories of her namesake's adventures in 'Wonderland'. Dodgson (Ian Holm), who wrote as, but disclaimed connection with, Lewis Carroll, 'because he shrank from the publicity that the acknowledged authorship would have brought him',[1] is depicted in the film as a reserved, mildly stuttering don, who likes photographing little girls. He is first seen making his way across a walled garden in which girls are playing croquet (though not, as in 'Wonderland', with flamingoes for mallets). As he approaches the Deanery, where Alice lives with her family, he hears her mimic his stutter as her mother, Mrs Liddell (Jane Asher) comes in. This Alice is an engaging little show-off, berating her sister Edith (Emma King) for saying 'Don't' ('Don't say don't, it's vulgar') and reciting bits of Tennyson's 'The Charge of the Light Brigade'. Mrs Liddell looks puzzled, possibly anxious, at the talk of Dodgson, when Alice says, 'He loves me of course', following this with, 'He loves us all – each and every one of us.'

   The relationship of this Alice to Dodgson is central to the film's agenda. As it explores the nature of the feeling on each side, it finds him tender and loving, offering his stories to her as a gift of love. Close-ups do suggest a suppressed sexual element, but the film is very far from wanting to suggest anything as ugly as paedophilia, at least not in practice. Alice is sharp, bright, teasing and fun-loving, and for the most part as little unnerved by the experiences she encounters as the Alice in 'Wonderland' is by the creatures she meets down the rabbit hole. In the film's beautiful evocation of an idyllic Oxford summer, director Gavin Millar focuses attention on this relationship but does so with sensitivity and restraint.

It is largely a matter of an exchange of tightly controlled close-ups. At the end of one such exchange, when Alice's family and Dodgson are on the river, she splashes him with water, breaking what must seem to her the tension of the moment. Mrs Liddell watches this with unease. Alice then apologises and goes to kiss Dodgson. I don't want to suggest that *Dreamchild* is offering a Victorian version of *Lolita*, and there is apparently no evidence of any improper behaviour on Dodgson's part, but the tensions are there: on the river and its banks on a later occasion when the boy Hargreaves (Rupert Wainwright) is present, with Alice almost leaning against him, and observed by the watchful Dodgson; and in Dodgson's darkroom where he is making photographic portraits of the kimono-clad Alice. In this latter episode, near the film's end, he asks her if she's thought about whom she'd like to marry, and warns her, 'Don't lose your head to the first spotted youth' who comes along. There is something undeniably creepy in utterances like this or, 'I hope you'll always remember our little moments together.'

Casting Ian Holm as Dodgson no doubt recalled his earlier performance of another author of ambiguous sexuality in relation to children: that is, J. M. Barrie in the 1978 miniseries, *The Lost Boys*. However, as one reviewer wrote: '*Dreamchild* manifestly does not revolve around the question of "did he/didn't he"… and while the film acknowledges both Dodgson's feelings *and* Alice's awareness of them, Potter is clearly more interested in the ways in which these feelings expressed themselves than in the feelings themselves.'[2] It is difficult to write about this aspect of the presentation of 'Alice 2' without over-stressing its place in the context of the film as a whole. It is there and it needs discussion but there is a great deal more to the film than this, important as it is.

Alice 3

At the heart of this film is Alice as an old woman (Coral Browne), who is coming to terms with the facts of her life as she makes her way to America in 1932 to receive an honorary doctorate from Columbia University to mark the centenary of Dodgson's birth. The first glimpse of her on the dark seashore before she is replaced by the child she once was is of an

29   Coral Browne (Mrs Alice Hargreaves).

apprehensive old woman wondering what to make of the strange fantasy creatures. The film then cuts to a long shot of the HMS Berengaria at sea and Mrs Alice Hargreaves, imperious and self-centred, stands on the deck with her timid young paid companion, Lucy (Nicola Cowper). This Alice is now a relic of Victorian England, preparing herself for 'whatever novelties lie ahead of us in the United States. At least they speak a form of English there', distinguishing between those Americans who travel to and from Europe on ocean liners and the rest – 'the great unwashed'. As she elects to go down to their cabin, she notes Lucy's lingering look at a kissing couple and says with some insight, 'It's not cheap music that disturbs you, it's your youth'. Lucy's responses to music, America and youth will have their part to play in the film's rich texture.

The 'facts of her [Mrs Hargreaves's] life' include marriage to a husband now dead and two sons, 'killed by the Hun', the notion of being identified with a child in a work of fiction *and* with the girl who gave rise to this 'Alice in Wonderland', and, as will become apparent, most importantly her affinity with the Rev. Charles Dodgson. Hers has not been the kind of life in which introspection has been encouraged but as she draws near its end she realises that there is some unfinished business. The experience of America unsettles her composure, the composure that till now has allowed her to make her wishes known and expect them to be obeyed. Asked on arrival in the US by the pushy reporter Jack (Peter Gallagher), 'to be the little girl you once were', she replies in words that link the three Alices: 'You mean the little girl Mr Dodgson made me out to be seventy years ago?... It would be difficult enough at my age for me to be what I once was but utterly impossible for me to be what I never was.'

Oxford and the happy summer days

As she finds herself grappling with the strangeness of America, she is increasingly unnerved by recollections of Oxford and Dodgson, and by the demands made upon her (the 'fuss' in her word) in this foreign location. The episodes in which the child Alice and her family are seen at play or on the river, backlit as they seem, are bathed in a soft glow and either perfect stillness or the gentlest breeze . These are not in any sense 'flashbacks' but are memories brought to the surface of Mrs Hargreaves' mind by this or that experience of the New World – and the term could hardly be more appropriate to her. So, the depiction of 'the happy summer days' (the last words of *Alice in Wonderland*) is not intended to be a realist evocation of mid-nineteenth-century Oxford, but a series of images recollected in something less than tranquillity.

Virtually every Oxford 'insert' has a trace of something disturbing for the old Alice. Only one of these involves knowledge that would have been denied to the child Alice. This is the first one, as she sits before the mirror in her cabin. It's easy to see the mirror's being used for reflection in other than the most literal way. She may have expected Mr Dodgson to visit, but she can't have *known* he was outside the window listening as she unkindly mimicked his stutter. On the other hand, in memory she might easily have recalled this and felt a pang of shame at her childhood cruelty. The look on his face as he listens hints at possible hurt and the look on Mrs Liddell's at some other sort of disquiet. In the scenes either on or by the river, the tensions on these beautiful summer days are clear, and there is something teasing on Alice's side, and some undefined withdrawn quality on his, especially as he observes the dreamchild moving into adolescence, with a not-so-spotty youth in attendance. So, 'the happy summer days' belong in their simplest form only to the Alice of the book, not quite to the real girl and, in memory, certainly not to the near-octogenarian Alice Hargreaves.

Alice in another wonderland

Between the flanking segments with various Alices at the glistening night-time seashore, the overarching story is that of Mrs Hargreaves's journey to New York. The narrative curve takes her from querulous, easily discomposed old woman to one who has, in the most affecting way, reconciled past and present, understanding the former and at peace with the latter. As she grapples with the unaccustomed brashness of New York, typified by the posse of pushful reporters, one of whom carries a large white rabbit, she finds herself grappling also with her own past and her own imaginative life. Used to giving orders, she is not used to introspection, and its onset finds her at a loss and motivates the film's fluid movement between past and present, reality and fantasy.

Although in the earlier episodes of her present-day self on its way to and in New York, she affects – or perhaps it comes naturally – a *grande dame* persona, there are even so fleeting suggestions that there may be more to her than this commanding surface. The quoted remark about Lucy's being disturbed by youth catches us off-guard with its perception. In her hotel room, when Jack arrives with flowers and the hope of the scoop interview that will get him his job back, she at first tries to dismiss him, then laughs more kindly at his flattery, saying, 'What a fraudulent young man you are!' He is, too, but not in the way she means. This more benign side to her nature is most touchingly in evidence near the film's end when she and Lucy are seated at a 'diner', another 'wonderland' aspect of her New York adventure. Jack rushes in with news of lucrative endorsement fees, then Mrs Hargreaves berates Lucy for not eating the meal her employer has paid for. Lucy explodes with, 'Shut up you nasty old cow!' and runs out into the rain. Jack follows and persuades her to go back. As she starts to apologise, Mrs Hargreaves beats her to it, and orders 'three Knickerbocker Glories': this Alice has come to some sort of terms with the new wonderland and, more crucially, with herself. What has happened is that her journey, to America and to self-understanding, has been partly influenced by those she comes in contact with, including these two young people.

But this is to jump ahead somewhat. The autocratic manner of this 'perfect Victorian', as Jack describes her, is partly the natural development of that confident, high-spirited child of the Oxford scenes, partly a way of inuring herself against a long-suppressed sense of something troubling. The New York of crowded, neon-lit streets, of radio recording-studios and so on may at first be daunting to her, but as in the diner sequence, there is also something liberating for her in this experience. In this wonderland she at first responds to the new sensations confronting her with either disdain or discomposure, but in the film's penultimate sequence in the hall at Columbia University it is clear that she has closed the gap between the child she was and the woman she is. By this time, she has come to accept the gift of love that Dodgson had offered, and is now prepared to face what she has so long been afraid to face in that gift – and to appreciate its value. In an image of her mother's face superimposed over a batch of letters, she has recalled how, 'My mother tore up his letters to me... Why should she want to do that unless there was something wrong, something I can't bear to think of?'

The wonderful sequence at Columbia opens on a close-up of Mrs Hargreaves's feet as she leads the academic procession in to the hall while the band plays 'Rule Britannia' in her honour. The chairwoman then introduces 'Alice herself' to the crowded hall while she sits there aware that she's not 'Alice herself' because (a) she's real and Carroll's Alice wasn't and (b) she's old and that other Alice wasn't. While awaiting her turn to speak, Mrs Hargreaves recalls the picnic tea by the river, with Dodgson singing 'Will you, won't you', and stuttering as he does. The child Alice laughs cruelly at this, as Dodgson watches, anguished. In the present time of 1932, the Columbia choir is singing this, and in the next moment of memory, as sister Edith reads the last paragraph of *Alice in Wonderland*, the young Alice goes to kiss Dodgson. Critic Andrew Sarris described this as 'the moment that Mrs Hargreaves finally realizes the great love and passion she was privileged to receive on behalf of the English-speaking world.'[3] This memory – 'true' or not – represents her acceptance of his role in her life. When she addresses the audience, she reads this last paragraph and finishes her speech with, 'At the time I was too young to see the gift whole and to see what it was, and the love that gave it birth, but I see it now at long last... Thank you Mr Dodgson, thank you.'

The standing ovation and cheers that follow give way to the symmetrical closing scene with a tracking shot like that which opens the film. The difference now is that Alice and Mr Dodgson are laughing on the beach, flanked again by the creatures of his imagination which in turn had fired hers. The anxious woman of the opening seashore scene is now replaced by the child who, in the older woman's understanding, is in serene companionship with the man who made her name famous.

Alice in Wonderland and the screen

Dreamchild is in no way an adaptation of Carroll's *Alice*; rather, it is really something much more daring and interesting. There have been over two dozen more or less predictable film or television versions of it, between a silent version in 1915 and Tim Burton's 2010 film starring Mia Wasikowska, who went on to play another spirited literary heroine, Jane Eyre, the following year. There had been British and American (Disney) animated jobs in 1949 and 1951, both with distinguished 'voice casts'. Joyce Grenfell, for instance, voices the Duchess and Pamela Brown the Queen of Hearts in the British combination of live-action and puppet-style animation, described by an online reviewer as maybe 'the most faithful adaptation of the story to date'.[4] It was of course eclipsed by the more popularly conceived US film.

The only one of all these adaptations that is really relevant to *Dreamchild* is the 1933 Paramount version with a wildly profligate all-star cast that includes Gary Cooper, Cary Grant, W. C. Fields and other big names of the period. When Mrs Hargreaves is sitting crossly in the diner, the big news that Jack runs in with is that Paramount will pay her one thousand dollars if she will endorse the film which is to be released shortly. This is worth noting in relation to *Dreamchild* because one of the strands that contributes to its richness of texture is the way it plays with the notion of narrative in so many forms, and across several media.

On one level, it is almost a film *about* narrative. Between the film's symmetrical opening and closing shots, it tells the stories of Mrs Hargreaves's visit to America, and the remembered 'interior' story of her childhood, of Oxford and Dodgson. These are the 'stories' that shape the film as a whole, but as well there are Dodgson's telling tales of Wonderland to the children, and the various creatures' telling their stories to Alice. In America, it's not only a matter of Paramount's re-telling the story of *Alice in Wonderland* as a movie, but there is also the radio play Mrs Hargreaves watches, as the performers tell an absurd story of a little girl lost on the prairie (an echo of Alice lost in Wonderland or even of Mrs Hargreaves in America?). This radio broadcast is very funny, with a soignée actress bleating as the little girl and a guy bouncing wooden balls on his bald head to create the sound of horse's hooves. It is all quite fantastic, but perhaps no more so than Carroll's imagining of Wonderland.

There is an emphasis on narratives throughout, of stories being told and enacted, listened to and watched, and all these strands are held together by Mrs Hargreaves's coming to terms with America, her childhood and Dodgson – even with the idea of the movie version and the tempting money involved. It is almost as if the film is suggesting that all life is a matter of narratives, of finding parallels and establishing causes and effects and learning to live with these – and, most important, of finding one's own place and one's own sense of self among what are often bewildering events and other people's motives.

Dennis Potter and others

Dreamchild was Potter's first feature as screenwriter, but he was already highly regarded for such television as *Pennies from Heaven* (1978) and *Cream in My Coffee* (1980), and would follow *Dreamchild* with the brilliant miniseries *The Singing Detective* in 1986. He was clearly fascinated with the way in which present and past, reality and fantasy, external and internal worlds can co-exist – as well as with 1930s American popular songs. All these predilections are called into play in *Dreamchild*, in which Mrs Hargreaves has to re-learn a child's capacity for moving easily between reality and make-believe and to readjust to her present in the light of a new understanding of her past. In Potter's screenplay, so deftly brought to life by director Gavin Millar, the film moves constantly between these oppositions of past and present, youth and age, Oxford and New York, real life and the life of the imagination. Millar had directed Potter's television movie, *Cream in My Coffee*, which was concerned with an elderly couple returning to the scene of a crucial moment in their past in search of present enlightenment. It is perhaps not surprising to find director and screenwriter so sympathetically at one in *Dreamchild*.

There are other major creative talents at work in the making of this luminous film. Multi-award-winning composer Stanley Myers, whose choice of known songs was plaintively integrated into the soundtrack for *A Portrait of the Artist as a Young Man*, achieves a similar harmony here. Crooners sing popular romantic numbers such as 'I Only Have Eyes For You', the Columbia orchestra strikes up with 'Rule Britannia', children are heard singing 'The Ash Grove' in the first Oxford sequence, and the whole is held together by a heartfelt soundtrack that stirs feeling but keeps it in its place. And the great cinematographer Billy Williams bathes the Oxford scenes in a glow of memory that contrasts with the glitter of New York. The Wonderland personnel are designed by Jim Henson's Creature Shop and voiced by the likes of Alan Bennett (Mock Turtle) and Julie Walters (Dormouse). Lighting, production design, location-shooting and music all collude to create the worlds encountered by the three Alices.

The sub-plot of the romance between the put-upon companion Lucy and the brashly opportunistic reporter Jack is attractively played by Nicola Cowper and Peter Gallagher. The observant and subservient Lucy finally has her moment of rebellion and in doing so elicits new understanding from Mrs Hargreaves. Jack moves from flattery and self-promotion to real concern for someone else when he runs out of the diner in the rain to rescue Lucy. Their little pasts ('little' compared with Mrs Hargreaves's) now give way to an embrace in the present which is more touching and less conventional than I've made it sound. Jane Asher gives Mrs Liddell an apt care for proprieties and a scrutinising caution in relation to Dodgson. As for Dodgson himself, Ian Holm makes him a properly enigmatic but likable figure, one whose feelings are difficult to be sure about but are expressed in the gift of the tale he told to Alice and bequeathed to generations of children.

Above all, it is Coral Browne's magnificent performance as Alice grown old that gives the film its centre. She resists playing for easy sympathy but as her Alice moves towards self-discovery and final resolution of past pain, she wins respect for this difficult woman. The frequent close-ups articulate her shifting responses: at times the face reflects the practice of dominance; at others it is lined with anxiety or confusion; there are moments when a benign smile plays about those chiselled features; and at the end it is suffused with the peace of acceptance. At her most dowager-like, she is never quite unaware of the absurdity hovering at the edges of her proclamations, her fear in alien worlds is properly disturbing, and her final reconciliation extraordinarily moving. Urging his readers to see this film which he'd previously overlooked, Sarris concluded his review by saying that 'the very thought of the film's conclusion comes perilously close to making me shed tears of cultural joy'.[5] The 'facts' of this tale of three Alices touch on the truth at various points, but it is a more important truth, an emotional truth, that makes the film an unforgettable experience.

Notes

1 Mavis Batey, *Alice's Adventures in Oxford* (London: Pitkin Pictorials, 1980), p. 4.

2 Julian Petley, '*Dreamchild*', *Monthly Film Bulletin*, January 1986, 8.

3 Andrew Sarris, 'The Film That Got Away', *Village Voice*, 6 May 1986.

4 Dave Sinclair, *Alice in Wonderland* (1949), http://scifilm.org/musing1865. html

5 Sarris, *Village Voice*.

16 Guests and others at
Four Weddings and a Funeral
(1994)

Plenty of comedy, but what about romance?

There's always been plenty of comedy in British cinema. In the 1930s for instance, George Formby and Gracie Fields were hugely popular; in the next two decades, 'Ealing comedy' became a brand name that still resonates with filmgoers of a certain age; and the 'Carry On' films, in one of the longest-running series ever, certainly tickled the national funny-bone. However, none of those three highly successful comedy runs could have been described as belonging to the 'romantic comedy' category. Formby and Fields may have ended up with partners (improbable as this was in his case at least), but their activities leading to this could hardly be thought of as romantic. Ealing comedy, though it remains one of the highlights of British cinema, was apt to be whimsical or satirical rather than romantic. As for the 'Carry On' films, on a good day you might laugh yourself into illness watching their antics, but you wouldn't expect the warm glow of a romantic pair fetching up together in the finale.

Whatever else is going on in romantic comedy, the one indispensable element is the movement towards a happy couple by its end. There will have been obstacles in the path of this outcome; the pair may have met in unlikely or difficult circumstances; they often have other attachments who will have to be got rid of, but in ways that won't reflect too badly on the star pair; and they must of course be attractive physically and, for preference, in other ways too. This was essentially an American genre, the films always moving towards the expected outcome but often touching on important realities along the way, as well as providing us with some dazzling entertainment. Think of titles like *The Awful Truth* (1937) and *The Philadelphia Story* (1940), to name but two masterworks from what now seems a golden age of the genre with stars like Cary Grant and Katharine Hepburn to dazzle us.

Somehow, British cinema never really made its mark in this genre. I'm aware of using some large generalisations here, but I think they do hold up. There are several quite charming pieces in the later 1930s, such as two in 1939 from director Robert Stevenson, starring his then wife Anna Lee, *Return to Yesterday* and *Young Man's Fancy*. In the latter Lee plays a 'human cannonball' at a circus who is fired into the lap of a young nobleman. There's 'meeting cute' for you, but these have never passed into film history as their Hollywood counterparts have. Have the English been too reserved, even inhibited, to take romance seriously as the best romantic comedy requires? If so, maybe the success of two 1990s hits, *Four Weddings and a Funeral* (1994) and *Notting Hill* (1999), both in part premised on the idea of a bumbling Englishman needing a beautiful American to get him moving in the right direction, had just the right idea – and just the right leading man.

Things begin to change...

I'm not looking for explanations here, but it can be noted that there was something of a resurgence of romantic comedy in Britain around the turn of the century. Apart from the two hit films named, there were also *Jack and Sarah* (1995), *Shooting Fish* (1997), *Shakespeare in Love* (1998, made in England, American money), *Sliding Doors* (1998), *The Very Thought of You* (1999), *Bridget Jones's Diary* (2001) and its sequel, *Bridget Jones: The Edge of Reason* (2004), *Love Actually* (2004), and *Wimbledon* (2004). There are others, but that's enough to give a sense of how things were moving. These are films of varying degrees of accomplishment and of commercial success, but their mere existence marked a shift in the output of British production, as often as not under the production banner of 'Working Title', one of the most successful companies of the period, and of course many of them are UK/US co-productions. This is reflected in their casting, especially in the importing of an American leading lady to lend lustre to the goings-on – and of course to increase their chances with the US box-office.

Four Weddings and a Funeral was in fact released in March 1994 in the US, two months before its UK release. An outspoken British

30   Kristin Scott Thomas (Fiona) and Hugh Grant (Charles) in a
promotional shot.

director, who shall remain nameless here, told me that, in his view, this indicated British over-caution (he used a more colourful term), as if exhibitors needed success in the US before venturing into the home territory. This may or may not be the exact case, but what is important is that the film succeeds utterly in a mode most often thought of as Hollywood territory. The film was a hit from the outset. It went on to win Oscar nominations and to scoop the pool at the 1995 BAFTA awards, as well as attracting numerous other awards and nominations. The names of director Mike Newell, screenwriter Richard Curtis and star Hugh Grant are the most commonly recurring in the awards lists, but there are plenty of others too. Somehow, Britain had got it right. In getting it 'right', it recalls that other impeccable British romantic comedy, *Genevieve* (1953): both films manage to be very funny and, at certain moments, touch a vein of real feeling.

A very busy film

The film's title suggests that there is a lot going on in *Four Weddings and a Funeral*. How are all these public events held together? There needs to be some underlying structural motif to ensure that the film is something more than just a succession of events. Typical of romantic comedy, this is likely to be found in the way in which two attractive people make their way towards coupledom. However, its strength is in the gradual move towards more serious adulthood by Hugh Grant's bumbling Charles. This is lightly but surely achieved; the film is not at all schematic about it. Each of the occasions mentioned in the title provides a little more evidence of his need to tidy up his life – as well as marking a stage in his dealings with the fetching American Carrie. We never doubt they'll be together at the end of the film; its skill lies in keeping us interested in the moves that show them apparently converging, then diverging, and ultimately converging for good.

Wedding 1
Getting to – and getting through – this takes nearly a quarter of the film's running time, in which a good deal about Charles is established, as well as a good deal about director Mike Newell's skill in the film's genre.

Getting there
While George Gershwin's 'They Can't Take That Away From Me' is heard on the soundtrack, Michael Coulter's camera first picks out the sleeping Charles who reaches out a hand to quell the alarm clock, without heeding its function. In a briskly edited sequence, various other wakenings are sketched, including those of elegant Fiona (Kristin Scott Thomas), and of a male couple, Gareth (Simon Callow) and Matthew (John Hannah), who are getting ready to tuck into a major fry-up. Charles is still asleep, and stays so as editor Jon Gregory cuts between this and Gareth and Matthew as they head off along the Thames Embankment and out on to a motorway. What follows is an alternation between one pair moving off as if they have a sense of purpose and another pair – Charles and flatmate Scarlett (Charlotte Coleman) – suddenly leaping about, desperately shouting 'Fuck!' over and over, then flinging on clothes before heading off to the countryside in Charles's somewhat battered car.

Two things above all matter from this introductory sequence. First, the sense of closeness between Gareth and Matthew: this will reach its end-point when Matthew recites a poem at Gareth's funeral. Second, and most crucial, we've been given a rapid insight into Charles's disorderly life. He is the best man at the first wedding, and as he

races out to his car, pulling his clothes on as he goes, he arrives at the
church just barely ahead of the bride (Sara Crowe), causing the groom,
Angus (Timothy Walker), some anxious moments. Not only is he late
in taking his place at the altar rail with Angus, it now turns out that
he – naturally – has forgotten the ring. However, disorganised as he
may be, he does manage to find a replacement for the ring and to have
it surreptitiously handed to him in the nick of time for passing it on to
Angus. It is actually a huge plastic, heart-shaped job in red and yellow,
generously lent by zany Scarlett, who is heard loudly letting go with
'Jerusalem' – out of tune.

Reception

While Charles is being established as an amiable bungler with plenty
of room for maturity to make itself felt, he catches a glimpse of the
beautiful Carrie (Andie MacDowell) among the guests in the church.
Afterwards, outside, he greets her with a comment about her hat. The
couple business has begun, but at this stage there is a lot of other comic
business competing for attention. Small children try to hide under the
bride's dress. Charles makes a terrible gaffe to an old chum John (Simon
Kunz), about John's old girlfriend's promiscuous habits and how right
John was to be shot of her. 'She's now my wife,' John replies succinctly.
Charles goes off to bang his head on a pole, as if that might help. There's
a very good sense of hordes of young people squealing and giggling, as
they are summoned into the marquee for dinner.

During the reception, Richard Curtis's comic invention stays at a
very lively pace and level. Scarlett kisses the guy seated next to her, then
introduces herself, adding: 'Don't let me drink too much or I'll get really
flirty.' Charles finds himself next to a mad old man (Kenneth Griffith)
whose confusion about Charles's identity leads him to demand: 'Are
you telling me I don't know my own brother?' As best man, Charles of
course makes a speech to the bride and groom that provokes a genera-
tional difference in the reception of its sexual blue jokes, the young ones
shouting with delight, their elders looking dubious. For one serious
moment, though, Charles has the insight to say: 'I am in bewildered awe
of anyone who can make this kind of commitment. I know I couldn't.' It
says something for Grant's playing that he can make such a line sound as
if Charles means it, and it is important as a small step in the necessary
development of a Charles in whose fortunes, romantic or otherwise, the
audience must take some interest.

Afterwards

In the interests of continuity, two more characters are introduced. They are short, balding Bernard (David Haig) and chatty Lydia (Sophie Thompson), who has hoped a sex encounter might happen at the wedding, but not with Bernard. 'I'm not that desperate,' she claims. Well, they will be the principals at Wedding 2. Carrie, who is not at all desperate but has the same idea in mind, makes a move towards Charles, asking, 'Where are you staying tonight?' As Lydia and Bernard are glimpsed frantically snogging, it seems as if the main by-product of a wedding is the making of further assignations. In spite of Charles's having other plans for staying the night, he leaves his friends and goes off to the pub where Carrie is staying.

But this is not to be plain sailing. Certainly Carrie is there in the lounge of 'The Boatman' when he arrives, but so is arch bore, George (Rupert Vanisttart), who, at least temporarily, thwarts Charles's plan for getting together upstairs with Carrie. In one of the film's many comic vignettes, Vansittart makes a memorable figure of George, very relaxed with, not a glass, but a *bottle*, of whisky. He is ready for a long chat with Charles, who shows just enough manners and patience to listen, as George talks first about his schooldays and someone's brother: 'head of my house – buggered me senseless but taught me a lot about life,' he says expansively. When Charles mentions his university days, George counters with (almost my favourite moment in the film), 'I couldn't see any point in going to university. If you work in the money market, what use are the novels of Wordsworth going to be?' This is a very brief scene, but Vansittart's utter command of the boorish and boring George makes it memorable.

Romantic comedy has come a long way since its golden era of the 30s and 40s. Not only is it much franker about sexual matters (though that can have its disadvantages) but also in how the female star might make the running in this respect. The enterprising Carrie has gone upstairs and sends a message down via the barman: 'Your wife is waiting for you'. This allows Charles to excuse himself to George and to find and hover outside Carrie's room where she invites him to 'come in and skulk for a while', and takes the lead in kissing. After a montage of limbs bathed in soft light, the film cuts to Charles waking to find Carrie dressed and ready to leave. She teases him about expecting an announcement of their engagement, and he replies with a film-savvy reference to Glenn Close, *Fatal Attraction*, and a fear for his pet rabbit. She may be teasing but she can't help one more serious comment as she leaves: 'I think we've both missed a great opportunity though.' Their 'passion', if that is the word, is sexually consummated before we've really got to know them, and, considering they will be the film's key 'couple', that is perhaps a point worth noting.

I've spent so long on this first wedding because it does much towards getting us interested in Charles, and in the couple that he and Carrie seem destined to be, and also in the sort of control that Newell's astute direction of Curtis's witty screenplay exhibits. It gets off to as satisfactory a start as any romantic comedy in recent decades, the central pair in place and surrounded by a host of engaging comic foils.

Wedding 2: three months later

This gets off to a rushed start that recalls the previous occasion. Charles and Scarlett are running late as before, racing around saying 'Fuck' again, and this time finding Charles's car has been clamped. Now it is Scarlett whose lateness is the issue, as she is bridesmaid to Lydia. In this role, arriving just in time, she absent-mindedly keeps her sunglasses on during the ceremony and, as she walks up the aisle, we – and the congregation – notice that her dress is not done up down the back, revealing that she is wearing blue knickers. The minister this time is Gerald (Rowan Atkinson), briefly glimpsed at the earlier wedding, and in his nervousness he invokes 'the Holy Goat' and pronounces Lydia the 'awful wedded wife' of Bernard.

Gareth opines at the reception that 'marriage is a way out of a deadlock' between two people, 'a way of getting out of an awkward pause in conversation'. His partner Matthew raises the possibility of 'true love', just before Carrie enters the frame again. This time she is accompanied by her fiancé, the considerably older Hamish (Corin Redgrave). The neat timing of the screenplay has just seen Charles pondering the issue of true love, when Carrie's entrance gives him serious pause of a kind essential to a firmly romantic comedy. 'Why am I always at weddings but never getting married?,' he asks Matthew reflectively. This momentary seriousness is followed by the usual giggling of the guests and Tom's (James Fleet) terrible best-man speech when he refers to Bernard's earlier girlfriends as 'complete dogs', leading one to wonder why best men always feel bound to be embarrassing.

The tone turns into something a little more muted here. Charles's earlier girlfriend, Henrietta (Anna Chancellor), unkindly nicknamed

'Duckface' by the soignée Fiona, has only to see Charles to burst into tears. Elsewhere, a girl tries to talk in sign language to Charles's deaf-mute brother David (David Bower), and subtitles translate her efforts as 'making tols of mistake' and, about dancing, 'that would be mice', recalling one's efforts at texting. But Charles has meanwhile shut himself away, as if the observing of what has passed has induced the beginnings of awareness – and of self-awareness – while 'Smoke Gets in Your Eyes' is heard on the soundtrack, the key line 'my true love was true' heard at an apt moment. Henrietta tells Charles, 'You're turning into a serial monogamist... you don't let anyone near you', warning him that he shouldn't start any relationship thinking 'I mustn't get married'. She goes off in tears again. The film may seem unkind in its attitude to Henrietta, but she will have her moment near the end. When Carrie, with bad timing, comes up to Charles to ask if he's having a good night, his reply is, 'Yes, right up there with my father's funeral'. This episode ends with Charles troubled by what he feels for her – and she for him.

Wedding 3: one month later

Charles is again found in bed, as before, when he gets an invitation to Carrie's wedding to Hamish. He goes off to buy her a present when, in one of those coincidences so unlike life but perfectly acceptable in romantic comedy, he runs into Carrie who takes him off to help her choose a wedding dress. They have a sexually charged chat over coffee, talking about her past affairs. Charles was number 32 for her, which leads him to say he's had 'nothing like so many. Don't know what I've been doing with my time'. When they part, he pursues her, saying, 'I think I love you', shambling his way through conversation, then running off.

   Wedding 3 takes place in Scotland, and Charles is routinely late, his arrival interrupting the service. The reception this time is replete with bagpipes and Highland dancing. Some of the regulars are there: Gareth and Matthew, Tom, Fiona and Scarlett – and Henrietta. Fiona unkindly asks Charles, 'How's Duckface?', but Duckface's time is coming. Bride and groom, Carrie and Hamish, are piped in as Charles watches them, and Fiona watches him. Carrie tells him, 'It's always been you... but there's nothing either of us can do ... such is life.' Odd moments like these give the film a surprising and satisfying depth that anchors the over-all lightness of tone.

During the post-wedding celebrations, Carrie, speaking for her late father, humorously imagines his referring to her marrying 'a stiff in a skirt', and Hamish makes a slightly pompous speech about how 'anyone involved in politics in the last twenty years [i.e. the Thatcher years] has got used to being upstaged by a woman'. Then a different sort of drama interposes itself: Gareth collapses while Hamish is speaking and is carried, dead, into an adjoining room.

The funeral

To introduce a funeral as a major sequence in a romantic comedy (and against an industrial townscape as a backdrop, at odds with the rest of the film) surely takes some daring, and to pull it off without either vulgarising the event or disrupting the over-all tone of the rest of the film is a significant achievement. Newell, Curtis and, among the actors, John Hannah especially, ensure that the occasion hits exactly the right notes emotionally.

As with the wedding episodes, this one also begins with a car waiting and then Matthew and others drive off. The recurring guests we've seen at the wedding are all in attendance: Charles and Carrie, Scarlett, Fiona, Tom, the first bride and groom, Laura and Angus, the second pair, Lydia and Bernard. What is being recognised are the bonds of friendship that keep this loosely disparate group together when it matters. Matthew delivers a touching and witty eulogy to Gareth, recalling his cooking habits (and we remember the fry-up he prepared for Matthew before the first wedding) and his 'enormous capacity for joy'. In Simon Callow's noisy, exuberant performance, this has been made palpable.

To clinch his recollections of Gareth and the mood of the sequence, Matthew quotes a poem by W. H. Auden, whom he describes as 'another splendid old bugger'. We may be used to romantic comedies popularising songs – think of 'Moon River' in *Breakfast at Tiffany's* – but it is considerably less common for such a film to inspire a revival of interest in a poem and a poet. John Hannah, as Matthew, reads with admirable feeling Auden's 'Funeral Blues', with its famous opening stanza:

> Stop all the clocks, cut off the telephone.
> Prevent the dog from barking with a juicy bone,
> Silence the pianos and with muffled drum
> Bring out the coffin, let the mourners come.

As he reads, the camera pans the faces registering their loss as Matthew arrives at the key lines:

> He was my North, my South, my East and West,
> My working week and my Sunday rest.

The publishing house of Faber & Faber, obviously believing it was on to a good thing, brought out later in 1994 a small collection of Auden's poems featuring a reflective Hugh Grant on the cover and the name of the film.[1] Among other references to the film's use of the poem, *The Daily Telegraph* ran a two-page piece about 'Why a hit film has inspired an Auden revival'.[2]

After the service, Carrie kisses Charles and the others comfort each other convincingly and touchingly. It's easy to start thinking that this has been after all a film about friendship. Proper feeling, though, has had its moment, and the episode finishes with Charles and the hapless Tom wondering if they'll ever find their 'right person'. Tom offers his philosophy and experience: 'I never expected the thunderbolt', and recalls how 'It [i.e., not expecting too much] worked for my parents, apart from the divorce'. The last line of the episode – 'Maybe waiting for this true love stuff gets you nowhere' – leads us smoothly into the final wedding.

Wedding 4

Ten months later it is Charles's turn. He is naturally running late again in arriving at the church where he is to marry Henrietta, aka Duckface, who has warned his friends, 'If any of you come near the house I'll set the dogs on you.' The guests pour in, including Bride and Groom 1 with their twins in arms; Scarlett leaps into the arms of 'gorgeous Chester', whom she's just met; the mad old man from the first wedding, asked by the usher, 'Bride or groom?', answers: 'It should be perfectly obvious I'm neither'. Then Carrie arrives, saying that Hamish 'wasn't the man for me after all'. This is a serious narrative troubler, and Hugh Grant is very good at dealing with the confusion of mind into which Charles is now thrown. And his conversation in the vestry with Matthew doesn't help the situation when Matthew tells him that marriage is, 'Really good – if you want the person with all your heart.'

Henrietta has arrived and the vicar jocularly asks Charles if he is 'ready to face the enemy'. The film's dilemma now is how to get

Charles out of marrying Henrietta without making him seem an irredeemable cad and without being too cruel to her. As the service starts, Charles is looking increasingly distant and when, following signs from brother David, he says, echoing Matthew, that 'you've got to marry the person you love with your whole heart'. This might have been saccharine if Henrietta hadn't then knocked him down with one well-aimed blow. The wedding is clearly off. Guests make the best of it: Scarlett says that Henrietta's 'lovely dress' will be useful for parties, and Tom says that 'at least people will remember it.' A little later, in the street and in the rain, Charles makes a characteristically bumbling overture to Carrie and there is a flash of lightning in recognition of something achieved.

As well as Henrietta's getting to deliver the knockdown blow to Charles in the church, the film also allows her, in a series of post-THE END shots, a glamorous wedding to a guards officer and they make their way through an avenue of raised and gleaming swords. It's important to the film's tone that some amends be made to the victim of Charles's earlier vacillation. There are other nice touches in these shots: Matthew has a new partner; Fiona is marrying Prince Charles (!); and the last one of all shows Charles and Carrie with a baby. In the end, everyone has more or less been looked after by the film's plot.

Credit where it's due

If *Four Weddings* seems to me the best British romantic comedy since *Genevieve* forty years earlier, the spread of credit is roughly the same. That is, in director Newell, screenwriter Curtis, star Grant (and delectable ensemble), the film has a lot going for it. Curtis was, for a decade or more, the unrivalled chronicler of middle-class comedy, but *Four Weddings* is arguably his finest hour. In *Love Actually*, he again writes a many-stranded narrative but in directing it himself he maybe took on more than was wise, whereas in the earlier film Mike Newell steers his way with utmost assurance through the five major plot events. Newell's grasp of the romantic comedy genre is obvious in the ways in which he maintains just enough underlying firmness of purpose without ever losing the lightness of touch so crucial to the genre. Curtis has provided him with a large cast of characters and Newell's direction of a choice bunch of British character players, as well as of his luminous stars, is exemplary. Everyone, even in small roles, gets a chance to sketch a character. There's a lot happening in and around the main events but Newell's control keeps it all in proportion.

There are songs from Elton John amongst the soundtrack; southern England looks ravishing in Coulter's cinematography; the laughs come where they should; and the film is not above touching our hearts at certain moments. *Four Weddings* may have initiated a run of successful romantic comedies, but arguably it remains the one that got everything right.

Notes

1 *Tell Me the Truth About Love: Ten Poems by W. H. Auden* (London: Faber & Faber, 1994).

2 Katherine Bucknell, 'Auden Regained', *The Daily Telegraph*, 11 June 11 1994, 2–3.

17   Families and other disasters:
Secrets & Lies (1996)

While absolutely *needing* to have a Mike Leigh film in this book, I had a problem in choosing which one. By *'needing'*, I mean something entirely personal, not intending any sort of objective claim about his status in the annals of British film. I'd earlier settled on *Secrets & Lies* (1996) because it deals with many characteristic Leigh preoccupations in masterly fashion. However, after seeing *Another Year* in 2010, I really want to sneak in a few asides about this equally eloquent, even heartbreaking film. One way and another, Leigh has become a phenomenon in British film. He started filming in 1971 with *Bleak Moments* (perhaps not the most inviting film title), then did only television, much of it notable, until the 1988 film, *High Hopes*. With this bracing and often abrasive study of family life and other relationships, he hit his stride and, in a far from stable film-industrial climate, has turned out ten often remarkable films since, as well as some more TV. When you consider that he is also responsible for the screenplay (the typical credit is 'Devised and directed by'), the achievement is the more extraordinary.

What is a Mike Leigh film like?

That question is not meant to suggest that his films are all alike, only that they do have recognisable recurring elements from one to the next. You're never going to expect him to fetch up in the multiplexes with a high-action thriller awash with special effects. And you're probably never going to emerge from a Leigh release saying, 'Laugh! I nearly died', though you may well have laughed quite often along the way.

There is actually a certain anarchic sense of humour that can lead to (in my view, misplaced) criticism of inconsistency of tone, and sometimes the comedy takes on an almost Swiftian ferocity. His films may be seen as belonging to British cinema's realist tradition, but he is not concerned about breaking from this. For instance, he won't shy away from giving a character a soliloquy which might seem more likely in the theatre (think of David Thewlis's tirade in *Naked* – there's actually someone present, so it's not quite a soliloquy, but he talks uninterrupted for a surprising length of time). Elsewhere Leigh doesn't mind turning a character into a caricature, as if aware that the latter can embody critique of a type, and in *Topsy-Turvy*, his beautiful valentine to Victorian theatre, he all but abandons realism for musical interludes as the plot requires.

Above all, his films are about relationships, especially as located in families but not always. He can be interested in the ways in which people work together, or how people simply establish friendships. Poppy (Sally Hawkins), the heroine of *Happy-Go-Lucky* (2008), for instance, has a colleague with whom she goes to salsa classes, and this has no effect on the narrative at large except that it shows us another aspect of how Poppy goes about organising her life. In *Another Year*, the stable, long-term marriage of Tom and Gerri (Jim Broadbent and Ruth Sheen) provides, without its being sentimentalised or idealised, a benchmark for considering how their friends are somehow not so successful in managing their personal lives. And the very poignant *Vera Drake* (2004) contrasts the loving accord between Vera (Imelda Staunton) and her husband Stan (Philip Davis) with the bleak lives Vera tries to help – and with the undoing of her own personal happiness. And even when he's exploring the most mundane set-ups, there's an ineradicable strain of the poetic: not in any self-conscious way but as a by-product of seeing things clearly and seeing them whole. For instance, there is a glorious long-shot of men playing golf on the horizon in *Another Year*, in which the beauty of composition and lighting creates a wonderful sense of a freedom at odds with the constraints of the men's lives. This is a shot to which I'd happily give the word 'poetry'. As for the last shot of *Secrets & Lies*, well, I'll save that till we've seen how it's been arrived at.

On a more businesslike or functional level, Leigh's films are the result of intense improvisation on the part of his actors. In 1996 he said:

> all my films evolve out of improvisation and the scripts come out of improvisation... But I'm a very precise director. If you look at my stuff it's very firmly and clearly directed... I'm not very excited by improvi-

sation *on camera*: the whole thing has evolved from improvisation; all
the joy and delight of that has gone on; and, for me, what it's all about
is distilling it all down to something that is coherent, ordered, dramatic
and cinematic.[1]

This was borne out by Brenda Blethyn: 'There's no script while we're
rehearsing', and one of the results of all the preparation is that 'what
follows is very specific, conventional filming. Much more specific than
ordinary filming actually, because we just know it so well'.[2] The effect of
the characters' having been worked out in the minutest detail over the
months before filming begins (five months in the case of *Secret & Lies*)
is an extraordinary sense of completeness about them, as individuals
and as people involved in relationships. The actors give a sense of *being*
rather than acting, of *inhabiting* a role rather than playing it. This effect
has no doubt been arrived at by other means in other filmmaking
set-ups, but it works for Leigh in a way that goes beyond any academic
concept of 'realism'.

Unleashing secrets and lies

Three households

The film opens with the camera prowling around a cemetery, with
gasometers in the background helping to place it socially, as the
steel-works backdrop did in the funeral episode in *Four Weddings*. As
the camera moves in on the mourners, it picks out several black faces
before settling on one in close-up. It then cuts to a wreath of white
flowers arranged to spell out the word 'MUM'. The next segment opens
on a bridal car outside a house, then moves inside where Maurice
(Timothy Spall) is photographing a bride while her father hovers in
the background. When the clients have gone, Maurice and his wife
Monica (Phyllis Logan) sit talking and drinking wine in their carefully
decorated home. They discuss the idea of inviting Maurice's sister
Cynthia and her daughter Roxanne for the latter's twenty-first birthday
celebration. There is a suggestion of Maurice's dutifully keeping up with
his sister – and of their no longer being of quite the same class. Monica's
question about what Roxanne is doing now: 'Is she back on the street?'
indicates that she is not enthusiastic about maintaining family ties. 'On
the street', as we will learn, refers not to the oldest profession but to the
fact that she works for the council, so there's a touch of the bitchy in
Monica's comment.

The second household the film enters is the shabby rented terrace where Cynthia (Brenda Blethyn) and Roxanne (Claire Rushbrook) engage in a bickering relationship. But, just as we were given a glimpse of Maurice's work before seeing him and Monica together, here there are brief shots of council worker Roxanne 'on the street' sweeping, and Cynthia dealing with flattened cardboard boxes as they come off the assembly line. In their home, at an address that will become significant, Cynthia talks about her younger brother Maurice with whom she's not in much contact and she blames him for this: 'He knows where I am if he wants me', and the terminally cantankerous Roxanne refers charmingly to Monica as a 'toffee-nosed cow'. Their conversation confirm the sense of class divergence between brother and sister. It then takes another turn when Cynthia instructs Roxanne, 'You want to get yourself a bloke... When I was your age I had the pick of the crowd'. She complains that she had got stuck at home looking after her mother and Maurice – and then Roxanne, who counters with 'I didn't ask to be born'.

The black girl seen at the funeral proves to be Hortense (Marianne Jean-Baptiste), an optometrist, and, in a sequence showing her at work, she is placed as a kindly professional in the brief scene of fitting a little girl with glasses. The film briskly cuts to her going through her late (adoptive) mother's papers upstairs in a house while her brothers (Brian Bovell and Trevor Laird) squabble down below. A reflective close-up of Hortense establishes her as thoughtfully inclined, benign. The house is well-kept, comfortable, unpretentious, and as always Leigh's concern with interior decor is a guide to the occupants in matters of class, taste and temperament.

These three households are worth spending this time on because they illustrate how beautifully constructed this film is. I don't mean that we are aware of an explicit schematism at work, but that we are being unobtrusively brought to the point of wanting to see how these three diverse households will be connected. Alison Chitty's production design quietly pinpoints the different social levels of each as well as the kinds of *living* that go on in each. As well, you don't have to be very knowledgeable about women's clothes to note the contrast between Cynthia's cheap flowered stretch-pants and, on the one hand, Monica's neat suburban outfit or, on the other, Hortense's stylishness. Along with the brief work inserts, a good deal has been set in place with unfussy precision about each of the three groups, and we are poised for further interaction among the three. There has been an edginess observed in each which contact between them may dispel – or exacerbate.

Finding things out

Hortense finds out

In her visit to social worker Jenny (Lesley Manville), Hortense reveals her wish to learn the identity of her biological mother. She has always known she was adopted, and makes clear that she is not trying to 'replace' her adoptive mother. 'My parents loved me and that was all that mattered.' When Jenny asks her, 'Why now?' – that is, why is she coming to this decision now? – Hortense replies simply, 'I just want to know.' Jenny offers conventional sympathy, epitomised by asking, 'Would you like a Rolo?' She explains that Hortense's birth mother may not want to see her, but gives her a folder of papers 'all about you' and leaves her to examine these. When Jenny returns, her earlier vague comment, 'Somewhere out there is your birth mother', has given way to the specificity of 'CYNTHIA ROSE PURLEY', the name on the Birth Certificate. If Hortense wants to follow this up, Jenny will 'get the ball rolling'. The key term on the certificate is 'Mother – white'. 'Could this be a mistake?,' Hortense wonders. This whole episode is a model of quiet naturalism, dialogue and body language, exactly defining Jenny's professional responsibility in putting her questions and Hortense's restrained feeling and honesty in her answers.

Cynthia finds out

After Hortense has located Cynthia's address and driven away without further contact, there are intervening sequences in which Hortense is seen at work or lunching with a friend, or Cynthia and Maurice meet to discuss having 'a bit of a get-together' for Roxanne's birthday. A casual remark of Cynthia's – 'I was carrying her when *I* was twenty-one' – is almost like a tiny signpost directing us to the next revelation. Just after Cynthia is having trouble with the daughter she didn't get rid of, the phone rings and it is Hortense talking of 'Baby Elizabeth Purley', the name she was registered with. This is the critical turning-point in the film. The sequence involves a series of alternations between Hortense, poised and controlled, and Cynthia, whose shock and anguish are made very real and moving in Brenda Blethyn's superb, award-winning performance. She weeps and slams down the phone. When Hortense tries to ring again, Cynthia begs her not to come to the house but takes Hortense's phone number, and the film cuts to Cynthia's calling her to arrange a later meeting.

This meeting is to take place outside Holborn Underground

31   Marianne Jean-Baptiste (Hortense) and Brenda Blethyn (Cynthia).

station, where Hortense walks straight past Cynthia who is standing by the entrance, each waiting, neither knowing whom she is looking for. Eventually Hortense produces the Birth Certificate to convince Cynthia and persuades her to go for a cup of tea. What most people no doubt remember from *Secrets & Lies*, and rightly so, is the astonishing nine-minute take in which Cynthia and Hortense sit at a table in a restaurant near the station. Not many films rely on such a long take. Some may remember Hitchcock's use of it in *Rope* (1948) in which he really wanted to tell the entire story in one long continuous take. This wasn't possible so he had to settle for a *series* of long takes. There is, though, in *Rope* an element of the gimmick, which is utterly missing from the café sequence in *Secret & Lies*. Here, it is as if any editing – say, to home in on the face of one of the women – would distract from the scene's purpose which is to show two lives coming into the most crucial contact with each other, and above all to register Cynthia's reactions.

Her first response is, 'I ain't never been with a black man in my life. I'd have remembered – wouldn't I?' Then, the camera having stayed absolutely still, we register the tiniest hint of recollection as it crosses Cynthia's face. 'Bloody hell,' is all she can say before dissolving into heartfelt tears. At the time of the birth, she had not been told the child was black. 'I didn't have no choice,' she tells Hortense, that is, about keeping or not keeping the baby. Hortense's parents had told her when she was seven that she was adopted. The interaction between the dignified Hortense and sloppy Cynthia is a triumph for the actors – and for Leigh's decision to settle for a single take after trying various other editing approaches. Brenda Blethyn recalled:

> Mike did shoot it in lots of other ways; he just chose to restrict the editing to one take. We did it all day long, until he decided, and it was exhausting ... but it was a wonderful scene. I remember one moment particularly, when I just said, 'Sorry darling' and reached over to touch Marianne and we both felt almost an electric shock from the touch.[3]

This tiny moment recalled is typical of the minimalist ways in which this great scene makes its impact. It is all done without any sense of melodrama, as the two women quietly talk their way into each other's lives. Hortense talks about her parents, her brothers (a computer salesman and a garage-owner); Cynthia asks her if she has a boyfriend, and giggles at the idea of herself having one: 'They [boys] got me into enough trouble in the past'. We've had reason to admire Hortense before this episode, but perhaps for the first time we can feel a real affection for Cynthia as she reaches into her past and emerges with some warmth into the present.

One small point worth noting was raised by Leigh himself. He is most often thought of as a realist director, and he does achieve some brilliant realist effects, but he is perfectly willing to work against this grain if he thinks it will make a different sort of meaning. He said that:

> the fact of the matter is that it is supposed to be a Saturday evening and it's near Holborn station and they go off in that direction, which, to be literal about it, must be somewhere in the direction of Covent Garden. Now, where on a summer evening on a Saturday would you find such a quiet, empty café? It's nonsense really, so there is a heightening poetic licence involved there [4]

This is only worth quoting to suggest that Leigh was less interested in surface realism in this sequence than in a more profound exploration of emotional realities.

Everybody finds out

The last of these three major revelations takes place at Maurice and Monica's home where the family has gathered for Roxanne's birthday

32   Timothy Spall (Maurice) and Brenda Blethyn (Cynthia).

party. Cynthia has asked if she could bring 'a friend from work', a small lie to avoid spilling a secret before she's ready to do so. Monica, who's shown Cynthia around her elaborately decorated house, can't believe that black Hortense can be Cynthia's 'friend', and there is the sense of a situation waiting to explode as everyone moves out into the backyard for the barbecue. Cynthia is working too hard at sweetness and light, while Maurice does his best with offering 'burgers or bangers', and there is a fine sense of reality, of conversation growing naturally out of a not too easy set of circumstances. After lunch, they move inside for birthday cake and Maurice's present for Roxanne, who's brought her boyfriend Paul (Lee Ross). The camera isolates Cynthia now as she's beginning to feel the strain of the day, and Hortense, also under a strain, needs a break in the bathroom. Everyone likes Hortense and says so while she's out of the room.

Cynthia now breaks the news about Hortense, about the secret she has only recently discovered, and the camera prowls the faces for reactions. The result of everyone's finding out is considerable disorder. Subtlety and sensitivity to atmosphere are not really Cynthia's strong points and we can feel for Maurice when he says, 'You don't half choose your moments, Cynthia'. Roxanne's response is a predictably aggressive,

'What the fuck's going on?', as she rushes out; her usual reaction to Cynthia's telling her something she doesn't want to hear. And to be fair, it is perhaps typical of Cynthia to wreck Roxanne's party, not out of malice but from emotional clumsiness. Her revelation leads to a surfacing of family resentments. Cynthia faces up to Monica with, 'You want to try bringing up a kid on your own', and challenging her with, 'Why don't you give him [Maurice] what he wants [kids]?' 'She can't have kids,' Maurice replies, and the air is now thick with exposed secrets and lies. There is a gradual sobering of the scene as Cynthia tries to comfort Monica; Maurice's assistant Jane (Elizabeth Berrington) tells him, 'I wish I had a dad like you'; Cynthia assures Hortense that her father was 'a nice man'; and Hortense goes to reassure Cynthia. While so much has been going on within and between characters in this skilfully orchestrated sequence, Leigh has maintained a restrained filming approach, as if not to let technique get in the way, and as if the explosive nature of the revelations and its aftermath would benefit from being seen in the context of the group at large without a lot of intervention of camera and editing.

Life goes on

Around the three big scenes of revelation there is a lot of other life going on. There is real attention to the everydayness of these lives for whom the emerging of secrets and/or lies is a major event but the film is interested too in what goes on when these people aren't dealing with crises. There's no sense of Leigh's wanting them – or the characters in his other films – to be seen as 'typical' working-class characters, as if people could be adequately defined in terms of where they stand in the social hierarchy. These are individuals who work certainly, and he is interested in what they do and even builds this into the fabric of the film's drama. Cynthia's job of making and stacking cardboard boxes is pretty much a mindless, repetitive affair and, given the suppressions of her life, there is perhaps something numbingly apt in this. Maurice, who has done well as a suburban photographer, is in the business of making people look their best, always exhorting them to look happy, to smile. He is a man who, in his private life, is always trying to damp down potentially fiery situations. Hortense's work as an optometrist is aimed at helping people to see more clearly, and she does so with professional kindness. As well as telling us something about the three personally, these glimpses of their work, and workplaces, also give pointers to class differences, as do the houses in which each lives.

It's not just this central trio whose lives, and how they fill them, are revealed, often in small but ·telling detail. For instance, Monica is first revealed making stencils to decorate her home. Has she been influenced by television programmes about home improvements? She is presented as very house-proud and the later implication is that, in her rather neurotic way, she is compensating for her childlessness. Her domestic habits contrast with Cynthia's more relaxed approach to housekeeping. Roxanne, 'on the street', doesn't seem to find much pleasure in her work and this is maybe not surprising, partly because sweeping streets and emptying bins is not innately rewarding, partly because her disgruntled temperament makes it unlikely that she will enjoy anything. Except perhaps her boyfriend Paul, who works as a scaffolder, and with whom she does throw herself into a snogging session. Even then she has to add, 'Just so's you know. I'm not staying the night every time I come round'.

Among Maurice's photographic clients is a blonde girl whose face has a disfigured left side to her otherwise good looks. The film is generous enough towards such characters as to give them just sufficient detail for them to make their presences felt. This young woman tells Maurice: 'I lost my job... I was a beauty consultant... My seatbelt was broken and I went through the windscreen.' This detail has no bearing on the *events* of the film, but, apart from establishing Maurice as sympathetic listener, it is typical of the way Leigh embeds the film in a wider sense of life. These other lives – along with welfare worker Jenny and Maurice's assistant Jane – fill out the texture of the film. The central trio exist in a context that includes their work, their families and the backlog of secrets and lies that, at various levels of consciousness, they live with. There is one other strange character who should be noted. A man seen hanging around Maurice's house proves to be another figure from the past, though of a different kind from Hortense. He is Stuart (Ron Cook), from whom Maurice has bought the photographic business. He is relentlessly downbeat. He's been living with his mother who has died, but he says, 'Didn't see much of her anyway. It's my dad I miss'. Here is another middle-aged person wondering about parents. He and Maurice quarrel when Stuart claims Maurice's success was due to his 'goodwill', while Maurice counters with 'Your clients were no use'. Stuart disappears as arbitrarily as he has appeared.

Leigh's team

Much of Leigh's work, including his late masterpiece *Another Year*, favours a plain style, or what *seems* to be a plain style. There is no sign of flashy cutting and, certainly not in *Secrets & Lies*, of much reliance on fades or dissolves as the narrative moves from one sequence to another. The characteristic cutting is about as unobtrusive as it could be, but in Jon Gregory's editing it keeps reinforcing the point about the inter-connectedness of these lives. Gregory had edited several films for Leigh prior to this and, after time in the US, would later edit *Another Year*. Alison Chitty had been Leigh's production designer on three previous occasions, and Dick Pope photographed all his films from 1990's *Life is Sweet* onwards. The point of mentioning these names is that they all contribute to the film's extraordinary sense of lives being lived, of people behaving rather than acting, in places and situations of palpable reality.

That last comment reminds one of the stable of actors on which Leigh has drawn over the last decade. Brenda Blethyn, a respected stage actress, had done little filming before *Secrets & Lies*, but Timothy Spall and, especially, Lesley Manville were more or less Leigh regulars. Spall, first noticed in television's *Auf Wiedersehn, Pet*, showed his range for Leigh in playing an opera singer in *Topsy-Turvy* (1999) and the taxi driver who makes a final, small but touching stand for self-respect in *All or Nothing* (2002). Manville, the snobbish yuppy in *High Hopes* (1988), reached heartbreaking heights as the motor-mouth Mary in *Another Year*. The fact that the cast of *Secrets & Lies* is peppered, in small roles, with the names of actors who had worked for Leigh before and would do so again – Ron Cook, Ruth Sheen and Philip Davis are just three of the best known – may indicate that he is a director who allows his actors to find their way into their roles, then provides them with the setting and the other collaborators to show them at their best.

Perhaps as a result of the overtly collaborative nature of his production habits, Leigh's best films give an extraordinary effect of catching actual moments as they are being lived. In a brief scene in which Cynthia and Hortense are sitting in a restaurant together, they are talking about how Hortense's adoptive mother was a midwife and Cynthia saying she'd 'like to have been one of those... I love babies – Oh, sorry darling.' A stage in their relationship has been reached when they can relax with each other, and the moment seems utterly natural, utterly spontaneous.

In the garden

After the disrupted birthday party in which everyone is at odds with the others before the storm passes, there is a brief scene of Maurice and Monica in bed, in which the often edgy Monica tells him, 'You don't know how much I love you'. In lesser hands this might seem soppy, but here there is a feeling of issues having been aired and basic affections can now be affirmed. The film's last sequence is set in the modest back garden of Cynthia's rented terrace house. There is an exchange between Hortense and Roxanne in which Hortense asks, 'Do you feel that we're sisters?', and the normally rough-tongued Roxanne replies benignly, 'Yes – it's a bit weird but I don't mind', and Hortense in turn sums up the meaning of the whole film with, 'Better to tell the truth. That way no one gets hurt'. Cynthia is lying on a reclining seat, and her comment, 'This is the life, ain't it', and a high overhead shot finishes the film on a poetic note. The situation may be prosaic but the decision not to deal in a lot of embraces and soulful talk but to leave the film on this note of at least temporary contentment looks like a poetic insight into the way things are – for the moment anyway.

Postscript

One of the many triumphs of *Another Year* is in its beautifully detailed evocation of Tom and Gerri's middle-class, professional, married contentment, their sense of comfortableness in each other's company, whether at home or at the allotment. They are a conventionally happy elderly couple at home with each other, able to understand each other through eye contact when there are others present, affectionately hugging each other, companionably reading in bed together. Structurally, they are the means of bringing to the fore the problems of assorted needy friends and colleagues. For instance, their son Joe is a worry in the background; Gerri's garrulous friend from work, secretary Mary, is welcomed in their home, however tiresome she may be, but sentimentality is warded off by allowing Gerri understandable impatience when the tiring Mary turns up unannounced on one occasion, and Mary's loneliness is set against the companionable Tom and Gerri. Then there's Ken, Tom's old friend, now overweight and more or less alcoholic; and finally Tom's taciturn brother, Ronnie, whom they take in when he is widowed. As in *Secret & Lies*, Leigh makes us privy to what makes relationships work – and what can make them difficult. And he ends both in such a way as to make us aware that this is only the beginning of a new phase in the lives of these people: for those in Cynthia's backyard, perhaps a less troubled period; for Mary, stilled into listening for once, perhaps a tiny access of self-knowledge. *Another Year* reinforces our sense of that profound, utterly unpatronising interest in and sympathy for what may seem unremarkable lives but which are far from seeming unremarkable to those actually living them.

Notes

1 'Mike Leigh' in Brian McFarlane, *An Autobiography of British Cinema* (London: Methuen, 1997), p. 361.

2 Interview with author, Melbourne, 2007.

3 Interview with author, Melbourne, 2007.

4 'Mike Leigh', McFarlane, *An Autobiography*, p. 363.

18   In search of
Wonderland (1998)

Wunderkind

Since the 1990s, director Michael Winterbottom has maintained a
prodigious output. After some superior television, including episodes
of *Cracker* in 1993, he made his feature debut with *Butterfly Kiss* (1995),
a road movie crossed with *amour fou*, and from then on has averaged
at least one feature per year, as well as the inspired TV series, *The Trip*.
He has not been merely more prolific than almost any director one can
think of, but has also tried his hand at so many different genres. Of
how many British, or any, directors could it be said that they have made
at least one each of road movie, Western, musical, romantic comedy,
romantic drama, documentary, science-fiction, sex film, war film, crime
drama and political thriller – as well as several of them being very
enterprising literary adaptations?

The answer is that he is almost certainly unique in this diversity,
and what is more remarkable is that he has maintained such a high level
of achievement across such a range and in the face of such venture-
someness. Can you imagine many filmmakers having the vision to
recast Thomas Hardy's *The Mayor of Casterbridge* as a Western, as
Winterbottom did in *The Claim* (2000) – or to have the sheer nerve to
make a film not just derived from but also *about* the filming of Laurence
Sterne's wildly idiosyncratic novel, *Tristram Shandy*, which emerged as
A Cock and Bull Story in 2005? Or road movies as dissimilar in tone as
Butterfly Kiss, In This World (2002) or the charming and funny *The Trip*
(2010), a compact version of the TV series in which two witty guys eat
their way round England? Choosing one film to write about here was

even more difficult in the case of Winterbottom than of most other directors. In opting for the humanist masterwork, *Wonderland*, I'm aware of all the other possibilities I'm denying myself.

One of the reasons for the amazing output over the last nearly two decades may be that Winterbottom has surrounded himself with a team of collaborators whose ways he knows. Also, when I talked to his producer Andrew Eaton, it was clear that they – i.e. their company, Revolution Films – was more interested in production than huge profits, so that they were able to keep filming regularly even though none of their films could be said to be major box-office hits. Eaton said in 2006:

> I think it's really good that we're the only directors of the company, and I'm a producer and he's a director and we don't want to swap places... I don't think either of us could have imagined doing films where the decisions about creative and financial matters didn't always go hand in hand.[1]

Eaton made it clear that they run a lean operation, with modest budgets, many regulars before and behind the camera, and they shoot fast. Revolution may have input from other sources on most of its films, but it is essentially the small tightly run outfit that has kept the supply going.

London and *Wonderland*

When a young couple have their first child at the end of the film, the husband wants to call it Alice, adding 'Alice in Wonderland', leaving us to ponder what he meant, since not too much in the film would have corresponded to the idea contained in this. And the film's title is at least partly ironic. The London we see in *Wonderland* is not the London of tourist guides. There are two brief shots in which the St Paul's dome is visible but essentially this is a London of undistinguished streets, often cluttered with rubbish, characterless cafés, crowded bars, tower blocks (and, once, a distant and dim Tower Bridge), and housing estates.

It is not a matter of looking for a deliberately scruffy underbelly but, rather, of providing a setting we can accept as merely ordinary and as a credible context for the film's ordinary lives. 'Ordinary lives' always sounds a bit patronising and isn't meant to be, here at least. It is intended to suggest that these are not lives in which anything very remarkable happens, though what happens to the people involved is certainly important to them. In the film's London, they are all too often seen to be jostling for places, and assignations in bars teeming with customers would seem to be off to a difficult start. As the hand-held camera follows characters out into the streets, there is most often an almost dizzying sense of activity, of people chatting with – or chatting up – other people, of vehicles jockeying for space and London's red buses weaving in and out of the traffic. This London seems a place of perpetual motion, and this is in line with the film's motif of people in constant quest, of life not going according to any plan, of trying vaguely to find some sort of satisfaction, in a densely crowded metropolis.

These people take their pleasures in such crowded places. For instance, one character is seen in a bingo hall where the camera picks out faces variously hopeful and disappointed; elsewhere, they are seen at a huge football arena where an estranged father takes his son, or later at a monstrous fairground where we fear for the safety of a child. Home, as we've seen, isn't always a refuge from all this, is in fact more often the springboard that propels the characters out into the milling throngs. Just once or twice, and notably almost at the end, there is a panoramic shot of the city which for a fleeting moment suggests a wonderland of possibilities.

Up close

The private lives of the main sets of characters don't generally give much grounds for such possibilities. It's not that *Wonderland* is a glum experience: its frequent alternation of scenes of kinetic activity and swarming masses with quiet interior moments ensures a constant attention to the lives depicted. We engage with their aspirations and/or disappointments and that means the effect is never merely downbeat. Perhaps it's as producer Eaton says: 'You get a sense that the characters, whatever their individual struggles, are after all surviving in the city.'[2] There are grounds for slivers of hope, but they have to be consciously on the lookout for these. The entire action takes place over four days, each boldly announced on a screen of different colour, and the focus is on one family. The parents are Bill and Eileen (Jack Shepherd and Kika Markham); the three daughters are Nadia (Gina McKee), Debbie (Shirley Henderson) and Molly (Molly Parker), and their son is Darren (Enzo Cilenti). The film chronicles the fractures that appear in their relationships among themselves and with others, and Winterbottom maintains a dazzling control over the many-stranded plot, though 'plot' sounds too contrived for the intense naturalness with which the action is played out.

Nadia and...?

The film opens with Nadia on the phone, giving her details to some sort of dating agency. 'I'm twenty-seven, five feet nine... I like to think of myself as honest, independent, self-aware', and indeed she does prove to be so. But she is not having much luck in finding a boyfriend, in spite of 'looking for someone after friendship, possibly romance'. Only in the film's last moments does she seem to have found something that looks like friendship as she walks off laughing with Franklyn (David Fahm), a depressed young black guy who lives near her parents' home. In the ninety minutes between these two moments, she is often seen walking solitarily through busy streets or on the phone looking out at an uninviting urban landscape or sitting alone in a bar or baby-sitting sister Debbie's little boy while Debbie is out on the town.

The first man she meets in response to her ad is quite a bit older, nice enough but not very interesting, not to Nadia anyway, and after a bit of chat she leaves and, disappointed, he watches her go. Like any number of characters in this film, *he* is left looking solitary. Her next answer is from Tim (Stuart Townsend), whose message has said, 'I like reading', and who is an advertising photographer. What this handsome young man is after is casual sex and, given his adeptness in this field and his looks, it is surprising – at first anyway – that he should need to be responding to an ad. When we know a bit more about him, it is less surprising. After he and Nadia have met, and gone back to his flat for sex, he prepares food, but just for himself without offering her any. He couldn't care less about her as a person, she is the merest sex partner, and when, as she is leaving and asks, 'Can I ring you, Tim?', there is a tiny movement of his eyes that suggests how little she has meant to him. He gives her a perfunctory kiss as she goes, and she is as lonely as before.

On the bus home, a man makes overtures to her, which she rejects, and the others in the bus are talking and laughing with raucous good cheer. Nadia sits alone, and in a large and eloquent close-up her face is stained with a single tear. There is something very affecting about Nadia as played by Gina McKee. In some scenes, it is a quality of stillness that compels our attention; in others, it is a sense of purpose as she walks

33   Gina McKee (Nadia) (Photo by Marcus Robinson).

as if looking for some kind of meaning. McKee convinces us of Nadia's essential decency and her laughter in the film's last moments as she walks with Franklyn seems to confirm this – and the fact that the film isn't taking a purely pessimistic view of what's available to people.

Debbie and Dan… and Jack

Debbie is the most abrasive of the three daughters. She is a single mum with a nine-year-old son, Jack, but she still wants a vigorous life of her own, and that includes a sex life. When we first see her, she is talking on the phone (oh, the nostalgia for those days when a phone was something attached to a wall – and was the major source of communication, as it is in *Wonderland*). While she is talking to her sister Molly, she is also urging Jack, who is watching something violent on television, to go to bed. She is a hairdresser and the salon she works in provides a handy rendezvous for her and a young black man to have some very noisy sex after hours, while Nadia is baby-sitting Jack. There is no explanation offered about how this pair have met, and this just adds to the notion of lives not planned but just hoping and trying, in some vague way, to find satisfaction of one kind or another.

There seems to be some real affection between Debbie and her sisters, especially with pregnant Molly, but there's barely even civility in her dealings with Dan (Ian Hart), her estranged partner and the irresponsible father of Jack. Jack is waiting on the housing-estate balcony for his dad on Saturday and seems pleased enough to see him. Unlike Debbie, who gracelessly rejects the flowers he has brought her and flinches when he goes to kiss her. We don't form a very warm picture of Debbie here, but as we'll see she may have reason not to expect too much from the superficially affable Dan. He first takes Jack to the football match and there's something very vulnerable in the individual faces picked out in the huge crowd, and particularly that of Jack sitting blank-faced alone. The way Winterbottom keeps taking in the crowds, here and there picking out an individual face, though not necessarily one of the main cast, points to the wider life of the film. The main characters are just those whom he has chosen out of the several million possibles in this vast metropolis.

Nevertheless, there is a brief moment of fearing for Jack as he sits alone before Dan returns with drinks. But, as weekend fathers go, Dan leaves a lot to be desired. When they leave the football crowd, they get involved in a wild traffic snarl which finds Dan shouting obscenities to the driver of an adjacent car in a way that can't be good for Jack's peace of mind, or his vocabulary. Back at Dan's place, he tidies himself up, leaves Jack with a video of Jim Carrey in *Dumb and Dumber*, then heads off for a spot of night life. By chance he meets Nadia sitting alone in a bar and she assures him, 'I'm not gonna spend the night with you', and 'No, we're not two old friends'. Next day, while Dan is sleeping off the night before, Jack wants to leave. Debbie has told him on the phone just to stay there till Dan wakes: in other words, neither parent is exercising any serious responsibility for this small boy, who finally heads off on his own. The camera tracks him through marketplaces and finally a fairground, where he looks up in wonder at the fireworks displays and, despite being alone, doesn't seem sad or afraid. Not, that is, till he is mugged and the muggers make off with his Walkman. Events are now moving towards a crisis, with pregnant Molly in hospital, Dan enlisting Nadia's help to look for Jack, and Jack showing the sense to go to a police station and try phoning his mum for help. A small boy in a Saturday night crowd in a big city is the film's ultimate comment on the bleaker chances of life. His retrieval by his angry mother who shouts abuse (admittedly deserved) at Dan telling him to 'fucking grow up' can't give him much consolation but in the taxi she hires to take them home he cuddles up to her. It is Dan's turn now to be left standing alone.

Molly and Eddie... and Alice

Though Molly's bitter mother Eileen claims, 'I never liked him', when he throws in his job at a crucial time, the film makes it clear that Eddie (John Simm) does have things going for him. He *does* love Molly; he *does* 'care about this baby we're having'. He is a decent man who panics about where his working life is going and throws in his job in 'kitchenware' without telling Molly and when the baby's birth is imminent. In Simm's quietly observant performance, we see into a man who wants to do the right thing but finds himself momentarily at sea in his life. Like all the other main characters in this densely populated film, he is given a series of revealing close-ups that make clear the inner conflicts he is trying to resolve.

His and Molly's relationship seems, at the outset, the only one in the film marked by real tenderness. He kisses her heavily pregnant belly as she talks on the phone to Debbie. Whatever Eileen says, he is plainly taking care of Molly who, alone of the sisters, has a devoted partner. In a poignant scene, he is walking on a bridge at night, arguing with himself. He is aware of his responsibility for Molly and the coming baby, but talks to himself, as if preparing his case to put before Molly, about doing a 'job you hate'. How long can you stick at this before the terrible onset of despair when you might buy a gun to end it all?

The crisis comes when Molly, having her hair done by Debbie at her salon, tries to phone Eddie at work and is told he is no longer working there. Eddie is at home practising what he is going to say, when Molly comes in stony-faced. In a film concerned with so many interlocking lives, it is impressive how sharply Winterbottom focuses on individual moments snatched out of the swirling dissatisfactions and hopes and anxieties that are the norm. This scene between Molly and Eddie is a prime example. Eddie talks persuasively about how he is going to cook them 'a great meal', while Molly stands still and silent. When he goes out shopping, there is a long, reflective close-up of Eddie's face as he makes his way by scooter through a street crowded with beggars or people making assignations of various kinds. Such close-ups have the effect of making us ponder some complex states of mind.

Some resolution is reached in the hospital where Debbie has rushed Molly when she suddenly goes into labour and where Eddie, who has fallen off his scooter and been injured, also fetches up, in a wheelchair. 'Where the fuck have you been?,' Molly berates him when he calls to her in the hospital corridor. He tries to explain: 'I don't know what happened. I just panicked. I just freaked out', then tenderly asks if the baby is 'OK' and then, to Molly, 'Are you all right?' He touches the baby's cheek and whispers, 'Alice... Alice in wonderland', and in this beautifully observed and gently played scene an authentic note of hope is struck without its ever descending into sentimentality.

Bill and Eileen

Behind the difficulties and disappointments of the three daughters and the missing son Darren, stand their parents Bill and Eileen in whose rancorous relationship no vestige of affection or kindness seems to remain. When Eileen makes her comment about never having liked Eddie, Bill, instead of maintaining his usual resigned silence, launches into an attack. 'You never liked anyone. Always carping, finding fault. It's never your fault is it? That's why Darren left.' And at this late stage in the film, we are perhaps near to understanding what has brought this unhappy pair to such a pass. Is the missing son Darren its cause? Eileen rejects any overtures of affection from Bill. If he tries to touch her in bed, she gets out angrily. She is so enraged by the barking of a neighbour's dog that she hurls some poisoned meat over the fence to kill it. When she and Bill are walking in the street they are, symbolically, never keeping pace with each other.

The film is too intelligent just to settle for the notion that this is a matter of faults on both sides. So there may be but it is Eileen's entrenched hostility to almost everyone that must take the larger share of blame for this now-loveless relationship. The only time she shows even a touch of affection is when she goes to see Molly and the baby in the hospital, but even then she can't repress her resentment when Eddie turns up. After she has poisoned the neighbour's dog, she is next seen in church (with an almost entirely black congregation), sitting stony-faced. Bill, on the other hand, is seen on several occasions to be capable of friendliness and affection. His moments with daughter Nadia suggest a real bond, and significantly they share the film's last sequence.

In an earlier episode, when he has locked himself out of his house and Eileen is not at home, he goes to the nearby home of neighbour Donna (Ellen Thomas) to wait. She gives him a drink, then encourages him to join her in dancing. She may have more on her mind than dancing, as she sends her children upstairs, but there is a core of decency in Bill which leads him to say, 'I should go now'. He may be tempted and going home to the taciturn Eileen is hardly an attractive prospect, but again and again Winterbottom makes us aware of how unclear-cut human relationships are. When the estranged Darren leaves an answer-phone message just to make contact and say 'I'm fine', it seems appropriate that Bill should be the one to receive it. He has 'earnt' a small moment of happiness.

In a film full of performances of remarkable truth and subtlety, perhaps most notable of all are those of Jack Shepherd and Kika Markham as Bill and Eileen. They bring this lacerating relationship to a sort of life that compels sympathy for Bill but pity for them both. The film doesn't spell out the cause(s) of Eileen's chronic bitterness but it makes us feel for anyone locked into such unhappy dealings with marriage and with the world at large.

Wonderland and British realist cinema

Of course in some ways *Wonderland* is in the tradition of realism that has been the dominant strand in British films, at least since World War Two, when the influence of the documentary tradition made itself felt in fiction films. And then the New Wave films of the late 50s and early 60s brought a more palpably socio-political edge to their realist depictions of working-class lives. There was about them an insistence on class matters, on taking seriously those working lives that had as often as not been the subject of comic relief in the prevailing middle-class mores of much preceding British cinema. In more recent times, Ken Loach has maintained a firmly committed political stance in relation to the lives he depicts, lives often lived at the margins of society, refusing to see these as purely individual but as cogs in an often unjust larger organism. Mike Leigh's interest is more primarily on those individuals who mess up their lives through clumsy interactions with those nearest to them, rather than indicting society at large for injustice.

In this way, *Wonderland* may have more in common with Leigh than with the others, but Winterbottom is persistently aware of the city at large and the pressures it exerts, even though it is the twisted strands of awkward human connection – and its failures – that most seem to preoccupy him. His protagonists may venture out into the busy world in search of gratifications of various kinds, but in the end realise these are most likely to be found within themselves or in those around them on an everyday basis. If the London of the film is any kind of a wonderland, this has to be actively sought. It may offer glimpses of hope and pleasure but it's up to individual personality to identify and claim these.

Winterbottom's sense of realism is partly influenced by a humanist interest in the way people behave and in a respect for their worth across a wide spectrum of impulse and behaviour. Even the least sympathetic characters such as Eileen are treated with enough concern for their complex humanity to stop us from merely dismissing them. How he goes about achieving his realist effect is the result of an entirely conscious approach to filming, not only on his part but through his collaborators and filming choices as well. For instance, he said in interview:

> The film is set in very specific parts of London – a section of south London between Vauxhall, Elephant & Castle and Brixton, and Soho. And because of the way we decided to film, we shot everything in what we felt was the 'real' location... What is more, because we shot in the real locations, without extras and when they were open, we had to shoot at the same time the events were happening... So really the whole method of filming came from the desire to be able to include in the film a real sense of the city, rather than a re-created version of it.[3]

This means that the film has taken realism a step further than is often the case with films judged as 'realist'. Winterbottom's cinematographer (Sean Bobbitt, who'd had a background in documentary) and sound editors would aim to catch the feel and sound of actual places, such as bars and café, at the time demanded by the screenplay. They didn't use 'extras' to populate such sequences and aimed to keep camera and microphones as unobtrusive as possible so as to disturb the habitués of these places as little as necessary. The aim seems to have been to capture 'behaviour' on screen rather than 'acting', and to a remarkable extent this has been achieved. Of course there is artifice involved – in for instance the speeded up shots of the streets at night in which Winterbottom's then-regular editor Trevor Waite cuts together images that, in frantic motion, evoke the city. So realism isn't just a matter of 'playing it like it is' but sometimes of using artifice to make us focus on what it *means* rather than just respond to the physical realities of time and place.

Faces

In the end, though, it is the faces that we meet that stay most potently with us, or with me at any rate. They can suggest reflectiveness, as in Eddie's case, or loneliness as Nadia sits on her own in a bar, or opportunism as when Tim sees her out the door, or the fierce combative anger that is corroding Eileen's soul. It may well be an effect of Winterbottom's decision to create images of the city at large, with all its noise and incessant movement, that, in contrast, the eloquent faces of his actors, often in close-up, haunt us in their moments of misery or of sudden joy. It is a film of huge vitality, but in its concern for the individual, epitomised in these memorable faces, it keeps surprising us with accesses of tenderness. I don't describe it as a humanist masterpiece for no reason.

Notes

1 Interview with author, London, 2006.
2 Production Notes, *Wonderland*, 1999, p.3.
3 Production Notes, p. 5.

19   Giving and taking
Last Orders (2002)

The way things are

Whenever British cinema seems to take an upward turn, it is almost invariably because of a new burst of realism. I raised this matter in the chapters on *Secrets & Lies* and *Wonderland* and it comes to the fore again in considering Fred Schepisi's beautiful and moving version of Graham Swift's award-winning novel, *Last Orders*. As in the best of realist filmmaking, it's not just a matter of pointing the camera at 'ordinary lives' here. There may be nothing remarkable in the lives of the main characters in *Last Orders*, but in evoking the way they live, what they have in common and what distinguishes them, director-screen-writer Schepisi always manages to suggest larger issues are at stake. He achieves this not by spelling out such significance but by his very precise attention to the details of the lives of five men and one woman. There is a powerful whiff of reality about it all and we end by suspecting that there are no such things as 'ordinary lives': all lives are particular, special in their own ways. Reality is not the same as realism, but realism, in relation to time and place for instance, is one of the ways by which we can be confronted with reality. So are, say, comedy or melodrama, but realism has most often been the British way.

Four for the road

In a pub called The Coach and Horses (the name already suggests a trip) four men gather for a drink. They are Ray Johnson (Bob Hoskins), a divorced and retired insurance salesman, in his sixties, Lenny Tate (David Hemmings) who runs a fruit-and-vegetable stall, undertaker Vic Tucker (Tom Courtenay), and, last to arrive, the much younger Vince Dodds (Ray Winstone), who runs his own secondhand-car salesroom. Vic arrives with a box containing the ashes of the old friend of the senior three and 'father' of Vince. It was the last wish of butcher Jack Dodds (Michael Caine) that his remains should be scattered to the winds off Margate pier, where he had always hankered to return. They are all used to meeting in this pub and Vic explains to their friendly barman Bernie (George Innes) the purpose of the trip they are about to make from the Bromley site of The Coach and Horses to Margate.

The shape of the film is dictated by this journey in the plush Mercedes that Vince has brought for the occasion. In spite of this narrative structure, *Last Orders* is not really a 'road movie' in the usual sense of the term. Certainly, we take in the changing settings along the way, and there are several important stops, but what essentially happen along the way are the recollections of the four. These take the form of memory sequences, rather than flashbacks. The term 'memory sequences' gives a more accurate sense of their sometimes fleeting nature, sometimes no more than a couple of moments set in train by a word from one of the men in the car. There's not a lot of action in the film's present, except on the occasion of a punch-up between Vince and the querulous Lenny in a muddy hopfield. The real drama is in the way bits of the various, sometimes interlocking, pasts of the four filter out of their rambling conversations. As one writer observed, the film 'relies for its cumulative power on flashbacks triggered by chance words or gestures – a comment on the handwriting on the dead man's will, for instance, sparks off a shot of him scrawling on a blackboard.'[1] I might quibble over the use of 'flashback', but the writer makes exactly the point about how the film is working.

Not many films adapted from novels keep so closely to the contours of the original as *Last Orders* does. On occasion, it comes near to transliteration, and yet there is nothing merely slavish about this. Schepisi has certainly adopted the novel's narrative trajectory. The journey for the execution of Jack's wishes still provides the film's framework. The recollections and reminiscences of the chaps in the Merc are still at the heart of the film's meaning, as they are in the novel. These are still what *happens* on the trip, but Schepisi takes full advantage of the cinema's effortless fluidity in time and place. Whereas the novel devotes a chapter to the memory flight of this or that man,

34   Ray Winstone (Vince Dodds) and Sally Hurst (Mandy).

the film can cut easily from the car's interior to, say, Jack's butcher's shop on the day he told Ray he was planning to sell up, or for a fleeting moment while Vince and wife Mandy comfort Amy (Helen Mirren) when she has just learnt that Jack's illness is terminal. If this mobility of present and past has any real comparison with literature, it is not so apparent in the novel or the drama as in poetry, where a word may evoke another time or place in a passing reference. A flashback in film is a more finite sequence for a special purpose, perhaps triggered by a specific act of story-telling by a character, but I think there is something nearly poetic in Schepisi's use of brief memory inserts. They illuminate the character doing the remembering as much as those being recollected.

The film retains the novel's reliance on such recollection and, without ever causing confusion, is not afraid to transport us from the present confinement in the Merc to the moment in the past – and *then* from that moment to another still further back in another past. Schepisi's technique is so sure that we are never in doubt about whose past we are inhabiting at any given moment.

Three stopovers and a punning title

Apart from when the four pull in for a boozy lunch – 'boozy' at least as far as the somewhat belligerent Lenny is concerned – there are three other major stopping-off places as the Merc makes its way across the Kentish countryside. I'd claim that in their own ways each has its bearing on the very resonant title of the film and novel. When they are finishing their lunch, Vic, who has been in the Navy during the war, suggests they make a small detour to visit the Chatham Naval War Memorial. There's been talk about Jack and Ray's army experiences over lunch and Vic has listened quietly. While standing there, Vic remembers a moment of naval action, and he also recalls how he was at first mocked for his job, in the family undertaking business, but later this had been found useful, for sea burials with some dignity. The visit requires them to climb a hill and Lenny complains predictably about this, and about the 'fucking navy', 'fucking army' and finally 'fucking tourists'. So how does this little excursion bear on the film as a whole? In one sense, the Memorial is a last order for those who didn't make it – or a last attempt to impose a sort of order on the awful randomness of wartime deaths.

The next stopover happens when Vince pulls the car off the motorway and on to a dirt road that leads to a large muddy hillside field. The clever editing doesn't allow any further lead-in to this detour but cuts instead to Amy and Ray talking on the London Embankment and she utters the words 'Wicks Farm', just as the Merc is coming to a halt. Vince offers no explanation for this as he gets out of the car and goes to scatter some of Jack's ashes there. Aggressive and never waiting for explanations, Lenny angrily calls Vince a 'toe-rag' and, ex-boxer that he is, he knocks Vince down, shouting that 'Jack's last orders have to be respected'. In fact, this was the place where, in the hop-picking season before the war, Jack and Amy had first made love and their daughter June was conceived. When the punch-slinging with Lenny is done, Vince stands in the field, recalling a conversation with Jack about June who is 'sort of yer sister' but not wholly so. This is where Vince learnt the fact of his parents' death in a London doodlebug bombing and how Amy had rescued the baby Vince. When Jack came back from the war, there was Vince, installed in the family. Jack has had a mentally disabled daughter he can hardly bear to contemplate and a son who was not really his son. Vince remembers saying to Jack, 'You're not really my dad', then scatters some of the ashes, and the juxtaposition of the memory and the gesture watched by the three old friends is suddenly very moving in the intense conjunction of past and present. Vince is here carrying out Jack's last orders in a wholly personal way, a way which brings him some real sense of reconciliation of his present and his past.

Back in the car, Vince and Lenny have got rid of the effects of their muddy scuffle as best they can, and there is then talk of Canterbury. Ray says he's never been there. 'Well, Canterbury doesn't have a race-course does it?,' is Lenny's inevitably needling reply. There are moments of rare beauty in the way the Cathedral rears up before them. This has nothing to do with so-called 'heritage' film-making; it is everything to do with a gnawing sense of mortality and eternity. Once inside the Cathedral, Vince picks up a tourist brochure and, while he and Lenny and Vic walk around the glowing interior, Ray elects to sit quietly on a pew at the back. This is a place full of effigies of the famous (Becket for instance), a place which is concerned with marking and honouring the dead, and those so honoured are there in compliance with someone's last orders. For Ray, kind and usually upbeat, it provides a time for reflection. He's on this trip to do what Jack has asked, but he is also recalling the time he has spent in loving Jack's wife, and, as Amy weeps at her recollections of the six weeks long ago when she let Ray love her, Ray sits quietly weeping in the Cathedral. The mutuality of their tears gently hints at a possible future, when both have paid their dues to others, a future that may include a trip to Australia to visit Ray's daughter Susie with whom he has been long out of touch.

The film starts in the Bromley pub where the four older men had been used to gather and where they must routinely have responded to barman Bernie's request for last orders. It's fitting that the film's journey begins there and ends on windswept Margate pier which we last saw in the bright sunshine of Jack and Amy's youth. Talk about the journey and stopovers isn't meant to suggest that *Last Orders* is a picaresque tale with interesting encounters along the way. The four in the car on their way to carry out Jack's last orders meet no one along the way, apart from people serving them in pubs; these are lives that have been shaped by World War Two and on this journey some of the things and people who have mattered to them come unbidden to the surface of their minds. The important journey is, for each of them, the inner one, as the film's meditative tone makes us privy to what it means to each. What happens on this journey is that, through the play of memories and reminiscence, about a dozen interconnected lives are gradually teased out, allusively but with great evocative vividness. What is recalled of their lives isn't whipped up into major dramas; their importance is for the men to

35   Bob Hoskins (Ray Johnson) and Michael Caine (Jack Dodds).

settle within and between themselves, as the penultimate shot of the
film suggests.

Schepisi's great cameraman, Brian Tufano, ends the film on the
most eloquent shots of the four men standing on the edge of the pier as
they discharge Jack's last orders. Somehow, the shots of the four from
behind as they face out to sea where the ashes have drifted are invested
with the most acute poignancy. Perhaps it's as if whatever tensions
have been observed along the way are now subsumed into this farewell
gesture. When they move back to the car, talking of having a drink
('Jack would expect nothing less'), the camera settles on a long shot of
the serene greyness of the sea. Schepisi has found a visual equivalent
for the novel's account of the four finally reaching the jetty: 'like all the
while we've been teetering and tottering towards some edge, and now
there ain't no more hanging back.'[2]

While these four are on the road to Margate there is a fifth character
making a journey at the same time and that is Amy. She has elected not
to be one of the party carrying out Jack's last orders because she has
some final business of her own to attend to. For fifty years, she has been
making a weekly journey by bus to visit Jack's and her daughter June
in the 'Home' in which June lives. All Amy has longed for from these
visits, which Jack has never made, is some sign of recognition from the

plump peaceful-looking girl who sits there oblivious to Amy. These trips
to see June have been built into the fabric of Amy's life. The mere fact
that Amy is most often wearing a red coat identical in colour to the bus
she always boards seems in its small way utterly to align her with the
purpose symbolised by the bus. On the day of the Margate venture,
Amy speaks to June eliciting no more response than usual: 'They must
be there by now.' And goes on to carry out her own 'last orders' to
herself by adding, 'I've got to think of me own future'. This is her final
goodbye to June who, of course, won't register any change.

Time passing

Even the notion of retirement carries with it some sense of 'last orders',
the last that will be given or taken, at least in working lives. Jack's
decision to sell up the 'Dodds and Son' butchery has a quality of
acceptance of time's inexorable hand. He has wanted Vince to join him
so as to carry on the name that Jack's father had established, but Vince
is more interested in running a car-yard, which he establishes with
Ray's help. No sooner has Jack decided to sell, wanting to set up in a
bungalow in Margate, than he takes ill and his next and final move is to
the hospital. Lenny, the least successful of the four friends, and envious
about this, still has to ply his business, but Ray is retired, more or less
contented with his lot and with doing things to help those who need
help. Only Vic is still in charge of his business but his sons are ready
to take it over when required, unlike Vince and the Dodds butchery.
Coming to the end of your working life isn't quite the same as last orders
but is perhaps a not uncommon step towards that finality.

The film gives a wonderful sense of the passage of time. It is
never confusing as it makes its way from the present of the journey
in the Merc or Amy's parallel bus trip to say goodbye to June, to the
recent past involving the progress of Jack's illness, to the much more
distant past of the war years and others in between. That there is no
confusion about the period in which the action is taking place at any
given time is doubtless due to Schepisi's orchestration of the whole
multilayered narrative. We know immediately where, or at least which
tense we're in, whether the Merc is making its progress through the
Kentish countryside, or whether we're in the memory sequences, or
the inserts within these. That this is clear is also partly the work of
the production and costume design, of lighting and even of hair and

make-up stylists. All of these keep us mutely informed. The Margate of Jack and Amy's honeymoon is bathed in the sunlight of a season other than the bleak one of the men's return. The bright red lips of the wartime women and their rolled hairstyles have become subdued by the time they've reached middle age, and so have their clothes, with Amy for instance later wrapped in warm overcoats and a knitted hat. In Ray's case, encroaching baldness is a help in placing him in various decades. The fact that the main characters are played by different actors at earlier stages is of course the most obvious informant about period, but all those other aspects of filmmaking work to persuade us about the authenticity of time and place in which they are set.

A major element of the film's skill in marking the passage of time is its cunning use of young actors to play the six leading roles in their twenties or earlier in Vince's case. For example, Vince (Stephen Cole, as a young man) has grown out of his 1960s ponytail and his shaggy 1970s locks by the time we see him behind the wheels of the Merc a couple of decades later. JJ Feild is a miraculously apt young Jack, not just because of his credible look of Michael Caine but also because he catches Jack's easy assumption of authority in any situation. As for the young Lenny, he is played by David Hemmings's son Nolan, so that the resemblance to the 60s star is not surprising. It is enough to say that all the youthful versions of the carload, of Amy and Jack, are spot-on as credible forerunners of those we see making their journeys to carry out last orders and this feeds our belief in the pasts that have made them.

Sorting them out

Whereas in Swift's novel, the reminiscences and memories of each of the protagonists is created in a recognisable voice, the film has its own means of differentiating them from each other. I'll start with the actors.

Who's who
The starring cast is virtually a compendium of British male film acting over nearly half a century. The careers of Michael Caine, David Hemmings and Tom Courtenay really got underway in the 60s (see what happens to various kinds of heroes in late middle age, in film and life), Hoskins' from the early 80s and Winstone's from the 90s, with the great Helen Mirren's spanning over forty years. Arguably none has ever been better than here; between them they are heartbreakingly real,

utterly true to their characters and to the film's large themes, which
have to do with nothing less than what life is worth, and on what sort
of terms it might mean the most. Caine, Hemmings and Courtenay are
now all much associated with fresh impulses in British cinema from the
1960s on.

Caine entered films in uncredited bits in 1950, was first noticed in *A
Hill in Korea* in 1956, but came to prominence with a string of versatile
displays in the mid 60s – starting with *Zulu* in 1964, improbably but
memorably cast as a posh officer doing his bit for the Empire at Rorke's
Drift, then more probably and again memorably as a serial womaniser in,
and as, *Alfie* (1966). Unlike many theatre-trained British actors he gave
an impression less of acting than of effortlessly *behaving* in whatever
role. Over the next forty-odd years, he acquired the sort of stardom that
enabled him to get away with quite a bit of rubbish (think of *Blame it on
Rio* or *Dirty Rotten Scoundrels*). In general, though, his range – and his
achievement within it – was remarkable, and as suggested in the chapter
on *Get Carter*, Caine seemed in line with that Hollywood tradition of
stars who often appeared to be doing nothing at all, but left you utterly
convinced about the lives they were enacting. In *Last Orders*, his Jack
rightly hovers over the whole film, whether he's there dominating the
company in a pub or lying flat on his back in a hospital ward or when
the chaps in the car are just talking about him. He is to the life the
working-class man who has happily inherited his dad's butcher shop
and is terse with his son Vince who doesn't want to maintain the line in
this matter. He is loud and confident most of the time and this makes
those moments when, for instance, he is concerned about 'seeing Amy
right' after he is dead all the more affecting.

The smoothly good-looking Hemmings was in films from 1954 at
the age of thirteen, and appeared in a number of largely forgotten films
often aimed at teenage audiences. He finally made his presence felt in a
big way in Michelangelo Antonioni's spectacularly successful art-house
hit, *Blow-Up* in 1966, as the modish London photographer who thinks
he's stumbled on something suspicious. Thereafter he worked steadily
until his death in 2003, increasingly in character roles as his youthful
looks gave way to somewhat pudgy middle age, a condition that suited
him admirably to the role of the stroppy, envious and disappointed
Lenny. He has a grudge against Jack's 'son' Vince, who had once got
Lenny's daughter pregnant, and he blames Vince for her having then
married a guy who is now in gaol. Hemmings brings to his playing of
Lenny a bitter edginess that is only kept in check by the odd pint or,

at the end, by the quartet's discharging of Jack's last orders as a group effort.

There was something pinched and inward-looking about the young Courtenay as he endured and made us understand *The Loneliness of the Long-Distance Runner* (1962) and the sense of entrapment felt by *Billy Liar* (1963). He was one of the 'icons', as they say, of the New Wave which produced a newly proletarian set of stars who had little in common with the previous traditions of British leading men. Like Caine, he came from a modest working-class background, and over the next half-century he was persistently in work across a wide social range, on stage, screen and television. His originally rather glum appearance has settled by the time of *Last Orders* (and in *Quartet*, a decade later) into a quiet contentment that is perfectly adapted to the character of Vic, the undertaker. He brings to the role the sense of a man at peace with himself, able to joke about his job and his name – 'I'm halfway to a vicar' – and the touch of dignity that the occasion calls for. Of the four older men, he is perhaps the one most satisfied with the cards life has dealt him, though without smugness, and in the visit to the War Memorial Courtenay brings just a flicker of something still stirring beneath the calm facade.

Bob Hoskins, a little younger than Caine and Courtenay but the same age as Hemmings, seems to belong to a different generation of British film. He did quite a bit of television in the 70s, most notably as the lead in Dennis Potter's *Pennies from Heaven* in 1978, but his film career really took off in 1980 when he played the wealthy gangster Harold Shand in *The Long Good Friday*. From then on, he became perhaps the major character star in British films, with side excursions into big-budget Hollywood jobs. There is something quintessentially English and stubbornly working-class about him, and his short, sturdy frame was ideally suited to the role of Ray, the most clearly benign of the *Last Orders* guys. He can play Ray as Amy's temporary lover without somehow compromising Ray's core of decency.

Youngest of the four on the road, Vince is played by Ray Winstone. Also from a working-class background and with several boxing championships to his name, he'd been active in film and television from the late 70s, but really came into his own as the hard man of British films in the 90s in such rigorous fare as *Nil by Mouth* and *The War Zone*. Everything about his physical presence – his stance, the way he wears his bulk (and his camel-hair coat) – feeds impressively into the way he brings Vince to life. He suggests a man capable of physical violence, though this is only called into play when he hits back at Lenny in the hopfield. He also suggests a man who may not be as sure of himself and his place in the world as we may at first believe.

I've wanted to stress the way these five actors represent decades-long strands of British filmmaking, because *Last Orders* is so patently an actors' film and because of the echoes they bring with them. As for the great Helen Mirren, she seems so much a star of today, appearing in film after film, that it is hard to accept that she first appeared, uncredited, in a Norman Wisdom farce, *Press for Time*, in 1966. She has contrived to be a major international star without surrendering her credentials as a major actress. As Amy, she has subdued her natural sexiness and glamour in the interests of playing a middle-aged, then elderly, housewife with a daughter who still doesn't know her after her fifty years of devoted and painful solicitude. While the men in the Merc are calling up their memories, Amy is quietly locked into hers on the top of the red London bus. Mirren ensures that Amy has aged as subtly and convincingly as the colour of her hair mutates. For those who knew, the fact that Caine's real-life mother regularly visited his disabled elder half-brother (unknown to Caine till after his mother's death) will perhaps add an extra note of poignancy to Amy's situation.

Telling them apart
Whereas the novel is able to give all the main characters access to a 'voice', the film relies on means to distinguish them other than just choosing distinctive actors. Those whose aspirations have been met – that is, Vince and Vic – have an air of self-possession (even if there are undercurrents hinted at) that is denied to Lenny, Ray and even Jack, who is unable to secure his dream of Dodds and Son. Their respective facial appearances and how they dress, how they have related to their children, the very vehicles which each is associated with: all these and more contribute to making *Last Orders* a telling study in approaches to masculinity. It may be as apparently confident as Vince's or as aggressive as Lenny's or as self-contained as Vic's or as kindly accommodating as Ray's. Bringing them together to carry out the last orders of breezy extrovert Jack is how the film goes about distinguishing them from each other as they approach a common goal.

When most films tend to focus on the younger demographic at which they are so often aimed, it is heartening to see one prepared to reflect on the challenges confronting these four men and one woman. *Last Orders* – and by film's end, everyone's last orders will have been carried out – is a humane and compassionate film. It understands what unites friends despite resentments and grudges nourished over the years, and the result is profoundly affecting.

Notes

1 Ryan Gilbey, 'Unmade Freds', *Sight & Sound,* January 2002, 12.
2 Graham Swift, *Last Orders* (London: Picador, 1996), p. 288.

20   In your face:
In the Loop (2009)

As time goes by

We – or at any rate British cinema – have come a long way since *Brief Encounter*. Celia Johnson had only taken off her scarf when her assignation with Trevor Howard was interrupted by the return of the owner of his friend's flat. Sex scenes of the kind routinely on show today would have been unthinkable, and were probably not even so common in life, prior to the spread of central heating anyway, but that's another matter. But it's not sex that comes to mind in relation to *In the Loop*. It's the language. At a rough guess, I should say that the word 'fuck' in its various permutations and tenses occurs about 976 times, or maybe more. It reaches the stage where we almost cease to be aware of it, as if we have become anaesthetised to its use. I don't raise this issue in a spirit of censorious noting of the decline in contemporary discourse, or even morals, but rather to register my sense of the film's literacy. It's not literary in any sense but I suspect – and the film convinces me about this – that it is *literate*: true, that is, to the way we can believe these people talk in the everyday hurl and burl of their lives. One critic finished his review of the film by announcing unequivocally: 'A magnificent film'.[1] I'm prepared to go along with this.

Screens small and large

Has there ever been a seriously good film derived from a television series? I haven't done the research that would enable me to answer to this question with authority. When I run my eye over the list compiled for 'Wikipedia', I am not at all inclined to viewing the big-screen likes of *The Beverly Hillbillies* or *On the Buses* just to be sure of my ground.[2] The notion of adaptation of one kind or another in filmmaking opens up many provocative issues. Filming would hardly have got off the ground without regular pillaging of novels, plays, short stories, even a few poems, as well as 'based-on-a-true-story' items, and many stimulating movies have resulted. So what is it about TV series that seems so endemically to resist the process of adaptation from the small to the big screen? Perhaps it is to do with running-time. Whereas a smartly written half-hour series can run satisfactorily on a single idea, dressed out with shrewdly calculated observation of milieu and the lives fleetingly glimpsed in it, the feature film, by inevitably having to stretch to about ninety minutes (if you're lucky) or (if you're not) two and a half hours, is constrained to go in for much more clotted plotting.

There must be exceptions to this depressing rule. I seem to remember *Sweeney!* (1977, David Wickes) managed the transfer with a rewarding share of tough action and tough insights. Indeed, as I write, a new version is scheduled for 2012 release, starring Ray Winstone and TV's *Homeland* hero Damian Lewis. Those with longish memories may also recall that some of the anarchic insanity of *Monty Python* made its way to the big screen with the original inspiration intact. And, Kevin Macdonald's 2009 version of the riveting British series *State of Play* (2003) didn't lose too much in having its investigation of the links between politics and press relocated from London to Washington. But we all know what exceptions can do to rules.

This preamble is really by way of saying that director Armando Iannucci, in his feature debut, has pulled off a major triumph with *In the Loop*, derived as it is from the TV series *The Thick of It*. He directed thirteen episodes of the programme between 2005 and 2012, as well as producing and co-writing most of them – along with the lethally deadpan *Alan Partridge* series, from which he has also made a feature film. He begins to seem like a polymath of early twenty-first-century television.

Why does *In the Loop* work so well when most of its predecessors in the small-to-big-screen transfer don't? We shall see.

36   A promotional poster featuring Peter Capaldi
(Malcolm Tucker).

Putting the boot into politics

Probably I should admit to a prejudice here. Political satire may well be my favourite genre – either that or Westerns. But there's not all that much in the way of political satire that comes our way, especially not when it is treated with such non-stop irreverence as it is in the big-screen spin-off from TV's *The Thick of It*. There have been enjoyable instances of what I more or less mean in such films as *Bob Roberts* (1992), *Primary Colors* (1998) and especially *Wag the Dog* (1997) in fairly recent times, but *In the Loop* may just be smarter and funnier than any of them.

As for political satire in British films, it has been sparsely present with varying degrees of ferocity over several decades. It inherited the Shavian attack on capitalism in *Major Barbara* (1941) and was a gentle element of *The Demi-Paradise* (1943). There was Ealing's cunningly political *The Man in the White Suit* (1951); the Boulting brothers gave both left and right a witty serve in *I'm All Right Jack* (1959); and Lindsay Anderson's 'Mick Travis' trilogy, *If...* (1968), *O Lucky Man!* (1973) and *Britannia Hospital* (1982), came up with something abrasive about the state of Britain through focus on several key institutions. These are all films of some distinction and there are others too, but even so no one could think of political satire as a dominant genre in British cinema.

For me *In the Loop* belonged to the nasty vein of television I most enjoy, though this may well show me in a poor light. I mean programmes like *The Thick of It* and *The Office*, and so on, which led me to write an article called *A Curmudgeon's Canon*,[3] specially dedicated to viewers who can sniff a feel-good ending from early on and who resolutely refuse to have their hearts warmed. It doesn't just mean 'nasty'; it means 'smart and nasty', with a finger on the pulse for the way things go on in life. In the case of *In the Loop*, this means the profession of spin-doctoring among assorted politicians on both sides of the Atlantic and the forces behind the push towards war in the Middle East.

Politics, politicians and the political life

Like all the best comedy, *In the Loop* is serious at heart. Not that you might have time to notice this while actually watching, the laughs come so thick and fast and the irreverence and profanity are almost breathtaking. Iannucci doesn't actually name political parties or actual politicians. If he did, the ensuing litigation would no doubt have impoverished him for decades. It is nonetheless clear that the political issue involved is whether or not the West – that is, essentially the US and the UK – will go to war against Iraq.

The machinations in both countries leading to 'the vote' are at the same time extremely funny and quite appalling in their lack of concern for what such intervention might entail. London's dim-witted Minister for International Development, Simon Foster (Tom Hollander), has been lured in a television interview to declare war as 'unforeseeable' without actually thinking about what he meant by this inanity. The Prime Minister's director of communications, the relentlessly foul-mouthed Malcolm Tucker (Peter Capaldi), berates him, yelling, 'You don't think that', in one of his few sentences devoid of a four-letter expletive. On this day they are joined by a new adviser, the somewhat hapless Toby Wright (Chris Addison), whose girlfriend Suzy (Olivia Poulet) works for the 'Director of Diplomacy', Michael Rogers (James Smith). These, along with Malcolm's aide, Judy (Gina McKee), are the Brits who will in one way or other become immersed in the politics surrounding possible intervention in the Middle East.

In the US, there is a comparable line-up. One of these, notably

Karen Clark (Mimi Kennedy), assistant secretary for diplomacy, has been in London where she's said, 'Military action is not a primary option at this point'. Her choice of words in itself suggests the sort of politics underlying anything as crucial as war; it's something you might or might not elect to pursue. However, Karen is at least trying to prevent war at this stage, unlike her hawkish opposite in Washington, Linton Barwick (David Rasche). The other key US figures are Karen's aide, Liza (Anna Chlumsky), author of a report on planning that gets leaked causing much vitriolic response, and General George Miller (James Gandolfini), an ally of Karen's and a man with some distinctive views on war. For instance, he tells Karen, in a private meeting conducted in a child's bedroom, 'At the end of a war you need some soldiers left or it looks as if you've lost.' And later, in the State Department, he offers this reflection: 'War – once you've been there, once you've seen it, you never want to go there again unless you fucking have to. Like France.'

The fact that Miller will eventually switch allegiances is just one among the film's myriad swipes at the nature of the political life. For virtually everyone involved, politics seems to be a sort of game where the rules are constantly changing at the whim of those who shout loudest or play dirtiest. Iannucci doesn't make the mistake of letting details of the plot overshadow the frantic interplay of characters in search of their own advancement. I'm not going into the ramifications of the political game as it is enacted by players on both sides of the Atlantic. It's enough to know that the over-all issue is whether or not the West will go to war in the Middle East, and that the relations between Downing Street and Washington's State Department are at least in part governed by mutual wariness and the effect of leaks to the media, as well as by utterly personal matters that rightly ought to have no place on the agenda. All of which, I'm aware, makes it sound a solemn business when in fact nothing could be further from the truth. It is serious only in the way that all great satire *is* serious: that is, its underlying critique of the political life is always present but not so as to compromise the irresistible flow of the film's verbal onslaught.

It is not just the politics of the war or non-war situation that the film addresses with such nimble wit and intelligence, contrasting rapier and the 'fucking great mallet of truth'. Again, there's the sense of what an appalling life so many of those involved lead. They are for the most part not concerned with getting to the actual nub of a problem but, rather, with wondering what sort of part they can play in it, and how the situation can be made to work in their favour. There is almost no sign of their private lives. We glimpse Toby's girlfriend Suzy, to whom Toby passes on the planning report PWPPIP, which she subsequently leaks to British television. She becomes his ex-girlfriend when she finds out that he has slept with Liza after a night on the town in Washington, and when he returns to London she sends him packing out of their shared flat. This is the nearest thing to a glimpse of private life the film offers. Judy, Malcolm's aide, is seen briefly asleep in bed with her husband when she gets a phone call from Washington in the early hours of the morning. Someone else's house in Washington has a child's bedroom upstairs, but the film resolutely rejects the idea of showing us that politicians might have a gentler, more domestic side. It's as if the very nature of the profession precludes this. It's an all-consuming business which leaves no time or mind room for anything not connected to the big goal of making your mark, of being seen to be important – even if, or particularly if, you're not.

War and wall

Whether or not war will be declared is the governing narrative motif. It provides more than enough scope for the plot's complexities as people jockey for positions, interviews are conducted, documents are leaked, high-level meetings are held, along with low-level shouting matches. This over-arching idea kick-starts the film's plot: the UK and US heads of state are keen to go to war; it emerges that Barwick has formed a secret War Committee. Karen Clark and the General are opposed to its machinations and pro-war leanings. All the manipulations, in and out of committee rooms (and in 'Restrooms' and in the UN 'Meditation Room' where Simon goes to suck a mint), about the possibility of such a war lead towards the United Nations Headquarters meeting-room. There, the British ambassador hovers, asking for 'a cheeky early vote', someone witters on about 'nibbles', Malcolm is trying to check out who was responsible for the leak, and finally the matter is put to a vote. Actually the lead-up to '30 Minutes till Vote' is really no more than a joke. This is not the kind of narrative interest that has kept us glued to the screen; it's just what gives a shape to the rich pleasures otherwise offered by the film.

There is too a sub-plot which keeps intervening to remind us of how absurd (as well as potentially lethal) all the main politicking is. This has to do with a wall in Northamptonshire. The wall belongs to Simon Foster's constituency office. At a meeting in the Town Hall, Foster and his assistant Ros (Joanna Scanlan) are listening to complaints from his electorate. One has to do with a faulty septic tank about which Simon bravely announces: 'I'm completely on board now.' Of course, he never is, even at this local level. The next complainant is Paul Michaelson (Steve Coogan), who claims that the wall is likely to fall down on his mother's garden. The final collapse of the wall is serendipitous for Malcolm Tucker who wants a reason to sack Simon, not giving him the chance to resign. He tells Simon, the wall having collapsed, 'The PM was very clear, you've got to go', and threatening that, if he doesn't go quietly, 'I will marshal all the media forces of darkness to hound you to suicide.' Malcolm, as we have seen, has a fine line in the rhetoric of threat. He has earlier warned Simon that certain information would 'make your blood clot – like a fucking black pudding in your guts'.

Simon is in fact the football kicked around by both war and wall. Tucker comes to Washington after him to prevent his being wooed by Karen Clark and Miller, as someone who might 'internationalise' the resistance to war. When Tucker arrives, finding Foster in his underpants eating burger and chips in his hotel room, he instructs him that he is to say nothing at tomorrow's meeting. Further, he's not to go to bed but rather, 'You're gonna stay here and rehearse saying nothing.' As far as the wall is concerned, Simon may be 'on board' but he's no match for Michaelson, played with hilarious deadpan solemnity by Steve Coogan in a knitted cap (or for Michaelson's mother who refuses to let her real age be announced on television when interviewed).The comparative triviality of the wall affair makes its point about the precariousness of a political career in the wild circumstances that the film depicts with such savage wit. As well, the mere fact of Simon's ineptitude on virtually every occasion, whether to do with war or wall, is a major swipe at what can be expected of politicians. How did he ever get to be a cabinet minister? How, indeed, did he ever persuade people to vote for him in the first place?

Mice and men

Actually they are all pretty much of the rodent species in one way or other. What makes them so memorable is the sheer brilliance of the dialogue that Iannucci and his team of co-writers (Jesse Armstrong, Simon

Blackwell, Tony Roche and Ian Martin) have produced. I remember the first time I saw this film in a cinema when I was trying to take notes in the dark, for review purposes. My jottings were largely unintelligible, I found later, because I was laughing too much for coherent note-taking.

When Toby first arrives at Downing Street he is greeted by people frantically talking on phones and Malcolm Tucker shouting abuse at almost everyone. Judy thinks Toby is 'Dan' because 'You chaps often *are* Dan'. 'Welcome to the madhouse,' Simon says not too reassuringly, later adding that Malcolm is 'a bit of an alpha male', a major understatement. The following exchange takes place when Judy suggests tentatively that the matter of Simon's 'screw-up' on television is perhaps not in Tucker's 'purview':

'Purview? Purview? Where do you think you are? In some Regency fucking costume drama?'

'Your language does not impress me. My husband works for Tower Hamlets and their language makes you sound like Angela Lansbury.'

The dialogue cracks along in this fashion, pretty much unabated, for the next hour and a half. But this is not merely a matter of ultra-smart one-liners. It carries the weight of characterisation throughout.

In Malcolm Tucker, archetypal spin-doctor, Iannucci and his associates have created one of the great originals of recent times. In the annals of British television, there has perhaps been none so brilliantly conceived and executed since John Cleese's Basil Fawlty, both unerringly true to a concept in every move and inflection. Peter Capaldi had been busy in films and television since the early 1980s but it was the role of Tucker that made him a household name, at least in those households who became addicted to *The Thick of It*. In a way, this could almost be seen as *Yes Minister* with four-letter words. The non-stop profanity was pretty much new in free-to-air television. Language had been loosening in film and television for a couple of decades, but the unending flow of colourful vituperation was something of a breakthrough. In the case of Tucker, it seemed to be done not to shock but to characterise this ruthless and unstoppable verbal force of nature – or of political manipulation. Somehow, too, Jamie Cairney's camera contrives to make Capaldi's face look like a cutting instrument as well. Combined with his lethal delivery of the dialogue, Tucker becomes one of the most alarming creations of modern film fiction, the more so because writers and actor contrive to make him seem all too like our suspicions of the real thing.

He is not alone though. Virtually everybody is given something – that is, dialogue – to get his or her teeth into and in the process they establish a memorable gallery of (mainly) venal portraits. Short Tom Hollander, who showed his comic paces as well as a touch of pathos in his playing of sycophantic Mr Collins in the 2005 *Pride and Prejudice* and found new fame in the TV series *Rev* (2010–11), is a wonderful foil to Capaldi. A mouse beside a rat, as it were. Where Capaldi's Tucker is in a state of constant motion and verbal aggression, Hollander's Simon Foster is in constant danger of quietly putting his foot in it. He can plead, 'I'm a cabinet minister and I didn't get here by screwing up every media appearance I ever had', but no one is really listening, let alone believing. He is there to be used, and for preference not to speak in important meetings. When he does utter some banality at a meeting in Washington, Toby's latest girlfriend sends Tony a message: 'Simon is behaving like a massive TIT'. Perhaps not so surprising when he's been spoken of as being, 'just the meat in the room – a fine cut, not offal'. Rather limited praise really. When he complains to Judy about how stressful his life is, her rather uncaring response is, 'You're not a lion-tamer'. If this had been a Hollywood movie, the filmmaker might well have felt he needed to tip the scales a bit in the little guy's favour at the end. Not Iannucci, though. Simon isn't even able to put his resignation in, over the collapsing wall, because Tucker sacks him first. This is not a film that wants to warm our hearts, for which we can only be grateful.

The other key figure in the British triumvirate is Toby, whose name Simon routinely abbreviates to 'Tobes'. As played by lanky stand-up comedian Chris Addison – at least he looks lanky beside Hollander's Simon – Toby emerges as a wittily conceived amalgam of naivety and opportunism. Mainly sexual opportunism, that is. From a balcony in the Foreign Office, he recognises a young woman in the hall below and confides to American Liza, 'I had a little thing for her. I don't think she remembers me.' Liza's reply is, 'No, that is one of the side-effects of Rohypnol.' When Toby is sent to Washington, he has a night on the town with Liza and ends up in her bed, which she vacates the next morning without waking him. As a result he oversleeps and is seen frantically pulling his clothes on as he races to a meeting. When Suzy, his Foreign Office civil-servant girlfriend back in London, learns of this latest 'little thing', he tries to argue his way out of it as 'an anti-war shag': 'On some level, just consciously, maybe it was a last-ditch attempt to stop the war.' Suzy is unpersuaded.

Suzy works for Michael Rodgers, the 'Director of Diplomacy', who has Bach or Debussy playing non-stop in the office. Suzy has to keep asking him to turn the music down when important calls come through. The point is nicely made: all this exquisite music is the accompaniment for all the political finagling in the foreground. Rodgers, a very buttoned-up type, later helps Toby with his packing when Suzy has ordered him out, showing him the right way to fold a shirt. Suzy sourly asks Toby about the size of Liza's breasts, only to be told they're, 'So big they've got their own postcode.'

The Americans are similarly distinguished from each other and from their British counterparts by the kind of language attributed to them. Linton Barwick, the bellicose State Department guy who wants to get the US into war, is ironically characterised by his profanity-free diction. He finally turns on Tucker in the UN's Meditation Room: 'You're a useless piece of s-star-star-t '. In a post-credits insert, Barwick is seen complaining, 'I can't see why *I Heart Huckabees* is on a list of DVDs for combat troops', a reference that at film's end seems to *place* the triviality of thinking that can co-exist with cataclysmic decisions. On the whole, the best lines go to the British but the General is gifted not only with the remark quoted about France and war: when Karen Clarke turns on him, calling him a 'fucking armchair general', he responds with, 'I've been a soldier all my life. Look at the uniform – you think I'm one of the Village People?'

A film to cherish

The temptation with this film, and one which I haven't wholly resisted, is to go on quoting its memorable lines. But what needs to be stressed again is that these are not just cleverly timed laugh lines. They are part of the whole raucous self-serving political scene, the seriousness of which is inextricably caught up in the verbal sniping and crossfire. It is wildly funny as almost no film in my recent memory has been. It also offers a lethal look at a dangerous world in which words can do irreparable damage. When I say that the film is enormously funny, I don't mean it trivialises important issues. Rather it subjects them, and the human venalities involved, to some savagely satirical scrutiny, at the end of which neither sentimentality nor cliché will have had a look in – except to be slapped in the face. Somehow, all the lines get their laughs without interrupting the film's mad zest. You can read all sorts of scabrous critique of Anglo-US relations into it, but it may be that you'll be laughing too much to do full justice to such high-minded political thinking. The only way to repair such an omission is to watch the film again. It repays re-viewing in spades.

Notes

1 Henry K. Miller, 'In the Loop', *Sight & Sound*, May 2009, 64.
2 *Wikipedia:* http://en.wikipedia.org/wiki/List_of_films_based_on_ television_programs
3 *Metro*, Issue 160, 2009, 134–8.

Cast and credits

The basic credits given are director, screenplay, cinematographer and main actors. On some occasions, other personnel of special interest are mentioned.

The Lady Vanishes (1938)
Director: Alfred Hitchcock. Screenplay: Sidney Gilliat and Frank Launder, based on Ethel Lina White's novel, *The Wheel Spins*. Cinematographer: Jack Cox. 97 minutes.

Cast: Margaret Lockwood (Iris), Michael Redgrave (Gilbert), Miss Froy (Dame May Whitty), Paul Lukas (Dr Hartz), Cecil Parker (Todhunter), Linden Travers ('Mrs Todhunter'), Naunton Wayne (Caldicott), Basil Radford (Charters), Mary Clare (Baroness), Googie Withers (Blanche), Sally Stewart (Julie), Catherine Lacey (the nun), Josephine Wilson (Madame Kummer), Philip Leaver (Signor Doppo).

Pygmalion (1938)
Directors: Leslie Howard, Anthony Asquith. Producer: Gabriel Pascal. Screenplay: George Bernard Shaw, W. P. Lipscombe, Cecil Lewis, Ian Dalrymple, from Shaw's play *Pygmalion*. Cinematographer: Harry Stradling. Editor: David Lean. 96 minutes.

Cast: Leslie Howard (Professor Higgins), Wendy Hiller (Eliza Doolittle), Wilfred Lawson (Doolittle), Marie Lohr (Mrs Higgins), Jean Cadell (Mrs Pierce), Scott Sunderland (Colonel Pickering), David Tree (Freddy Eynsford Hill), Everley Gregg (Mrs Eynsford Hill),

Leueen McGrath (Clara Eynsford Hill), Esmé Percy (Kaparthy), Violet Vanbrugh (Ambassadress).

The Way Ahead (1944)
Director: Carol Reed. Screenplay: Eric Ambler, Peter Ustinov. Cinematographer: Guy Green. 115 minutes.

Cast: David Niven (Jim Perry), Raymond Huntley (Davenport), William Hartnell (Sergeant Fletcher), Stanley Holloway (Brewer), James Donald (Lloyd), Jimmy Hanley (Stainer), John Laurie (Luke), Hugh Burden (Parsons), Penelope Dudley Ward (Mrs Perry), Renee Asherson (Marjorie Gillingham), Mary Jerrold (Mrs Gillingham), Eileen Erskine (Mrs Parsons), Esma Cannon (Mrs Brewer), Peter Ustinov (Rispoli), Leo Genn (Company commander), Raymond Lovell (Garage owner), Tessie O'Shea (ENSA entertainer).

Brief Encounter (1945)
Director: David Lean. Producers: Anthony Havelock-Allan, Ronald Neame. Screenplay: Noël Coward, David Lean, Anthony Havelock-Allan, from Coward's play, *Still Life*. Cinematographer: Robert Krasker. Music: Rachmaninov Piano Concerto No. 2 played by Eileen Joyce. 86 minutes.

Cast: Celia Johnson (Laura Jesson), Trevor Howard (Alec Harvey), Cyril Raymond (Fred Jesson), Stanley Holloway (Albert Godby), Joyce Carey (Myrtle Bagot), Everley Gregg (Dolly Messiter), Marjorie Mars (Mary Norton), Margaret Barton (Beryl Waters), Valentine Dyall (Stephen Lynn), Nuna Davey (Mrs Rolandson), Irene Handl (organist).

Great Day (1945)
Director: Lance Comfort. Screenplay: John Davenport, Wolfgang Wilhelm, from Lesley Storm's play, *Great Day*. Cinematographer: Erwin Hiller. 79 minutes.

Cast: Eric Portman (Captain Ellis), Flora Robson (Mrs Ellis), Sheila Sim (Margaret Ellis), Philip Friend (Geoffrey Winthrop), Isabel Jeans (Lady Mott), Marjorie Rhodes (Mrs Mumford), Walter Fitzgerald (Bob Tyndale), Margaret Withers (Miss Tyndale), Maire O'Neill (Mrs Walsh), Beatrice Varley (Miss Tracy), Irene Handl (Miss Tomlinson), Kathleen Harrison (Maisie), Leslie Dwyer (Maisie's friend), Ivor Barnard (pub customer).

Temptation Harbour (1947)
Director: Lance Comfort. Screenplay: Rodney Ackland, Victor Skutezky, Frederic Gotfurt, from Georges Simenon's novel, *Newhaven-Dieppe*. Cinematographer: Otto Heller. Music: Mischa Spoliansky. 104 minutes.

Cast: Robert Newton (Bert Mallinson), Simone Simon (Camelia), Margaret Barton (Betty Mallinson), William Hartnell (Jim Brown), Marcel Dalio (Inspector Dupré), Joan Hopkins (Beryl Brown), Charles Victor (Gowshall), Irene Handl (Mrs Gowshall), Leslie Dwyer (Reg), George Woodbridge (Frost), Kathleen Boutall (Mrs Frost), Gladys Henson (Mrs Titmuss).

It Always Rains on Sunday (1947)
Director: Robert Hamer. Screenplay: Robert Hamer, Angus MacPhail, Henry Cornelius, based on Arthur La Bern's novel, *It Always Rains on Sunday*. Cinematographer: Douglas Slocombe. 92 minutes.

Cast: Googie Withers (Rose Sandigate), John McCallum (Tommy Swann), Edward Chapman (George Sandigate), Susan Shaw (Vi Sandigate), Patricia Plunkett (Doris Sandigate), David Lines (Alfie Sandigate), Detective-Sergeant Fothergill (Jack Warner), Sydney Tafler (Morrie Hyams), John Slater (Lou Hyams), Betty Ann Davies (Sadie Hyams), Jane Hylton (Bessie Hyams), Jimmy Hanley (Whitey), Alfie Bass (Dicey), Michael Howard (Slopey Collins), Hermione Baddeley (Mrs Spry), John Salew (Neesley), Gladys Henson (Mrs Neesley), Grace Arnold (landlady).

The Third Man (1949)
Director, producer: Carol Reed. Screenplay, story: Graham Greene. Cinematographer: Robert Krasker. Music: Anton Karas. Art director: Vincent Korda. 104 minutes.

Cast: Joseph Cotten (Holly Martins), Alida Valli (Anna Schmidt), Orson Welles (Harry Lime), Trevor Howard (Major Calloway), Bernard Lee (Sergeant Paine), Paul Hoerbiger (the porter), Ernst Deutsch (Baron Kurtz), Eric Ponto (Dr Winkel), Siegfried Breuer (Popescu), Crabbin (Wilfrid Hyde-White), Hansl (Herbert Halbik).

Genevieve (1953)
Director, producer: Henry Cornelius. Screenplay: William Rose. Cinematographer: Christopher Challis. Music: Larry Adler. 86 minutes.

Cast: Dinah Sheridan (Wendy), John Gregson (Alan), Kenneth More (Ambrose), Kay Kendall (Rosalind Peters), Joyce Grenfell (hotel proprietress), Geoffrey Keen (first speed cop), Harold Siddons (second speed cop), Edie Martin (hotel guest), Michael Medwin (expectant father), Arthur Wontner (elderly gentleman).

Private Information (1952)
Director: Fergus McDonell. Producer: Ronald Kinnoch. Screenplay: Gordon Glennon, John Baines, Ronald Kinnoch, from Glennon's play, *Garden City*. Cinematographer: Eric Cross. 66 minutes.

Cast: Jill Esmond (Charlotte Carson), Jack Watling (Hugh Carson), Carol Marsh (Georgie Carson), Norman Shelley (Freemantle), Brenda de Banzie (Dolly), Mercy Haystead (Iris), Gerard Heinz (Alex), Lloyd Pearson (Mayor).

Cash on Demand (1963)
Director: Quentin Lawrence. Screenplay: David T. Chantler, Lewis Greiffer, based on Jacques Gillies' play, *The Gold Inside*. Cinematographer: Arthur Grant. 66 minutes.

Cast: Peter Cushing (Fordyce), André Morell (Hepburn), Richard Vernon (Pearson), Norman Bird (Sanderson), Barry Lowe (Harvill), Edith Sharpe (Miss Pringle), Kevin Stoney (Detective-Inspector Mason).

A Kind of Loving (1962)
Director: John Schlesinger. Screenplay: Keith Waterhouse and Willis Hall, from Stan Barstow's novel, *A Kind of Loving*. Cinematographer: Denys Coop. 112 minutes.

Cast: Alan Bates (Vic Brown), June Ritchie (Ingrid Rothwell), Thora Hird (Mrs Rothwell), Gwen Nelson (Mrs Brown), Bert Palmer (Mr Brown), Pat Keen (Christine), David Mahlowe (David), Jack Smethurst (Conroy), James Bolam (Jeff), Leonard Rossiter (Whymper).

The Servant (1963)
Director, co-producer: Joseph Losey. Screenplay: Harold Pinter, based on Robin Maugham's novella, *The Servant*. Cinematographer: Douglas Slocombe. Music: Johnny Dankworth. 115 minutes.

Cast: Dirk Bogarde (Hugo Barrett), James Fox (Tony), Sarah Miles (Vera), Wendy Craig (Susan), Catherine Lacey (Lady Mountset), Richard Vernon (Lord Mountset), Ann Firbank (society woman), Doris Knox (woman in restaurant), Patrick Magee (bishop), Alun Owen (curate).

Women in Love (1969)
Director: Ken Russell. Screenplay: Larry Kramer (also producer), based on D. H. Lawrence's novel, *Women in Love*. Cinematographer: Billy Williams. Costumes: Shirley Russell. 130 minutes.

Cast: Gudrun Brangwen (Glenda Jackson), Oliver Reed (Gerald Crich), Alan Bates (Rupert Birkin), Ursula Brangwen (Jennie Linden), Eleanor Bron (Hermione Roddice), Vladek Sheybal (Loerke), Christopher Gable (Lupton), Alan Webb (Mr Crich), Catherine Wilmer (Mrs Crich), Michael Gough (Mr Brangwen), Norma Shebbeare (Mrs Brangwen), James Laurenson (minister).

Get Carter (1971)
Director: Mike Hodges. Screenplay: Mike Hodges, based on Ted Lewis's novel, *Jack's Return Home*. Cinematographer: Wolfgang Suschitzky. Editor: John Trumper. 112 minutes.

Cast: Michael Caine (Jack Carter), Britt Ekland (Anna Fletcher), John Osborne (Cyril Kinnear), Ian Hendry (Eric Paice), Bryan Mosley (Cliff Brumby), Geraldine Moffatt (Glenda), Dorothy White (Margaret), Alun Armstrong (Keith), Petra Markham (Doreen), John Bindon (Sid Fletcher), Tony Beckley (Peter).

A Portrait of the Artist as a Young Man (1977)
Director: Joseph Strick. Screenplay: Judith Rascoe, based on James Joyce's novel, *A Portrait of the Artist as a Young Man*. Cinematographer: Stuart Hetherington. Music: Stanley Myers. 92 minutes.

Cast: Bosco Hogan (Stephen Dedalus), T. P. McKenna (Simon Dedalus), John Gielgud (Preacher), Rosaleen Linehan (Mrs Dedalus), Maureen Potter (Dante), Niall Buggy (Davin), Brian Murray (Lynch), Desmond Cave (Cranly), David Kelly (Dean of Studies), Susan Fitzgerald (Emma Daniels).

Dreamchild (1986)
Director: Gavin Millar. Screenplay: Dennis Potter. Cinematographer:
Billy Williams. Jim Henson's Creature Shop for *Alice in Wonderland*
characters. 94 minutes.

Cast: Coral Browne (Mrs Alice Hargreaves), Ian Holm (Reverend
Charles Dodgson), Peter Gallagher (Jack Dolan), Nicola Cowper
(Lucy), Jane Merrow (Mrs Liddell), Amelia Shankley (young Alice),
James Wilby (Baker), Rupert Wainwright (Hargreaves), Caris Corfman
(Sally).

Four Weddings and a Funeral (1994)
Director: Mike Newell. Screenplay: Richard Curtis. Cinematographer:
Michael Coulter. 116 minutes.

Cast: Hugh Grant (Charles), Andie MacDowell (Carrie), Kristin Scott
Thomas (Fiona), Simon Callow (Gareth), James Fleet (Tom), John
Hannah (Matthew), Charlotte Coleman (Scarlett), Anna Chancellor
(Henrietta), Corin Redgrave (Hamish), Rowan Atkinson (Father
Gerald), Rupert Vansittart (George), David Haig (Bernard), Sophie
Thompson (Lydia), Kenneth Griffith (mad old man), Jeremy Kemp
(Lord Delaney), Rosalie Crutchley (Mrs Beaumont).

Secrets & Lies (1996)
Director, screenplay: Mike Leigh. Cinematographer: Dick Pope.
Production design: Alison Chitty. 140 minutes.

Cast: Brenda Blethyn (Cynthia), Timothy Spall (Maurice),
Phyllis Logan (Monica), Claire Rushbrooke (Roxanne), Marianne
Jean-Baptiste (Hortense), Leslie Manville (Jenny), Ron Cook (Stuart),
Elizabeth Berrington (Jane), Lee Ross (Paul), Brian Bovell, Trevor
Laird (Hortense's brothers).

Wonderland (1998)
Director: Michael Winterbottom. Producer: Andrew Eaton. Screenplay:
Laurence Coriat. Cinematographer: Sean Bobbitt. 108 minutes.

Cast: Shirley Henderson (Debbie), Gina McKee (Nadia), Molly Parker
(Molly), Ian Hart (Dan), John Simm (Eddie), Stuart Townsend (Tim),
Kika Markham (Eileen), Jack Shepherd (Bill), Enzo Cilenti (Darren),
Sarah-Jane Potts (Melanie), David Fahm (Franklyn), Ellen Thomas
(Donna).

Last Orders (2002)
Director, co-producer: Fred Schepisi. Screenplay: Schepisi, based on Graham Swift's novel, *Last Orders*. Cinematographer: Brian Tufano. 109 minutes.

Cast: Michael Caine (Jack Dodds), Tom Courtenay (Vic Tucker), David Hemmings (Lenny Tate), Bob Hoskins (Ray Johnson), Helen Mirren (Amy Dodds), Ray Winstone (Vince Dodds), JJ Feild (young Jack), Cameron Fitch (young Vic), Nolan Hemmings (young Lenny), Anatol Yusef (young Ray), Kelly Reilly (young Amy), Laura Morelli (June Dodds), Meg Wyn Owen (Joan), George Innes (Bernie).

In the Loop (2009)
Director: Armando Iannucci. Screenplay: Armando Iannucci, Jesse Armstrong, Simon Blackwell, Tony Roche. Cinematographer: Jamie Carney. 105 minutes.

Cast: Peter Capaldi (Malcolm Tucker), Tom Hollander (Simon Foster), Gina McKee (Judy Molloy), James Gandolfini (General Miller), Chris Addison (Toby), James Smith (Michael Rodgers), Anna Chlumsky (Liza Weld), Paul Higgins (Jamie MacDonald), Mimi Kennedy (Karen Clark), David Rasche (Linton Barwick), Steve Coogan (Paul Michaelson), Eve Matheson (new minister).

Further reading

For those who would like to read what others have said about some of the films highlighted in this book, the following list is suggested. Some are biographical studies, some focus on particular films, others are more wide-ranging surveys that have extended references to one or more of the twenty films.

Armes, Roy, *A Critical History of British Cinema* (1978, Secker and Warburg)

Barr, Charles, *Ealing Studios* (1977; 1993, University of California Press)

Barr, Charles, *English Hitchcock* (1999, Cameron and Hollis)

Brownlow, Kevin, *David Lean: A Biography* (1996, Richard Cohen Books)

Chibnall, Steve, *Get Carter: A British Film Guide* (2003, I. B. Taurus)

Chibnall, Steve and Robert Murphy (eds), *British Crime Cinema* (1999, Routledge)

Ciment, Michel, *Conversations with Losey* (1985, Methuen)

Coldstream, John, *Dirk Bogarde* (2004, Weidenfeld & Nicholson)

Drazin, Charles, *The Finest Years: British Cinema in the 1940s* (1998, I. B. Taurus)

Drazin, Charles, *In Search of The Third Man* (2000, Methuen)

Durgnat, Raymond, *A Mirror for England* (1970; 2011, BFI Publishing)

Dyer, Richard, *Brief Encounter* (1993, BFI Publishing)

McFarlane, Brian, *Lance Comfort* (1999, Manchester University Press)

McFarlane, Brian and Deane Williams, *Michael Winterbottom* (2008, Manchester University Press)

Mackenzie, S. P., *British War Films, 1939–1945* (2001, Continuum)

Mann, William J., *Edge of Midnight: The Life of John Schlesinger* (2004, Hutchison)

Mayer, Geoff, *Guide to British Films* (2003, Greenwood)

Minney, R. J., *Puffin Asquith* (1973, Frewin)

More, Kenneth, *More or Less* (1978, Hodder & Stoughton)

Murphy, Robert, *Realism and Tinsel: Cinema and Society in Britain 1939–1948* (1989, Routledge)

Murphy, Robert (ed.), *British Cinema of the 90s* (2000, BFI Publishing)

Perry, George, *The Great British Picture Show* (1974; 1985, Little, Brown)

Russell, Ken, *Fire Over England* (1993, Hutchison)

Ryall, Tom, *Anthony Asquith* (2005, Manchester University Press)

Slide, Anthony, *Fifty Classic British Films* (1985, Dover Publications)

Spicer, Andrew and A. T. McKenna, *The Man Who Got Carter* (2013, I. B. Taurus)

Taylor, B. F., *The British New Wave* (2006, Manchester University Press)

Taylor, Phillip M., *Britain and the Cinema in the Second World War* (1988, Palgrave Macmillan)

Vermilye, Jerry, *The Great British Films* (1978, Citadel Press)

Wapshott, Nicholas, *The Man Between: A Biography of Carol Reed* (1990, Alfred A. Knopf)

Whitehead, Tony, *Mike Leigh* (2007, Manchester University Press)

Index

39 Steps, The 8, 10, 15, 20

Accident 135, 136
adaptations 11, 32, 50–4, 147, 155, 172–3, 188, 217, 240
Addison, Chris 243, 248
Adler, Larry 106, 107
Agate, James 54
Agee, James 54, 58, 109
Alan Partridge 241
Aldridge, Michael 20
Alfie 166, 236
Alice in Wonderland 181, 185, 187, 188
All or Nothing 214
Ambler, Eric 36, 37, 39
Amis, Kingsley 124
Anderson, Lindsay 131, 134, 242
Another Year 204, 205, 214, 215
Ante-Room, The 56
Antonioni, Michelangelo 236
Appointment in London 105
Arms and the Man 23
Armstrong, Alun 162, 168
Armstrong, Jesse 246
Army Kinematograph Service 36
Arnold, Grace 78
Arrighi, Luciana 155
Asher, Jane 182, 190

Asherson, Renee 44
Asquith, Anthony 9, 24–5, 27, 29, 30, 32, 67
Associated British Studios 72
Atkinson, Rowan 198
Attenborough, Richard 39
Auden, W. H. 200–1
Auf Wiedersehn, Pet 214
Auric, Georges 84
Awful Truth, The 193

Baddeley, Hermione 78
Bailey, Robin 20
Baines, John 111
Balcon, Michael 80
Balcony, The 172
Bank Holiday 87
Barnard, Ivor 25, 27, 32
Barr, Charles 82
Barrie, J. M. 183
Barry, Joan 18
Barstow, Stan 124, 130
Barton, Margaret 68, 71, 72, 73
'Basement Room, The' 87
Bass, Alfie 78
Bates, Alan 125, *126*, 128, 130, 150, 152–3, 154, *155*
Baxter, John 20

Beckwith, Reginald 105
Bennett, Alan 190
Bennett, Compton 8
Berrington, Elizabeth 212
Bête humaine, La 73
Beuer, Siegfried 92
Big Sleep, The 161
Billion Dollar Brain 148
Billy Elliot 160
Billy Liar 128, 131, 237
Bindon, John 161
Bird, Norman 116
Blackwell, Simon 247
Blame It on Rio 236
Bleak Moments 204
Blethyn, Brenda 206, 207, 208, *209*,
        211, 214
Blithe Spirit 50, 51, 52
Bloom 172
Bloom, Claire 106
Blow-Up 236
Blue Lamp, The 85
Bob Roberts 242
Bobbitt, Sean 226
Bogarde, Dirk 105, 106, 135, 136, *141*,
        144, 166
Bolam, James 128
Boulting, John and Roy 39, 87, 131,
        242
Boutall, Kathleen 69
Bovell, Brian 207
Bower, David 199
Braine, John 122, 124
Brassed Off 130
Breakfast at Tiffany's 200
Brennan, Kevin 164
Brick Lane 47, 48
Bridget Jones's Diary 193
Bridget Jones: The Edge of Reason
        193
Brief Encounter (1945) 5, 32, 47–60,
        83, 240

Brief Encounter (1974) 48
Brief Encounter (play, 2000) 52
Brighton Rock (1947) 68, 87, 158
Brighton Rock (2010) 87
Britannia Hospital 242
British 'B' films 2, 5, 8, 109–20, 158
Broadbent, Jim 205
Bron, Eleanor 153
Brook, Clive 82
Brown, Pamela 188
Browne, Coral 183, *184*, 190
Browning Version, The 24
Buchan, John 10
Burden, Hugh 40, 43
Burstall, Tim 147
Burton, Tim 188
Bute, Mary Ellen 172
Butterfly Kiss 217
Bye Bye Birdie 119

Cadell, Jean 26, 32
Caine, Michael 148, 160, 162, 166–8,
        229, 233, 235, 236, 237
Cairney, Jamie 247
Callow, Simon 195, 200
Calvert, Phyllis 80
Cannon, Esma 44
Canterbury Tale, A 65, 66, 67
Capaldi, Peter 242, 243, 247
Cardiff, Jack 147
Carey, Joyce 56
Carmichael, Ian 20
Carol, John 78
Carroll, Lewis *see* Dodgson,
        Charles
'Carry On' series 98, 192
Carstairs, John Paddy 8
Cash on Demand 2, 110, 115–19
Cass, Henry 25
censorship 154–5
Challis, Christopher 99, 103, 106
Chancellor, Anna 198

Chandler, Raymond 161, 165
Chapman, Edward 75, 84
Charteris, Leslie 12
Charters & Caldicott 20
Chitty, Alison 207, 214
Chlumsky, Anna 244
Christie, Julie 128
Christmas Carol, A 115
Cilenti, Enzo 219
Cineguild 49, 51
Citizen Kane 95
Claim, The 217
class 39–40, 56–7, 62, 122, 123,
    124, 125, 129–31, 134, 135, 137,
    138–43, 207, 213, 225
Cleese, John 247
Close, Glenn 197
Cock and Bull Story, A 217
Coetzee, J. M. 177
Cole, Stephen 235
Coleman, Charlotte 195
Collier, John W. 77
comedy 2, 192
    romantic comedy 2, 14, 98,
        106–8, 192–3, 199
Comfort, Lance 3, 61, 63, 64
Compton-Burnett, Ivy 133
Conrad, Joseph 11
Coogan, Steve 246
Cook, Ron 213, 214
Cooper, Gary 167, 188
Cornelius, Henry 75, 84, 101, 107
Costello, Donald 23, 31
Cottage on Dartmoor, A 24
Cotton, Joseph 88, 89, 94, 95
Coulter, Michael 195, 203
Courtenay, Tom 128, 130, 229, 235,
    236, 237
Coward, Noël 35, 39, 49, 50–4, 56,
    57, 58, 121
Cowper, Nicola 184, 190
Cox, Jack 18

Cracker 217
Craig, Wendy 138, 144
Crawford, Anne 39
Cream in My Coffee 189
Creature Shop 190
Crooks' Tour 20
Cross, Eric 111
Crowe, Sarah 196
Crowley, Dave 70
Curtis, Richard 194, 196, 198, 200,
    202
Cushing, Peter 116, 119

Daldry, Stephen 160
Dane, Lois 116
Darling 131
Davenport, A. Bromley 41
Davies, Betty Ann 77
Davis, John 105
Davis, Philip 205, 214
De Banzie, Brenda 112
Dead, The 172
Dead of Night 80, 82, 84
Dear Octopus 48
Dearing, R. E. 18
Deep Blue Sea, The 105, 121
Del Giudice, Filippo 37
Delaney, Shelagh 123
Deutsch, Ernst 93
Dickens, Charles 50, 88, 115, 118
Dirty Rotten Scoundrels 236
Dixon, Campbell 73
Dockery, Michelle 22
Doctor's Dilemma, The 25
documentary film 35, 36, 37, 38, 147,
    167, 225, 226
Dodgson, Charles 181, 182, 184, 185,
    187, 188
Donald, James 41, 42, 44
Donat, Robert 8, 36
Donner, Clive 107
Double Indemnity 158

Doyle, Conan 8
Drazin, Charles 49, 95
Dreamchild 2, 181–91
Dr Syn 19
Dudley-Ward, Penelope 44
Duffy 135
Dwyer, Leslie 41, 44

Ealing (Studios) 36, 74, 79, 80, 84,
        98, 107, 192, 242
Eaton, Andrew 218, 219
Edwards, Glyn 162
Ekland, Britt 161, 168
Elizabeth Costello 177
Elvey, Maurice 35
Enemy of the People 110
Englishman Abroad, An 131
Erin Brockovich 110
Erskine, Eileen 40, 44
Esmond, Jill 111, *112*, 114

Fahm, David 220
Fallen Idol, The 87, 90
Far from the Madding Crowd 131
Farewell My Lovely 161, 165
Fatal Attraction 197
Feild, JJ 235
Fergusson, Guy 8
Ferran, Pascale 147
Field, Shirley Anne 128
Fields, Gracie 34, 192
Fields, W. C. 188
Figgis, Mike 160
film noir 58, 66, 68, 69, 73, 84, 158
Finest Years, The 49
Finney, Albert 127, 130
Fish Called Wanda, A 107
Fitzgerald, Susan 179
Fitzgerald, Walter 64
Fleet, James 198
Fleischer, Richard 8
Flight Plan 9

Flying Scot, The 8
For Better, for Worse 107
Forde, Walter 8
Formby, George 34, 81, 192
Foster, Jodie 9
Four Weddings and a Funeral 2, 5,
        107, 192–203, 206
Fox, James *137*, 137, *141*, 144
French, Harold 23, 28
French, Philip 98
French Dressing 147
Frend, Charles 79
Friend, Philip 64
'Funeral Blues' 200

Gainsborough Films 50, 58
Gallagher, Peter 185, 190
Gandolfini, James 244
gangster films 158–9
Gangster No.1 158
Garden City 111
Gavron, Sarah 47
Genet, Jean 172
Genevieve 2, 98–108, 194, 202
Genn, Leo 39
Gentle Sex, The 35, 36
Georgy Girl 107, 134
Gershwin, George 195
Get Carter (1971) 2, 158–69, 236
Get Carter (2000) 160
Ghost Train, The 8
Gielgud, John 8, 177
Gilliat, Sydney 8, 9, 12, 18, 20, 35
Gillies, Jacques 115
Glennon, Gordon 111
Go-Between, The 135
Gold Express, The 8
Gold Inside, The 115
Gone with the Wind 88
Good-Time Girl 79
Gotfurt, Frederick 72
Gow, Ronald 25

Granger, Stewart 166
Grant, Arthur 116
Grant, Cary 188, 193
Grant, Hugh 194, *194*, 195, 201, 202
Grass Is Greener, The 107
Gray, Sally 81
Great Day 3, 61–7
Great Expectations (film) 50, 57
Great Expectations (novel) 170
Great Train Robbery, The 7
Green, Guy 38
Greene, Graham 86–7, 96
Greenwood, Joan 81
Gregg, Everley 26, 27, 32, 59
Gregory, Jon 214
Gregson, John 98, 104, 105, 106
Grenfell, Joyce 105, 188
Grey, Clifford 19
Grierson, John 35
Griffith, Kenneth 196

Haig, David 197
Hamer, Robert 74, 75, 79–80, 81, 84
Hammer Film Productions 119
Hanley, Jimmy 41, 43, 78
Hannah, John 195, 200
Happy-Go-Lucky 205
Hardy, Thomas 217
Harker, Gordon 18
Harrison, Rex 22
Harry Brown 167
'Harry Lime Theme, The' 90, 95
Hart, Ian 221
Hartnell, William 41, 70
Harvey, Laurence 127
Hatter's Castle 71
Havelock-Allan, Anthony 49, 57
Hawkins, Sally 205
Hayers, Sidney 160
Haystead, Mercy 112, 114

Heinz, Gerard 112
Heller, Otto 69, 73
Hemmings, David 229, 235, 236
Hemmings, Nolan 235
Henderson, Shirley 219
Hendry, Ian 162, 168
Henry V 50
Henson, Jim 190
Hepburn, Katharine 193
Hetherington, Stuart 171
High Hopes 204
Hill in Korea, A 236
Hiller, Wendy 8, 23, 24, 25, 27, 28, 29, 30
Hillier, Erwin 65
Hird, Thora 126, *128*
History Boys, The 48
Hitchcock, Alfred 2, 4, 7–24, *13*, 34, 209
Hobson, Valerie 81
Hodges, Mike 158, 167, 168
Hoerbiger, Paul 92
Hogan, Bosco 172, 179
Hollander, Tom 243, 248
Holloway, Stanley 41, 44, 56
Holm, Ian 182, 183
Homeland 241
Honorary Consul, The 167
Hoskins, Bob 228, 233, 235, 237
House Un-American Activities Committee (HUAC) 107, 133, 134
How He Lied to Her Husband 23
Howard, Leslie 24, 27, 28, 30, 35
Howard, Trevor 47, 48, 49, 51, 53, 59, 88, 90, 240
Huntley, Raymond 38, 40, 43
Hurst, Sally 230
Huston, John 172
Huth, Harold 18
Hyde-White, Wilfrid 92
Hylton, Jane 78

I Know Where I'm Going! 25
I'm All Right Jack 242
Iannucci, Armando 241, 243, 244, 246, 247, 248
If... 242
Importance of Being Earnest, The 24
In the Loop 2, 5, 240–50
In This World 217
In Which We Serve 35, 36, 39, 48, 50, 67
Independent Producers 50
Innes, George 229
Ipcress File, The 166
Irving, Laurence 29
It Always Rains on Sunday 74–85, 122
Italian Job, The 167
Ivanov, Yevgeny 134

Jack and Sarah 193
Jack's Return Home 167
Jackson, Glenda 149, 150, 151
James, Henry 147
Jaws 110
Jean-Baptiste, Marianne 207, 209
Jeans, Isabel 62
Jefford, Barbara 172
Jerrold, Mary 42, 44
John, Elton 203
Johnson, Celia 47, 48, 49, 51, 53, 59, 81, 83, 240
Johnstone, Luke 179
Jones, Ken 155
Jour qui lève, Le 158
Joyce, James 170, 171, 172–3, 176

Kangaroo 147
Kanin, Garson 37
Karas, Anton 95, 96
Keeler, Christine 134, 139
Keen, Geoffrey 105
Keen, Pat 125

Kelly, David 178
Kendall, Kay 100, 103, *103*, 104, 105
Kennedy, Mimi 244
Kent, Jean 81
Kind Hearts and Coronets 74, 80, 84, 107
Kind of Loving, A 4, 121–32, 134, 160
King, Emma 182
King and Country 136
Klinger, Michael 167, 168
Knack, The 135
Korda, Alexander 34, 87, 88
Korda, Vincent 96
Kramer, Larry 152
Krasker, Robert 95, 96
Kunz, Simon 196

La Bern, Arthur 77, 79
Lacey, Catherine 17, 143
Lady Chatterley (1993, TV miniseries) 148
Lady Chatterley (2006) 147
Lady on a Train 12
Lady Vanishes, The (1938) 2, 7–24
Lady Vanishes, The (1979) 20
Ladykillers, The 74, 79
Laird, Trevor 207
Lancashire Luck 25
Last Journey, The 8
Last Orders 228–39
Lavender Hill Mob, The 74
Launder, Frank 9, 12, 18, 20, 35
Laurenson, James 155
Laurie, John 41, 44
Lawrence, D. H. 146–8
Lawrence, Quentin 115, 117
Lawson, Wilfrid 31–2
Lean, David 4, 27, 32, 35, 49, 50–4, 57, 88, 105
Leavis, F. R. 146

Lee, Anna 9, 193
Lee, Bernard 91
Leigh, Mike 204, 210, 212, 213, 225
Leigh, Vivien 105
Lejeune, C. A. 54
Lewis, Cecil 23
Lewis, Damien 241
Lewis, Ted 167
Lexy, Edward 69
Life Is Sweet 214
Lillie, Beatrice 82
Linehan, Rosaleen 174, 176
Linden, Jennie *149*, 150, 153
Lines, David 77
Lisztomania 146
literary sources 5, 10, 19, 50, 88, 123, 124, 170
Loach, Ken 122, 225
Lock, Stock and Two Smoking Barrels 158
Lockwood, Margaret 12, *13*, 17, 19, 22, 50, 80
Lodger, The 10
Logan, Phyllis 206
Lohr, Marie 31
Lolita 183
Lom, Herbert 19, 93
London to Brighton 98
Loneliness of the Long-Distance Runner, The 122, 123, 134, 237
Long Good Friday, The 237
Look Back in Anger (film) 123
Look Back in Anger (play) 121
Lorna Doone 19
Losey, Joseph 133
Lost Boys, The 183
Love Actually 193
Love on the Dole 25
Lovell, Raymond 41
Loves of Joanna Godden, The 80, 82, 84

Lowe, Barry 116
Lucky Jim 124
Lukas, Paul 15, 19
Lumet, Sydney 8

McCallum, John 74, *76*, 76, *81*, 82, *83*, 84
McCarthy, Michael 8
Macdonald, Kevin 241
McDonell, Fergus 111, 115
MacDowell, Andie 195
McGrath, Leueen 26
McKee, Gina 219, 220, 221, 243
Mackendrick, Alexander 79
McKenna, T. P. 172, 176
McLaren, John 66
McPhail, Angus 75, 84
Mahlowe, David 125
Major Barbara 23, 28, 50, 242
Man in Grey, The 19
Man in the White Suit, The 242
Man Who Knew Too Much, The (1936) 10
Manville, Lesley 208, 214
Markham, Kika 219, 225
Marsh, Carol 111, *112*
Martin, Edie 106
Martin, Ian 247
Mason, James 166
Matheson, Muir 107
Matter of Life and Death, A 67
Matthews, A.E. 44
Maude, Joan 62
Maugham, Robin 136, 139
Mayor of Casterbridge, The 217
Medwin, Michael 105
Michael, Ralph 22
Middleton, Guy 106
Midnight Cowboy 131
Miles, Christopher 147
Miles, Sarah 138, 143, 144
Miller, Gavin 183, 189

Millionairess, The 25
Millions Like Us 20, 35, 39
Mills, John 50
Ministry of Information 37
Mirren, Helen 230, 235, 238
Mitchell, Leslie 101
Modesty Blaise 136
Mona Lisa 167
montage 26, 28, 29, 30, 112, 154
Monty Python series 241
More, Kenneth 98, *100*, 104, 105, 106
Morell, André 117, 119
Mosley, Bryan *162*, 162
Mount, Peggy 111
Murder on the Orient Express 8
Murphy, Pat 172
My Fair Lady 22, 27
My Pal Wolf 114
Myers, Stanley 178, 189
Mystery Junction 8

Naked 205
Narrow Margin, The 8
Neagle, Anna 80
Neame, Ronald 49
Nelson, Gwen 126
New Lot, The 36
New Tricks 168
'New Wave, the' 121, 127, 128, 130, 131, 134, 159, 160, 163, 225, 237
Newell, Mike 194, 195, 198, 200, 202
Newhaven-Dieppe 68, 71
Newton, Robert 67, 70, 71, 72
Night and Day 86
Night Darkens the Streets 79
Night Train to Munich 20
Nil by Mouth 237
Nine Men 35
Niven, David 37, 38, 41–3, 42
No Orchids for Miss Blandish 158
Non-Stop New York 9

Nora 172
Norton, Richard 24
Notting Hill 107, 193

O Lucky Man! 242
O'Brien, Kate 56
Office, The 243
Oliver! 88
Oliver Twist 50
Olivier, Laurence 114
On Approval 82
... one of our aircraft is missing 35, 81
O'Neill, Maire 62
Osborne, John 121, 160
O'Shea, Tessie 44
O'Toole, Peter 22
Out of the Past 158

Page, Anthony 20
Palmer, Bert 126
Parker, Cecil 12, 17, 19
Parker, Molly 219
Pascal, Gabriel 23, 26, 28, 50
Pascal, Valerie 23
Passages from James Joyce's Finnegan's Wake 172
Passport to Pimlico 74, 107
pastoral 65–6
Patch, Blanche 24
Payroll 160
Pearson, Lloyd 111, 114
Pennies from Heaven 181, 189, 237
Percy, Esmé 29, 32
Philadelphia Story, The 193
Pigott-Smith, Tim 22
Pinewood Studios 24
Pink String and Sealing Wax 80, 82
Pinter, Harold 135
Plunkett, Patricia 75, 76
Ponto, Eric 93

Pope, Dick 214
Portman, Eric 39, 61, 63, 65, 66, 66
Portrait of the Artist as a Young Man, A (film) 4, 170–80, 189
Portrait of the Artist as a Young Man, A (novel) 170
Potter, Dennis 181, 237
Potter, Maureen 174
Poulet, Olivia 243
Powell, Dilys 54
Powell, Michael 1, 9, 25, 35, 65, 66, 67, 81, 109, 148
Press for Time 238
Pressburger, Emeric 35
Pride and Prejudice (2005) 248
Priestley, J. B. 121
Primary Colors 242
Private Information 2, 110–15
Profumo, John 134
propaganda 35, 36, 37, 38
Pulp 168
Pygmalion 5, 22–33

Quai des brumes 73, 158
Quartet (1948) 19
Quartet (2012) 237
Quiet American (2002) 87
Quiet Wedding 24
'quota quickies' 109

Rachmaninoff's 2nd piano concerto 51, 59
Radford, Basil 12, 17, 20
Radio Telefís, Éireann 170
Rainbow, The 148
Rank, J. Arthur 50
Rank Organisation 107
Rasche, David 244
Rascoe, Judith 175
Rattigan, Terence 121

Raymond, Cyril 52
realism 58–9, 74, 79, 88, 117, 159, 206, 210, 225–6, 238
social realism 110–11, 205
Redgrave, Corin 198
Redgrave, Michael 13, 17, 19
Reed, Carol 4, 20, 34, 37, 38, 87–8, 95, 96
Reed, Oliver 150, 151, 154, 155
Reisz, Karel 131
Rev 248
Revolution Films 217
Rhodes, Marjorie 62
Richardson, Tony 131
Rigby, Terence 161
Right True End, The 124
Ripley, Arthur 8
Ritchie, June 125, 126
Roberts, Rachel 127, 130
Robinson, Bernard 116
Robson, Flora 62, 63
Rocking-Horse Winner, The 146
Rome Express 8, 18
Room at the Top (film) 57, 122, 123, 127, 134, 160
Room at the Top (novel) 122, 124
Roome, Alfred 18
Rope 209
Rose, William 104, 106
Ross, Lee 211
Royal Court Theatre 121
Ruddock, John 41
Rushbrook, Claire
Russell, Ken 146, 147–8, 151, 152, 154, 155, 156–7, 170–1
Russell, Shirley 156

Sabotage 10, 11
St Joan 25
Salew, John 78
San Demetrio, London 35, 79
Sarris, Andrew 187, 190

*Saturday Night and Sunday
    Morning* 123, 127, 134
Savage Eye, The 172
Saville, Victor 9, 10
Scanlan, Joanna 246
Schepisi, Fred 228, 229, 233, 234
Schlesinger, John 124, 125, 127, 130,
    131
Scott, Avis 51
Scott Thomas, Kristin 194, 195
Searchers, The 167
Sears, Heather 127
Secret Agent 11
Secrets & Lies 5, 204–16, 228
Selznick, David O. 88, 91, 96
Servant, The (film) 133–45
Servant, The (novella) 136, 139
sexuality 143–4, 150–4, 176, 183,
    197, 220, 240
Shakespeare in Love 107, 193
Shanghai Express 8
Shankley, Amelia 182
Sharpe, Edith 116
Shaw, George Bernard 22, 23, 26,
    31
Shaw, Susan 75
Sheen, Ruth 205, 214
Shelley, Norman 111, 114
Shepherd, Jack 219, 225
Sheridan, Dinah 99, 104, 106
Shilling for Candles, A 10
Shooting Fish 193
Shooting Stars 24
Signoret, Simone 127
Silkwood 110
Sim, Sheila 65, 66, 66
Simenon, Georges 68, 69, 71
Simm, John 223
Simon, Simone 69, 70, 72, 72
Singing Detective, The 189
Skutesky, Victor 72
Slater, John 77

Sleeping Car to Trieste 8
Sliding Doors 193
Slocombe, Douglas 84, 139, 144
Smith, James 243
Smith-Wood, Jackie 22
So Long at the Fair 9
Sons and Lovers (film) 147
Sons and Lovers (novel) 147, 170
Sound Barrier, The 104
Spall, Timothy 206, 211, 214
Spectator, The 86
Spoliansky, Mischa 71, 72
Stallone, Sylvester 167
Stars Look Down, The 87
State of Play 241
Staunton, Imelda 205
Sterne, Laurence 217
Stevenson, Robert 9, 193
Stewart, Sally 12, 13
Still Life 50, 51–2
Stock, Nigel 77
Storm, Lesley 62
Stormy Monday 160
Story of Gilbert and Sullivan, The
    105
Stradling, Harry 29
Strick, Joseph 170–1, 172, 174–6, 177,
    178, 179
Strick, Terence 174, 179
Sunday Bloody Sunday 131
Sunderland, Scott 27
Suschitzky, Wolfgang 160
Sweeney! 241
Sweet, Bob 66
Swift, Graham 228
'swinging London' films 134, 135

Tafler, Sydney 75, 85
Taste of Honey, A 122, 123
Tate, Reginald 39
Tell England 24
Temple, Shirley 86

Temptation Harbour 61, 67–73
Terminus 131
Terror by Night 8
Tey, Josephine 10, 11
Theatre 70 series 115
Thewlis, David 205
They Made Me a Fugitive 68, 158
Thick of It, The 241, 242, 243, 247
Third Man, The 2, 86–97
This Happy Breed 48, 49, 51
This Sporting Life 122, 123, 134
Thomas, Ellen 224
Thompson, Sophie 197
thrillers 2, 7, 15, 16, 70, 92, 110, 115, 117
Time Gentlemen Please 110
Topsy-Turvy 205, 214
Touch of Class 48
Townsend, Stuart 220
Travers, Linden 12, 16, 19
Trip, The (film, TV) 217
Tristram Shandy 217
Trouble Brewing 81
Trouncer, Cecil 30
True Glory, The 37
Truffaut, François 10
Truly Madly Deeply 48
Tufano, Brian 233
Twentieth Century 7
Two Cities 37
Tynan, Kenneth 121

Ulysses 172
Ulysses Film Company 170
Upstairs and Downstairs 107
Ustinov, Peter 36, 37, 39, 44

Valli 89, 91, 96
Vanbrugh, Violet 32
Vansittart, Rupert 197
Vera Drake 205
Vernon, Richard 116, 143

Very Thought of You, The 193
Vetchinsky, Alex 18
Victor, Charles 69
Virgin and the Gipsy, The 147
Von Sternberg, Joseph 8
Vorhaus, Bernard 8, 109

Wag the Dog 242
Wainwright, Rupert 183
Waite, Trevor 26
Walker, Timothy 196
Wallace, Edgar 34
Walsh, Sean 172
Walters, Julie 190
Wanted for Murder 68
Wapshott, Nicholas 37
War Zone, The 237
Ward, Stephen 134, 139
Warner, Jack 84, 85
Wasikowska, Mia 188
Watchers on the Shore, The 124
Waterloo Road 35
Watling, Jack 39, 111
Watt, Harry 35
Way Ahead, The 5, 34–46, 48, 67, 87
Way to the Stars, The 48, 67
Wayne, John 167
Wayne, Naunton 12, 17, 20
Welles, Orson 88–90, 94, 95
Welwyn Studios 72
Wheel Spins, The 7, 11
Where No Vultures Fly 104
Whisky Galore! 74, 79
White, Dorothy 162
White, Ethel Lina 7, 11
White Peacock, The 147
Whitty, Dame May 12, 17, 19
Wicked Lady, The 19, 50, 58
Wickes, David 241
Williams, Andrew 98
Williams, Billy 152, 189

Wimbledon 193

Winslow Boy, The 24, 50

Winstone, Ray 229, 230, 235, 237, 241

Winterbottom, Michael 217–18, 219, 222, 225, 226, 227

Wisdom, Norman 238

Withers, Googie 12, 13, 19, 75, 76, 79, 80–4, *81*, *83*

Withers, Margaret 62

Wodehouse, P. G. 142

Women in Love (film) 2, 5, 146–57, 170

Women in Love (novel) 148–9

Women's Liberation Movement 144

Wonderland 5, 217–27

Wontner, Arthur 104, 105

Wood, Robin 11

Working Title 193

World in Action 167

Wright, Basil 32

Yes Minister 247

Young and Innocent 10, 15, 20

Zulu 166, 236